HOPE for the CHURCH

contemporary
strategies
for growth

CHURCH HOUSE
PUBLISHING

...b Jackson

Church House Publishing
Church House
Great Smith Street
London SW1P 3NZ

ISBN 0 7151 5551 2

Published 2002 by Church House Publishing
Second impression 2003
Third impression 2004

Typeset in Rotis by Vitaset, Paddock Wood, Kent

Printed by The Cromwell Press Ltd, Trowbridge, Wiltshire

Contents

List of tables   iv

List of maps   iv

List of figures   v

Foreword   vii

Preface   viii

Author's preface   xi

1   Facing the truth   1

2   Bums on seats – why they matter   17

3   Church growth – mission possible   27

4   Bringing growth out of decline   33

5   Why should the future be any different?   46

6   The Church after Christendom   56

7   Using figures   70

8   Nurturing faith   80

9   Welcoming all   86

10 Taking risks   94

11 Acting small – whatever your size   108

12 Planting churches   132

13 Growing younger   146

14 Supporting the clergy   157

15 The vital role of the diocese   168

16 Renewing the spiritual heart   183

Notes   191

Index   193

List of tables

1.1 Decline in the Church of England, 1980–2000   2

4.1 Percentage change in the uSa of adults, 1989–99:   37
diocesan league table

4.2 Percentage change in the uSa of children, 1989–99:   38
diocesan league table

4.3 Examples of parish churches reversing adult attendance   43
decline, 1989–99

7.1 The relationship between numbers attending and type of   74
service in larger churches in one diocese

8.1 The soul of Britain, 1987 and 2000   84

11.1 Adult attendance in the Diocese of York, 1988–94   112

11.2 Adult attendance at the 32 largest churches in St Albans   116
Diocese, 1991 and 1999

12.1 Growth of Anglican church plants   138

List of maps

Map 1 Percentage change in the uSa of adults by diocese,   39
1989–99

Map 2 Percentage change in the uSa of children by diocese,   40
1989–99

List of figures

1.1 Usual Sunday Attendance, 1999, October 2000 Sunday 9
count and October 2000 all-week count

1.2 Percentage change in adult attendance over successive 11
three-year periods, 1989–99

1.3 Percentage change in child attendance over successive 12
three-year periods, 1989–99

1.4 C of E attendance projections to 2030 13

1.5 Adult attendance in selected denominations, 1999 and 2000 14

4.1 Adult uSa in the Diocese of Wakefield, 1990–2000 44

4.2 Adult attendance decline in northern dioceses, 1996–9 45

5.1 Annual loss of adult Sunday attendance in the Church of 48
England (three-year moving average), 1991–9

5.2 Percentage of Anglican churches of different traditions 50
with static or growing attendance, 1989–98

7.1 St Mary's: adult attendance at different services, 1989–92 72

7.2 Average total attendance at St Mary's, 1993–2001 72
(October counts)

7.3 Total attendance at Christ Church, 1990–2001 73
(October counts)

8.1 The effect of Alpha on church attendance, 1989–98 82

9.1 The impact of ethnic mix on church attendance, 1989–98 88

10.1 Usual Sunday Attendance of children (under 16) in the 97
Church of England, 1910–2000

10.2 Percentage change in the uSa of children in East Riding 99
deaneries, 1998–9

10.3 Usual Sunday Attendance of children at large churches with 102
and without a professional youth and children's worker,
Diocese of St Albans, 1995 and 1999

10.4   Growth and decline in churches with and without a youth   104
        service, 1989–98

11.1   Church growth and decline in all denominations, 1989–98   109
        (grouped by size of church in 1989)

11.2   Adult attendance growth in the Diocese of Sheffield, 1982–8   111
        (grouped by size of church in 1982)

11.3   Diocese of York: annual percentage change in attendance at   113
        the larger churches and in the diocese as a whole, 1996–2000

11.4   Diocese of Lichfield: attendance growth and decline in   114
        parishes in different settings, 1995–8

11.5   Diocese of Guildford: percentage change in adult attendance,   115
        1997–9 (grouped by size of church in 1997)

11.6   Diocese of St Albans: change in adult uSa, 1991–9   115
        (grouped by size of church in 1991)

11.7   Diocese of Coventry: percentage change in adult attendance,   117
        1997–2000 (grouped by size of church in 1997)

12.1   Southern Baptist churches in the USA: baptisms p.a. per   134
        100 members (grouped by age of church)

12.2   Old churches shrink, new churches grow   136

12.3   Composition of newly planted churches in the UK   137

12.4   Percentage growth of church plants (by size of   139
        planting team)

13.1   Church growth and decline, all denominations, 1989–98,   147
        by percentage of congregation aged over 45

14.1   Age profile of recommended ordination candidates, 2000   158

14.2   Attendance growth and decline in C of E churches,   159
        1989–98, by age of incumbent in 1998

14.3   Attendance growth and decline in C of E churches,   160
        1989–98, by length of incumbency by 1998

15.1   Seven marks of a healthy church: expressing the life of   182
        Christ through the local church

Foreword

Most of us have an ill-defined but oppressively real sense of belonging to a Church in steady but inexorable decline. This book carries us, not into yet more vague and scary speculation, but into a more substantial world of the quantifiable and the verifiable. The sharp corners of this reality are every bit as painful but, given new shape and definition, our previously amorphous anxieties are robbed of their overpowering dread.

The statistics as a whole may still present a dismal picture, but closer analysis – and this is where Bob Jackson really comes into his own – reveals some genuine signs of hope and encouragement. Yes, the decline is real, but it is neither universal not is it inexorable. One church in five actually *grew* in the closing decade of the twentieth century, and among these were many of the tiny country churches which are generally perceived as being most at risk. Other churches whose congregations experienced serious decline have managed to reverse the trend with spectacular success.

However, there is no 'one size fits all' strategy for this success. Many different approaches have, in varying situations, helped turn things around, and their strength and their limitations are usefully evaluated in this book.

But most telling of all is the reminder that we can all learn from, and help, each other. Indeed, we must, for it is as unreasonable as it is unchristian to expect a diminishing and demoralized congregation to pull itself up buy its own bootstraps. But *together* – parish with parish, parish with deanery and parish with diocese – it can be done. It *can* be done and I am confident that it *will* be done – if, at the heart of what we are and of what we offer, there lies a vision of the mystery and majesty of the God whose love encompasses our every moment.

✠ David Ebor:
Archbishop of York

Preface

This book is full of surprises.

The first surprise is that it should have taken the Church of England so long to begin to address openly the subject of this book – namely, the decline in church attendance. That decline began back in 1904, so at least Bob Jackson cannot be accused of rushing things by addressing what the Church has, for a century, studiously avoided facing.

The next surprise is that a book about statistics – and church statistics at that – should be enjoyable to read. For many, statistics are dull, baffling or dubious. Some would use all three words. Yet this book makes those statistics not just understandable but full of insight and practical relevance – and not just for the Church of England but for all denominations, and further afield than the British Isles.

A further surprise is that a book about the decline in church attendance in the Church of England should be one shot through with hope. Its in-depth look at the facts of a century of declining church attendance does not end up daunting or depressing the reader but rather makes one aware that things can be different. This is not a book that bemoans the past or can see nothing but gloom in the future. Rather, facing the facts of decline, Bob Jackson develops a whole raft of seriously achievable options, drawing lessons from the 20 per cent of Anglican churches that have been growing in the last decade. These options are not wild dreams or 'if onlys' but specific and possible actions which some churches have already taken.

There has been a spate of books about the Church in recent years – I know, I have tried to keep up my reading of such works – but few can match the practical down-to-earth ideas communicated in this book. As the author himself puts it, 'there is no point in presenting the Church of England with an agenda it is incapable of delivering'.

I should not really have been surprised in all these ways since I have known Bob for over 20 years and have learned during that time to respect and enjoy his stimulating work on church statistics. We first met in the Sheffield Diocese when he was serving his first curacy in a nearby parish and I had just been made a rural dean. Since then I have read his articles in the Church press in which the patterns of growth and decline, first in the Sheffield Diocese, then in the York Diocese to which he moved, have been explored in some detail. When our paths have crossed I have been fascinated by the insights gained from his various pieces of research.

We first did a piece of work together for the larger churches of York Diocese, which was eventually published as a Springboard Resource Paper (*There Are Answers*) and is developed and expanded considerably in this work. We now find ourselves working for the same organization, namely Springboard, the Initiative for Evangelism of the Archbishops of Canterbury and York.

One of the key reasons for the stimulating nature of this book is Bob's great ability to read statistics well. Having studied economics and statistics at university and then spent six years as a civil servant handling the statistics of British Rail and devising railway policy out of them, it is perhaps not surprising. Yet it does surprise me and will no doubt have the same impact on many readers. This is probably because statisticians tend to treat facts – and the trends indicated by them – as fixed. This can make for a fatalistic and depressing reading of the figures.

Bob's approach is very different: 'history rarely proceeds in a single straight line and it is dangerous to forecast the future by extrapolating recent trends'. He is continually asking what the statistics are telling us and what we can do about them, seeing them as challenges rather than statements of the inevitable. This was brought home to me in a discussion I had with him about the research finding that whilst 27 per cent of churches with an incumbent aged *under* 55 were growing, only 16 per cent of churches with incumbents aged *over* 55 were growing. Being in the latter age bracket myself I made some comment about this giving me a whole new understanding of what it meant to be in my 'declining years'. Bob's response was creative and very different: 'Rather,' he said, 'it shows how important it is for dioceses to invest more time and support in older clergy and not just focus on the newly ordained – it is possible to keep the best wine for the end.'

It is that sort of positive, practical and achievable attitude that colours this whole work, which is why I am really pleased to have the opportunity to commend it to a wide readership. My hope is that it will go some considerable way to helping the Church – at all levels of its life – to dare to look the facts in the face. With the help of the thinking in this book, we should then be able to discover appropriate responses to the challenges we face.

Not everyone will agree with everything in this book. However, if it stirs up some to address the facts from a different perspective and to develop other courageous, mature and purposeful reflections on them, it will have served the Church well. For little is gained by denying that the facts matter, or whistling to keep our spirits up; and much – as this book so clearly indicates – is to be gained by honestly addressing uncomfortable facts and doing something about them.

It might even result in the biggest surprise of all – a turnaround in the fortunes of the Church.

Canon Robert Warren
Springboard Missioner

Author's preface

This book contains much practical detail, but just one simple argument: that the Church of England is in decline, and may die if it fails to acknowledge and address the seriousness of the situation. But decline is neither desirable nor inevitable. The power of the gospel always transcends the culture of society. In fact, some parts of the Church have already discovered ways to grow today. The book identifies a whole range of good practices that, if adopted widely, could turn around not just individual parishes but the whole Church of England. However, just as important as the discovery of 'technical' answers to the decline of the Church is the need for the spiritual heart and the underlying culture of the Church to respond to the challenges of the times. The Church of England is changing in many hopeful ways, but its decline will only be reversed if appropriate changes are pursued energetically in the coming years.

In offering statistical evidence for the effectiveness of good practices in the growth of the Church, I am conscious that I may appear to be suggesting that the fate of the Church is purely a matter of human effort or mechanical policy. Where do God or prayer come in? In fact, I once wrote a book about a church which had no strategy at all for good practices but seemed to grow through prayer and self-sacrifice,[1] and another which described the explosive growth of a whole national Church out of persecution, healings and charismatic revival.[2]

This present book does mention God from time to time, and it assumes that good Christians will continue to pray as though prayer was all that mattered. But primarily it urges Christians to use our God-given intelligence to analyse our situation logically, and so to seek out the pathways for growth that God has already excavated, and some have pioneered. In this way, the book seeks not merely to be technical but also to be prophetic. Although it is primarily about the Church of England, my hope is that other Churches may find that both the conclusions and the methodology are relevant to them. In addition, it is important to recognize that whereas *Hope for the Church* does dip both into the sociology of religion (in Chapter 6) and into ecclesiology, it is primarily intended as a practical tool for the working Church, turning facts and figures into operationally useful conclusions.

I am enormously grateful to a large number of people who have given their time and encouragement to helping me shape this book. In particular, I would like to thank Canon Robert Warren, who began this process with me in the writing of the Springboard booklet *There Are Answers*, which gave rise to this present volume. He has also contributed a number of important insights – and a preface – to this book. I am also grateful for the helpful comments and contributions of a number of people, including Professor Leslie Francis, Revd Dr Alison Morgan, Revd Robert Freeman, Revd Lynda Barley, Martin Cavendar, Revd George Lings, Peter Brierley, Katy Coutts, my daughter, Revd Ruth Jackson, and my wife Christine Jackson, and my publisher Kathryn Pritchard of Church House Publishing. I am also grateful to my teenage son, Joe, for his help in teaching an old man new tricks on the new-fangled laptop thingy that has recently replaced my quill pen. Needless to say, all contentious opinions and all mistakes are entirely my own responsibility!

1

Facing the truth

'You will know the truth, and the truth will set you free.' (John 8.32 NIV)

This chapter should not be read by Anglicans of a nervous disposition, because it gives the statistical evidence for an unpalatable truth: the Church of England is in decline, and has been for nearly a century. This truth is paraded in the newspapers and perceived by the populace. The Church is also, it would seem, prone to scandal and open to ridicule. It need be taken seriously no more – it is an outdated, discredited, dying institution that the country is walking away from without a backward glance. Or so it would seem. But truth is a slippery thing. Even Pontius Pilate knew that. Some Anglicans are tempted to ignore or deny the truth that everyone else 'knows'; others get depressed by it. Decline is hard to face and seems impossible to do anything about. Confidence is low and morale is fragile. Facing the possible demise of the Church they know and love, Anglicans are prone either to fall into a state of denial, or, if they do accept the truth about what is happening, to succumb to despair.

But there is another way. We can face the truth of decline head on. We can examine it, learn from it, and know it thoroughly. And then we can apply the lessons we have learnt and the encouragements we have discovered to break free of the cycle of decline. Courage to face the facts and confidence in God to set us free – that is the Christian way.

The statistical truth about decline is not as awful as the newspaper truth, but it is still bad. Those who like their Easter Sunday without their Good Friday should move straight on to the later chapters now. However, these may then make as little sense as did the Resurrection to those who had been out of town two days before. The Christian faith is all about good news arising out of bad news. Even Jesus had to face his crucifixion before he could be raised again. But if the start of this chapter is our book's Garden of Gethsemane, its destination is the hope of glory to come.

The Church of England measures its own size and activities in a number of ways. Table 1.1 shows the change in a number of these measures for the 1990s compared with the 1980s. Some official figures for 2000 had not been released at the time of writing. (Figures are often a year or two out of date by the time they are prepared and released, which makes it difficult for the Church to respond to them effectively.) So, in order to be able to compare the figures across the decades here, a few of those for the year 2000 are based on extrapolation of the 1990–99 trend.

Table 1.1 Decline in the Church of England, 1980–2000

	% change 1980–90	% change 1990–2000
Baptisms	−13	−24
Confirmations	−39	−43
Marriages	−11	−46
Stipendiary clergy	0	−15
Churches open	−3	−1
PCC voluntary income*	+42	+30
Electoral rolls**	−10	−13
Easter communicants	−11	−16
Christmas communicants	−14	−24
Adult attendance	−5	−14
Child attendance***	−17	−28
Total attendance	−8	−17

*At constant 1999 prices
**Adjusted for position in the six-year cycle
***Children are defined as under 16 years of age
Source: *Church Statistics and Statistics of Licensed Ministers*, annual official Church of England publications (various years) published by Church House Publishing.

Baptisms

As with most of the other figures, the number of baptisms fell faster in the 1990s than the 1980s. This is only partly due to the falling birth rate: the number of live births in England fell by 13 per cent between 1990 and 2000 and the number of infant baptisms per 1000 live births by 25 per cent. But the number of baptisms of children over one and of adults actually increased. The numbers of children may have risen because more and more babies are over twelve months old before their families get around to organizing their baptism. The number of 'adults' (aged 13 and over) baptized rose steadily, with a big jump from 8,380 in 1998 to 10,130 in 1999. This partly reflects the fact that a growing proportion of adults and teenagers were not baptized as babies, but may also be an encouraging sign that increasing numbers of people are willing to take the very public step of believer's baptism in the Church of England.

Confirmations

The number of confirmations fell away even more rapidly than infant baptisms. From 98,000 in 1980 they dropped to around 34,000 in 2000. Partly this may reflect a decline in the number of 'social' child confirmations, which have little to do with a quickening of Christian faith in the young person. However, this vast and continuing drop in the numbers of people willing to become members of the Church through confirmation has serious implications for its long-term future.

Marriages

The decline in the number of marriages conducted accelerated rapidly in the 1990s. The Church of England now marries only half the number of people it did ten years ago. Partly this is due to the falling number of marriages being contracted, but it is also due to a declining proportion being solemnized in the Church of England, mainly because of the rise in second marriages, few of which are conducted in church. During the decade the proportion of marriages conducted in the Church of England fell from over a third to about a quarter.

Stipendiary clergy

Following a period of stability in the 1980s, there was a significant fall in the number of stipendiary clergy in the 1990s. The number of full-time stipendiary clergy fell from 11,072 in 1990 to 9,538 in 2000, a fall of 14 per cent. The net decline is connected mainly to the age profile of the clergy, which meant a large number of retirements, but there was also a fall in the number of ordinations to the stipendiary ministry, from 361 in 1990 to 313 in 2000. Also, some stipendiary clergy – 395 by the year 2000 – resigned following the decision to ordain women to the priesthood. This represents about 25 per cent of the total net fall in the numbers of stipendiary clergy. It is important to note, however, that the decline in stipendiary clergy was offset by increases in the numbers of non-stipendiary clergy and of Readers. For example, in the three years 1997 to 2000 there was a net loss of 356 stipendiary clergy, but a net gain of 153 non-stipendiaries and Ordained Local Ministers, and a net gain of 422 Readers.

The fall in the number of stipendiary clergy was accompanied by a change in their age profile. Following the 1976 Synod Act, clergy have had to retire at 70, so there are far fewer elderly clergy in post. However, whereas in 1968 19 per cent of the (all-male) clergy were under 35, by 1999 this had fallen to under 7 per cent. The clergy have become more middle-aged, and some 52 per cent of the existing clergy are now over 50. One consequence of this demographic fact of life is that numbers of stipendiary clergy are forecast to continue falling for some years to come, perhaps at the rate of about 0.75 per cent per annum.

The rapid recent decline in the number of paid clergy has had various consequences. Pastoral reorganization has been needed to share out the ministry between fewer clergy, and many clergy have reported increased workloads and stress levels. Impetus has been given to the development of diocesan-sponsored local ministry teams in order to transfer ministry and workload to people who are unpaid but trained. The pensions bill of the Church has increased to such an extent that the net flow of funds from the central authorities to the dioceses has dried up. In fact, parishes are now making increasing net contributions to the pension fund each year. Clergy are beginning to be urged to invest in their own supplementary private pensions, though how this can be afforded out of a carefully calculated stipend that makes no allowance for such spending is one of life's mysteries. Finally, the fall in the number of paid clergy has also meant that an even greater financial crisis has been averted. Not only are there fewer stipends to find, there have also been many redundant parsonage houses to sell. At least some of the proceeds from parsonage sales, or the annual income from the capital invested, eventually find their way into unrestricted diocesan accounts and so into stipend provision.

The number of churches open

It is a striking fact of recent Anglican history that, although total church attendance has fallen by a quarter in the last 20 years, the number of churches open has hardly fallen at all. *At the start of the twenty-first century we do not have fewer churches, we have smaller congregations.* This may be connected with the fact that decline has been much more rapid in larger churches than in smaller ones (see Chapter 11). In fact very small congregations appear, on average, to have grown in the 1990s. This is the reason why those in the Church charged with the care and disposal of redundant churches have so far had far less work to do than they had imagined. Very few small congregations have dwindled sufficiently to close down. Rather, the traditionally strong have borne the brunt of the losses. However, sooner or later the process of decline must result in a much higher rate of church closures. An ever-dwindling number of Anglicans cannot keep the same number of buildings going indefinitely. Eventually, fewer and fewer Anglicans will have no time left for anything else – we will be crushed by our own heritage. Any future decline will increasingly mean fewer as well as smaller churches. And management of decline must increasingly involve the planned closure of many thousands of buildings.

When British Rail was privatized, the planning assumption was that the long-term decline in passenger and freight traffic would continue. Track capacity and the number of routes open, both of which had been dwindling for years, were expected to continue to decline. But, unexpectedly, traffic volumes began to rise again strongly. This has led to capacity problems – lack of space on the track for the new trains that operators would like to run. This is not the Church of England's problem. No Beeching Axe has yet fallen on the Church of England's branches. Although a lot of it may be in the wrong places, the spare capacity in the churches of the land is large enough to absorb the wildest of revivals. The point will need to be considered whether a future reduction in that capacity will leave the Church better able to respond to new demands and possibilities, or whether, like the railways, its withdrawal from many areas will weaken its capacity to respond to future growth in demand for its services.

Giving

The increase in the voluntary income of PCCs (mainly from congregational giving) is in complete contrast with the decline in other measures of the strength of the Church. *More and more money is being given by fewer and fewer people.* This, together with the fall in the number of clergy and the sale of several thousand vicarages, is the reason why the Church of England survived financially through the period. If giving had not risen in real terms and if the number of clergy wanting a post had not fallen there would perforce have been many unemployed clergy by now. Even in present circumstances many dioceses are starting to cut back on their stipendiary clergy for purely financial reasons. Moreover, it is unlikely that the rise in giving can continue at the rate of the recent past for very much longer because more and more Anglicans are now giving at realistic levels. Indeed, the increases are already showing signs of levelling off. From 1990 to 1995 voluntary income rose 19 per cent in real terms, but from 1995 to 2000 it rose only about 9 per cent. *The Church of England can only rely on increased congregational giving to keep on coming to the rescue in the future if the numbers in its congregations start to rise again.*

Membership

The Easter and Christmas communicant figures each give a sort of high water mark of adult church adherence. In both cases, decline in the 1990s was more rapid than in the 1980s. Electoral rolls are not very accurate measures of church membership because some attenders never bother to join rolls while some non-attenders do join them. For example, couples wanting to get married at a certain church will attend for a short while to join the roll and then remain on it until the next re-signing in six years' time. However, the roll is the best measure of current membership we have and it is possible when making comparison between years to make allowance for the different stages in the six-year cycle. The year everyone has to re-sign (1990, 1996, 2002, etc.), numbers go down dramatically, and then creep up again until the next re-signing year. The best estimate on this basis is that the number on electoral rolls went down by 13 per cent during the 1990s, compared with 10 per cent in the 1980s.

A wider measure of membership of the Church of England is that of the numbers of people baptized as Anglicans. It is estimated in *Religious Trends 2000/2001*[1] that there were 25.8 million baptized Anglicans in 1990, and 24.8 million in 2000, a drop of 4 per cent. However, this level of 'membership' holds little meaning for many of these people. It is surprising, for example, how many people today don't even know whether they have been baptized, let alone where. The number of baptized Anglicans still alive will, of course, continue to drop steadily for many years into the future in response to the reduction in the number of baptisms.

Frequency of church attendance

In the 1980s, numbers on electoral rolls actually declined faster (10 per cent) than adult attendance on a usual Sunday (5 per cent). In other words, membership fell faster than attendance. This suggests that, on average, the remaining people were coming more often, perhaps because those who left were the infrequent attenders. In the 1990s, however, the two figures showed a similar decline – 13 per cent for electoral rolls and 14 per cent for adult attendance. The numbers of Christmas and Easter communicants declined rather faster than the usual attendance figure – by 24 per cent and 16 per cent respectively. The fact that usual Sunday attendance fell at the same, or perhaps a slightly slower, rate as these three membership indicators is significant because it is often asserted that recent falls in Sunday attendance result not from fewer people being involved in churchgoing but from the same number coming less often. Busier lives mean people miss more Sundays than they used to. There has been a dramatic change in the nature of Sunday behaviour patterns among the population in general in recent years. A survey for the *Sunday Express* suggested that 55 per cent of the population now go shopping each Sunday. Many clergy have the sense that their people are coming to church less frequently than in the past. This can only be true globally if membership is falling less rapidly than attendance. But it is not – comparing the national statistics of membership and average attendance suggests that there has been no reduction in the average frequency of church attendance.

This theory of declining frequency has arisen partly as a result of certain deaneries and churches taking registers for a period of a couple of months or so and finding that more individuals were each coming less often than they had imagined. From this important finding some people have made the erroneous assumption that attendance frequency must have dropped because in the golden age of the past we know that everyone came every week. But we don't know that. Only a repeat survey can establish whether there is a trend or 'it was ever thus'. Almondbury Deanery in Wakefield Diocese conducted their first census in 1997, and then a repeat in 2000. The result was that there had been no significant change in attendance frequency. The one piece of evidence so far available from a repeat survey therefore tends to confirm the message of the global figures: falling attendance frequency is not the cause of declining average Sunday attendance. Yet many clergy believe from their own experience that frequency is certainly falling.

There is one possible explanation that reconciles the anecdotes with the statistical evidence. It may well be that people do not leave the Church suddenly. Few people move all at once from one steady state – attending every week – to another steady state – never attending. Rather, they erratically slide down the slippery slope from regular attendance to non-attendance. The average attendance frequency does not fall because other people who used to be occasional attenders (Christmas, Easter, etc.) stop coming altogether. But their disappearance has not been noticed as much by the clergy as has the more high-profile slide of regulars into infrequent attendance. So, in a declining Church many are getting less frequent and some are falling off the bottom. Perhaps younger adults with their more complicated lives are the most likely of all to drift away due to increasing infrequency. Both clergy anecdotes of falling frequency and the statistical fact of no average decline are correct in their own terms. Declining frequency, far from being an alternative explanation to that of people leaving the Church altogether, is in fact a description of the way they leave. It was ever thus. Doubtless the writer to the Hebrews had good and urgent cause to beg his church members, 'Let us not give up meeting together, as some are in the habit of doing' (Hebrews 10.25 NIV).

Even if there were an element of declining frequency in the overall attendance figures, this would not be joyous news. In fact it could be even more of a problem than having fewer numbers involved. Low frequency attendance makes pastoral care very difficult. It becomes impossible to know who is not in church because they are ill or in trouble. By the time someone has noticed that a person has not been around for a few weeks, the damage to the relationship could have been done. Intermittent churchgoers are easily lost. It is similarly difficult to teach systematically or to develop coherent fellowship or working groups. Gideon preferred to work with 300 reliable men rather than 32,000 unreliable ones, and it seems God may have put him up to it.

Usual Sunday Attendance and October counts

The measure used in Table 1.1 to provide the adult and child attendance figures is known as the Usual Sunday Attendance (uSa). For many years every parish has provided these figures on a standard form at the end of each year as their best estimate of their average attendance on an ordinary Sunday when there were no special features such as a festival or a baptism. This has been the principal statistic used to measure the size and the speed of decline of the Church. It is the one that makes the biggest newspaper headlines, and it has registered a national decline every year in recent times. The average rate of fall in the 1990s was just under 1.5 per cent per annum.

There are problems with the uSa measure, however. For example, there may be inconsistency in the way parishes interpret an 'average' Sunday: some may just make a guess, some may underestimate their figures in order to reduce their parish share. Most diocesan share allocation formulae take adult attendance into account when determining shares. This may tempt some hard-pressed parishes to be pessimistic in their average attendance estimate. Also, not all dioceses collect the figures in exactly the same way. Far more people come to church than is suggested by the uSa figure because not everyone comes every week, and because some people worship midweek. Perhaps the biggest problem is that uSa went down every year and so generated unwelcome 'decline' publicity for the Church. In 2000 the uSa question in the annual questionnaire to parishes was replaced by a count of people attending services on both Sundays and weekdays for each of four weeks in October. However, the uSa figure was still collected and used by some dioceses to help them calculate parish shares, and it was reinstated nationally in 2001 alongside the October count questions.

It is undoubtedly true that uSa is not a good measure of the total number of Anglicans. But it was never meant to be that. It measures the size of congregations. Worship is the central activity of the Christian Church, and uSa measures the worshipping strength of the Anglican Church. But more important than the actual numbers is the trend. The uSa appears to be a solid and reliable trend indicator because it is very stable year to year when all the parishes have been aggregated. Aggregation cancels out the random errors made by parishes. It is intrinsically unlikely that parish returns underestimate their real attendance by a bigger and bigger proportion with each succeeding year. There is no evidence that an October count or any other measure would have produced a different trend in the 1990s from that of uSa. Its trend is very much in line with the other indicators in Table 1.1. The downward trend of children attending, who do not count towards parish share, is steeper than that of adults. It is safe, therefore, to take uSa as a reasonably reliable measure of the past trend in church attendance. To ignore or deny the trend because of claimed flaws in the statistical series is to ignore or deny the truth it is telling us.

The Octoberr count carries with it the advantage of measuring midweek attendance as well as Sundays, but also allows us to view fluctuations in attendance from week to week. Parishes are asked to take care in actually counting attenders on specific occasions, rather than simply invited to estimate an annual average.

The results of the first October count, for 2000, were published in spring 2002. The numbers of adults attending church were higher than the 1999 uSa by 10 per cent, partly because October is a slightly better than average month for churchgoing. Also, numbers attending 'special' services such as harvest are included in the October count, though they were excluded from the uSa figures up to 1999. Total numbers also rose because midweek churchgoing, including weddings and funerals, was included for the first time. The results are summarized in Figure 1.1, and compared with the uSa figures for 1999. The most significant extra midweek churchgoing appears to be that of children – an extra 35 per cent on top of the Sunday numbers. However, most of this seems to have come from the week of maximum attendance, when there were 300,000 children on the Sunday and an extra 155,000 midweek. It is likely that this large extra number is connected with annual school harvest services rather than with worship events that take place every week or even every month.

It is important to be clear that this definitional change does not mean that the numbers of people attending church in the real world have gone up. The

Figure 1.1 Usual Sunday Attendance, 1999, October 2000 Sunday count and October 2000 all-week count

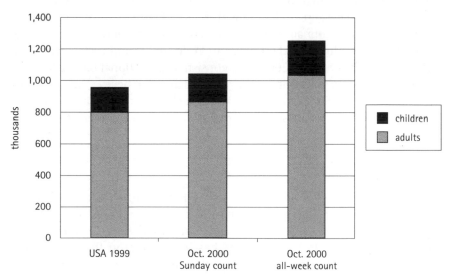

downward movement may well be resumed in 2001 when like is again compared with like. However, the trend may not become apparent for some years because October counts may be more volatile than annual averages. In a year when 1 October is a Sunday there may be more harvest festivals than when the 7th is a Sunday. In some years school half term will fall on the third and fourth Sundays, in others on the fourth and fifth. Weather patterns make a small difference – autumn gales and floods can reduce churchgoing on certain Sundays. One-off events can also skew the count in individual years. It is thought that churchgoing rose in response to the events of 11 September 2001, and this may have inflated the October 2001 count.

When the results of the first October count were announced, some were tempted to say, 'Good news, there are more of us on the *Titanic* than we thought'. But we can only announce the end of decline when uSa itself, or the October count, start to turn round.

Midweek churchgoing

It is sometimes suggested that the actual decline in church attendance is not as steep as the Sunday figures suggest because there has been an increase in churchgoing on other days of the week. There is much talk of changing patterns rather than declining totals. However, there is little evidence at the moment to support this. Midweek attendance is nearly 14% of the total, and so is not insignificant. There must be considerable scope in today's seven-days-a-week twenty-four hour world for more weekday worship. Many people now work on Sundays. But equally there may be many traditional midweek 'Prayer Book Communion' services in decline, offsetting the rise of the new. The net picture is as yet unknown because of definitional changes between the 2000 and 2001 October count questionnaires, which have asked about midweek attendance for the first time. However, the Church in Wales did record a 4% increase in midweek attendance 2000–2001 on a consistent definitional basis and some survey results show significant numbers of churches that believe their midweek attendance is rising. So far the scale may be small and the facts uncertain, but there must clearly be future scope for growth in midweek church attendance.

The disappearing children

The decline shown by the uSa figures in the number of children (defined as under-16s) attending church in the 1990s was double that of adults. *Between one in three and one in four children disappeared from Sunday church between 1990 and 2000.* This decline has been going on for so long that there are now also far fewer younger adults in church life. For every 100 children in Church of England churches in 1930, today there are 9. Congregations across the land who once found themselves with no one in their twenties now have no one in their thirties or forties either. According to *Religious Trends* the average age of Anglicans in 1980 was 36, today it is about 47. In 1980, one in five Anglicans was aged 65 or over, today it is one in three. The ageing of Anglicans is both a major consequence of and a contributor to decline in church attendance. A major research finding (reported in Chapter 13) is that older congregations are far more likely to be in decline than those with a mix of ages. And there is also a demographic time bomb built into the age structure of the Church of England nationally. Very few adults without a Sunday school background become worshippers in later life. Most people who begin churchgoing as adults are returning to the Church of their childhood. The massive missionary challenge posed by generations growing up without childhood involvement has not so far been met. The age structure of congregations today, and in particular the absence of children, therefore appears to have future decline already built into it unless this missionary challenge can be met.

What does the future hold?

Decline in church attendance was more rapid in the 1990s than in the 1980s. But what was the trend through the 1990s? Figures 1.2 and 1.3 show a similar pattern for both adults and children. Using a three-year total smoothes out annual variations and allows trends to be seen more clearly. The rate of decline

Figure 1.2 Percentage change in adult attendance over successive three-year periods, 1989–99

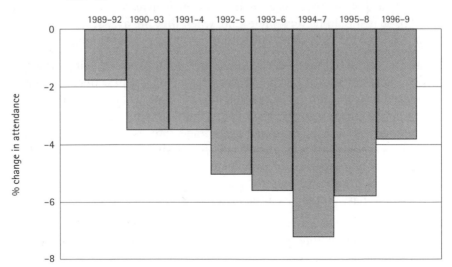

Figure 1.3 Percentage change in child attendance over successive three-year periods, 1989–99

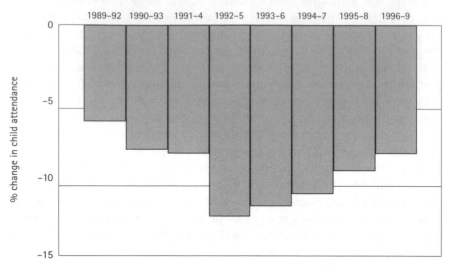

seems to have accelerated up to the mid-1990s, but decelerated again at the end of the decade. The Church is still getting smaller, but at a somewhat slower rate. What the decline rate will be from 2000 onwards will be quite hard to estimate from the October counts. Apart from the problem of estimating the change from 1999 to 2000, October counts, as explained above, will be more volatile from year to year. It will be some years before it will be clear what the October counts are telling us about the long-term attendance trend. Evidence from eight dioceses which continued to collect uSa figures for adults in 2000, however, suggests that the slowing down of attendance decline has continued. In fact, these dioceses together even showed a small increase in adult attendance in 2000. So it should be very interesting, when they are available, to compare the uSa figures for 1999 and 2001 with the 2000–01 October count changes.

Given the recent history of decline in church attendance, it is important to consider how much the Church of England will shrink if past trends continue unchecked into the future. Figure 1.4 shows the projections for attendance of adults and children on the assumption that in future decades attendance decline will continue at the same percentage rate as in the 1990s. These projections are not forecasts, they simply show what would happen if future decades were like the one just completed. They are simply illustrative of the sort of future decline we might expect if the future is rather like a certain period of the past. In practice it hardly ever is.

They suggest an adult attendance figure in 2030 of about 500,000, less than two-thirds of the number going to church in 2000. Child attendance would fall to almost nothing. Total attendance in 2030 would be under half what

Figure 1.4 C of E attendance projections to 2030 (at a constant percentage rate of decline)

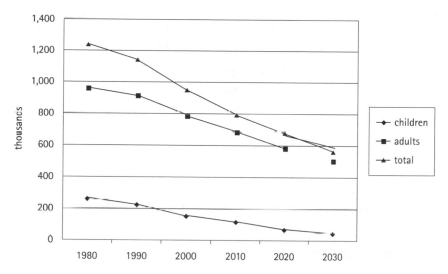

it was in 1980. Different assumptions would produce different projections, with decline being either more or less rapid. Whatever the details, however, such a reduced Church of England would look radically different from that of today. One possibility is that thousands of churches and many dioceses would have disappeared altogether. However, as we will see in Chapter 11, the very smallest congregations usually cling tenaciously to life, so it is possible that few church buildings would actually be closed even if total numbers were half what they are today. Instead, as we have already suggested, the Anglicans of 2030, in a myriad tiny congregations, could be struggling to maintain their buildings in a thinly spread church crushed by the weight of its own heritage. Unless the Church of England successfully tackles its decline problem, one of these outcomes is likely. In any organization, to have no strategy with which to counter decline is to follow a recipe for its continuance. *Given that church attendance has been declining for nearly a century, it could be argued that the formulation of an anti-decline strategy by the Church of England is somewhat overdue.*

It could, however, also be argued that decline will plateau out without any need for strategy. Perhaps God will never let the Church of England decline unto death. Unfortunately, history does not support this theory – it is littered with defunct churches. The attitude of the Spirit to the churches of Asia was that he would send them on their way to extinction unless they mended their ways (Revelation 3.1-3,14-16). Their salvation was in their own hands.

Or perhaps the spirit of the age will change back in the Church's favour. People will flock back to an unreformed Church of England as postmodernism loses its grip. Unfortunately, all the signs are that our society will continue to move away from the traditional, institutional Church. The times never adapt to the Church, the Church always has to adapt to the times.

Or perhaps, when only hard-core Christians and the successful churches are left, then decline will cease. Unfortunately, the evidence suggests the reverse will be the case. Areas of the country where the decline in church attendance has gone furthest are declining just as fast as areas that still have high church-going rates. For example, the place with the lowest proportion of Anglicans, and of churchgoers in general, is Hull. Only about 0.7% of the population of Hull is to be found in Anglican churches on an average Sunday. This is less than half the national average. Yet adult attendance in Hull in the 1990s fell by about 21%, which is half as fast again as the national average.

But there is still hope

It is important to set the decline of the Church of England in the context of general church experience in recent years. In the 1980s, total adult attendance in all denominations fell about 8 per cent, compared with only 5 per cent for the Church of England. In the 1990s, however, the Anglican decline (14 per cent) was about average. Roman Catholic and Methodist decline was rather faster, and other denominations' rather slower, as shown by Figure 1.5. There

Figure 1.5 Adult attendance in selected denominations, 1990 and 2000

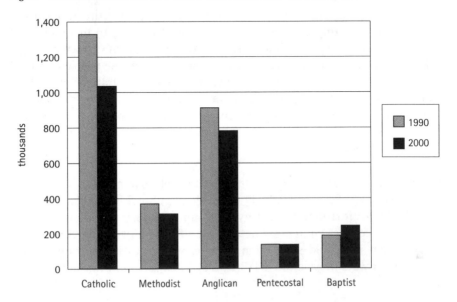

14

are, however, a number of exceptions to the general rule of decline. The Baptists saw their attendance figures rise slightly during the 1990s. They live in the same world and culture as Anglicans, so if cultural change made decline inevitable, the Baptists would have been in decline as well. In fact, at the start of the 1990s the Baptist Church framed some clear policies for future growth, including organizational reform and church planting, which have seen them through to something like success.

Other reasons for hope of growth in the future come simply from examining the Church of England's own statistics in a little more detail. Each of these will be dealt with more fully in later chapters, but it is worthwhile summarizing them at this stage in order to show how knowing the truth of decline can start to set us free from its grip. *The general finding is that decline is not uniform. It is patchy.* The English Church Census data for 1989 and 1998 suggest that one in five Anglican churches grew their attendance by more than 10 per cent between those dates. One in twelve grew their attendance by over 60 per cent. The Church of England's own attendance statistics, further-more, show huge variations in trends between different dioceses. If decline were inevitable due to a changing world then it would be fairly uniform as the whole world changes together. But it is not. Some categories of church, and churches in some denominations, areas and dioceses, are doing better than others. This means that parts of the Church are performing differently in today's environment than are other parts. This in turn means that some churches are finding answers to the question of how to grow. Perhaps those answers can be discovered and disseminated to help the rest of the Church grow as well.

In summary, the three main concentrations of contrasting growth and decline within the Church of England are:

1. *Some dioceses*: from 1989 to 1999 London Diocese gained an extra 4 per cent in child attendance and 12 per cent in adult attendance, while Durham lost 42 per cent of its children and 28 per cent of its adults.

2. *Younger people*: in the same period, Truro Diocese lost 48 per cent of its children but only 12 per cent of its adults.

3. *Larger churches*: six out of ten tiny churches (average attendance ten or less) grew their attendance between 1989 and 1998, but three out of four of the largest churches (400+) were in decline.

If something is broken, you must find out where it is broken before you can mend it. Sometimes this is difficult, but it is never impossible. If your bucket leaks, there is no point trying to mend the whole bucket. You look for the hole and mend that. If your bicycle tyre is flat, it can be tricky to find the puncture in the inner tube with the help of a bowl of water, but then you only need to patch one hole rather than buy a new inner tube. If a chain of shops – Marks & Spencer, for example – is losing custom, their head office will quickly track down which shops, products, customers and local managers are associated with the decline. Remedial action, an anti-decline strategy, will have to follow if the chain of shops is to survive.

The Church of England's bucket has been leaking for years. Some, averting their gaze, have said, 'I see no leaks.' Others have said, 'The leaks don't matter, it's the bucket that counts.' Others have said, 'It's only a slow leak and there will still be some water in the bucket when I retire.' Still others have said, 'There is nothing you can do to stop a postmodern bucket leaking.' *Surprisingly, few have thought to find out where the holes are with a view to mending them.*

'The people of this world are more shrewd in dealing with their own kind than are the people of the light' (Luke 16.8 NIV). We have much to learn from Marks & Spencer. The Church of England is not shot through with a myriad of unmendable small holes. It has certain specific large holes that can be tackled – some dioceses, children and large churches being perhaps the most obvious. And some areas of the bucket are in good shape. If the rest of the bucket can become like them, the Church will grow strongly. This is how knowing the truth will set us free.

•

2

Bums on seats – why they matter

'The harvest is plentiful but the workers are few. Ask the Lord of the harvest, therefore, to send out workers into his harvest field.' (Matthew 9.37,38 NIV)

There has long been resistance within the Church to giving priority to addressing its decline in membership and attendance. The peak year for church attendance per head of population was 1904, and since then the Church has rarely given the impression that it is working on a new strategy for growth. Part of the resistance to addressing the issue of decline comes from distrust of the statistics. The contention that they are either unclear or unimportant or not the whole picture was dealt with in the first chapter. It should no longer be possible to be in denial of the basic fact that the Church is shrinking. But there are also some theological objections, which suggest that the study of the growth and decline of the Church is not a proper subject for the Church's scrutiny. The core task of the Church is to serve the kingdom rather than recruit people to its worship services. This gives rise to that classic piece of oft-repeated conventional wisdom, 'I'm not interested in numbers of bums on seats.' At least four arguments are used to justify this lack of interest:

Argument 1: the kingdom matters, not the Church

Jesus came proclaiming the kingdom of God. It was the great theme of his ministry and preaching. The Church, so the argument runs, should pay more attention to God's work in the world than to matters of parish shares, attendance returns, and the counting of heads. This raises the question of the relationship between the Church and the kingdom. Part of the low view of the Church expressed in the phrase 'bums on seats' is also evident in the contrast between 'Church' and 'kingdom'. The kingdom is seen as the good thing, the Church as the dubious commodity. Yet in the New Testament the Church is seen both as a sign of the kingdom and as a means of the kingdom of God doing its work in the world around us. The writer of Revelation sees the seven frail churches to whom Christ sends his letters in this way. They are called to embody something of his truth and revelation, but also to share in his wider purposes in the world.

So, although the Church is not the same as the kingdom, it is not irrelevant to the kingdom. It is more like a pilot project or base camp for the kingdom. It is a community called to engage with God in the work of building his kingdom in the world. Christ called his disciples to preach and to live the kingdom. To that end he called them into the community of faith that is the Church. The smaller and more dispirited that community becomes, the fewer the people who enter it, the less use it is to the kingdom. The Church is also the Bride of Christ – a loving partner in whom the risen Christ takes a deep pleasure, whose worship he revels in, and whose co-operation in the work of the kingdom he covets. How can Christ take pleasure from the wasting away of his Bride? How can he fail to rejoice in her growth and rejuvenation?

Today, it is reckoned that many people come to Christian faith and conviction through a long process that begins with some initial contact with the Church. This may be by coming to a church service with a friend, or just by attending a parent and toddler group in the church hall. The attraction that began with the church community leads eventually to a living faith. In a secularized society where Christian values and morality are no longer normative, living like a Christian is likely to come only after believing as a Christian. In other words, the typical sequence is belonging ... believing ... behaving. The kingdom of heaven as the rule of God in the hearts of humans is evidenced by their behaviour. Kingdom behaviour can only be expected of those who have started to belong to the Church and to believe the faith. Most people only become subjects of the kingdom once they have become members of the Church.

Christ spent his earthly ministry holding in tension the building of the twelve into a prototype community of faith, the communication of God's truth and love to the crowds who hung upon his words, and a prophetic challenge to the centres of power. It was this last element that led to his crucifixion. He understood the vital strategic importance of his frail community of disciples, and devoted himself to nurture and prepare it for the mission that lay ahead. Too exclusive a focus on the kingdom is as antithetical to the practice of Christ as is too narrow a focus on the Church. We must focus on both the Church and the kingdom.

Argument 2: quality, not quantity

What matters most in the coming of God's kingdom, it is argued, is the quality of what is done and said, not the quantity. Jesus was a lone voice crying out for justice and peace in a hostile world. It was the quality of his commitment to that cause which, in the providence of God, won the day. So too, runs the argument, should those with responsibility in the Church pay more attention to the quality of what is done than to the number of people participating.

Jesus taught us to see the mustard seed – the smallest type of seed – as a sign of the kingdom. He spent a disproportionate amount of time with the twelve he had chosen. He seemed uninterested in popular acclaim – in fact he often escaped from the crowds. He went for quality every time.

That is true, of course, but Jesus' mission was to prepare his followers for the harvest to come. The point about the mustard seed is that this tiniest of seeds is capable of extraordinary growth. His focus on quality was not due to indifference to how many heard and responded to what he had to say, rather it was the fruit of his recognition that quality is the best way to achieve quantity. The prayer he taught us to pray for the harvest was all about quantity: 'The harvest is plentiful but the workers are few. Ask the Lord of the harvest, therefore, to send out workers into his harvest field' (Matthew 9.37,38 NIV).

Healthy organizations are concerned about falling numbers. They have to be. Sometimes there is a limited amount that can be done: the Miners' Union decline in membership, for example, was the inevitable result of pit closures. It may be that the decline in the number of marriages conducted in Anglican churches falls into a similar category, and that, at least in the short term, it may not be sensible for the Church to devote a lot of resources directly to reversing a trend that is so strongly driven by social change. More often, however, if an organization is to survive it has to make major adjustments. Not so long ago, the cinema industry was facing extinction. It reversed its long-term trend of attendance decline by building cinemas that were more attractive and had more screens. No longer did people simply have to take or leave the one show that was on offer, they could make their own choice of what to watch. And they could watch in comfort as well. 'Cinemas as we knew them' have largely gone to the wall, but a new, and better, sort of cinema has taken their place. As a consequence, cinema attendances have been rising again for a number of years.

It is possible that 'church as we knew it' will go to the wall. But it is equally possible to prevent the demise of the Church by offering a better-quality product with greater choice. Quantity matters, and quality is the solution to it.

Argument 3: small is often beautiful

It is estimated by those who have studied these things that not more than 7 or 8 per cent of the Roman Empire professed faith in Christ prior to the Constantinian settlement. That is less than the number of churchgoers in the UK today. A relatively small number, by the sheer quality and courage of their faith, turned a whole empire upside down. Then, after Constantine established

Christendom, thousands more flooded into the churches. Yet that growth seems to have been achieved at the cost of quality. In Nazi Germany it was the small, despised and persecuted 'Confessing Church' that held fast to the faith when the great majority of churchgoers succumbed to the seduction and pressure of Nazism. Examples like these fuel the argument that small is beautiful where the Church is concerned.

It is also the case that church attendance is very high in certain parts of the world today, yet from the outside, those societies seem surprisingly unaffected by this phenomenon. In Rwanda leading up to the atrocities, in apartheid South Africa, and in Northern Ireland there have been very high levels of church affiliation yet striking amounts of injustice and division. Uganda and South Africa have the highest rates of churchgoing in Africa, and also the highest incidence of AIDS. The United States has about the highest level of churchgoing in the West, yet it is not obviously any more Christian in its values than anywhere else. Attendance at church seems to have only a limited impact on the morality and values of the culture in which it takes place.

Yet the fact that churchgoing on a large scale may not transform a nation does not mean that it does no good. A larger, more dominant 'Confessing Church' might have been a more effective countervailing force against Nazism. The strength and weight of the numbers involved in the Jubilee 2000 Campaign has had considerable impact on international debt reduction. How many Anglicans would seriously argue that a smaller Church is preferable because it will have greater influence on society? We do not have to choose between a Church that is large and a Church that is faithful – we should work for one that is both large *and* faithful.

Argument 4: the Church for others

William Temple famously remarked that 'the Church is the only organization that exists primarily for the benefit of non-members'. The Church of England believes itself called to exercise a mission for the whole 'parish', irrespective of whether or not people come to church. The primary concern in the conduct of weddings and funerals is to make the service a meaningful reflection on that particular rite of passage for those taking part. Getting people at vulnerable points in their lives to 'sign up' for regular churchgoing can simply be taking advantage of them. Similarly, the pastoral care expressed by visiting the sick in hospital would be abused by a direct challenge to them to attend church next Sunday. This would be a distortion of the task, which is – without strings attached – to help the person come to terms with their current experience of life. The true calling of the church, so our fourth argument goes, is to care for others, not to market itself.

And yet, though the Church is called to stand alongside other caring bodies in service to all, it is also an agent of the kingdom. The greatest benefit the Church has to offer non-members is that which is most precious to Christians – the eternal love of God in Christ found in the worshipping, kingdom-building life of the Christian community. Where is the care for others in not inviting them to find this joy, and join in this ministry, for themselves?

Many Anglicans enjoy the old adage that clergy are like manure: pile them up in one place and they will create a stink, but spread them thinly over the ground and they will do a lot of good. But imagine a country without any clergy to teach the faith, lead the Church, comfort the distressed, and bury the dead. Such a country, where the churches are too weak to support paid clergy, would also have so few lay Christians remaining to be salt in society that their influence, too, would be lost. Bishop Nigel McCullough, on arriving in Wakefield Diocese in 1992, took a careful look at the attendance figures for the diocese over recent years and concluded that, if such a rate were to continue, there would be no 'Diocese of Wakefield' by 2014. Hence the call to become a 'Missionary Diocese'. This is a diocese that decided that its own future was important. It has shown it *does* care that it may soon cease trading as 'the Church for others', and the steps it has taken appear to be arresting its decline.

Underlying motives

Having examined these four arguments in more detail, we now need to look at what may be a more fundamental attitude behind them. It may be that the reason some people refuse to take the problem of the decline in church attendance seriously is not because of theological conviction at all but because of despair – despair that anything can be done about it. This can lead to a fatalistic attitude: 'This is the way things are so there is no point in thinking or worrying about it – it is a fact of life that bums disappear from seats.' Or they try to persuade themselves that the problem that cannot be cured does not matter so much after all: 'We may be thinner on the ground, but we can still fulfil our calling', they say. Either way, it seems that denying the seriousness of the situation may be the best protector of morale there is when remedies seem unavailable. This may be understandable, but it represents a serious lack of confidence in God, the faith, the Church and the good news of Jesus Christ. The way to help the Church regain its confidence is not to shield it from the truth but to lead it into growth.

There has also been a tendency recently to emphasize the good news about the Church and downplay the bad, in order to promote a good image of the institution in the press and in the country. This is an understandable temptation, but it doesn't work, partly because the press are not stupid, and partly because it is still failing to address the problem. We need to face up to our problems, not spin away from them. It is most encouraging that the report *Statistics for Mission* was adopted by General Synod in July 2000, for that acknowledges that paying attention to the number of bums on seats is important to the future mission of the Church.

Parish clergy sometimes find it hard to face up to the reality of decline in church attendance because it feels like personal failure, when in fact it is more likely that the system has failed and the clergy are some of the victims of that failure. Rather than avoiding confronting uncomfortable truths, it is much healthier for clergy and church councils honestly to face the trends and tackle them together.

Serious consequences

Ironically, it is often the case that Church leaders who downgrade the importance of bums on seats actually spend vast amounts of their time dealing with the retrenchment and reorganization that result from fewer people belonging to and attending church. They daily handle the consequences of decline yet shy away from fighting the decline itself. Instead, denying the importance of numbers becomes a way of not having to face up to corporate failure. It can sometimes be all too easy to allow the *urgent* problem of attending to the consequences of decline (e.g. pastoral reorganization, financial crisis) to squeeze out any attention to the *important* problem of reversing it.

But this book demonstrates that decline is not inevitable. We know this because it is not universal. There are many things that churches do do, and that the Church as a whole can do, that will make a difference. Overall growth is a realistic possibility. However, the fact remains that one of the most serious impediments to growth in the Church is the Church's failure to look decline in the face and do something about it.

In the business world, it is reckoned that the moment a company abandons its research and development work and stops trying to improve its product, its days are numbered. The Church of England has yet to set up its R & D department. It is, of course, true that the Church is not a business operation, and in one sense the product is God-given and immutable. But it is not less than a business. It is much more than one. It has a profound duty to the people it serves and would like to serve. Therefore, it needs not less but more courage than a business to research its problems and opportunities and develop solutions to them. Only a Church that faces up to its problems and opportunities will be able to do this. Before it is too late, the culture of the

Church needs to change to make research and development of its own life a priority.

Why numbers are important

It is true that fixation with numbers per se is unhealthy. Evangelism is about sharing the good news of God's love and his care for all creation, but if the Church uses evangelism purely as a means to the end of church growth, the message proclaimed can easily get distorted. It has been said that the best thing that ever happened to evangelism in the 1990s was the Church Commissioners' loss of £800 million, because it forced the Church to go out and look for alternative means of finance. It is actually impossible to establish whether this event had *any* effect on the work of evangelism. But if it did drive some to a desperate recruiting drive to pay the bills, it was not good news. Churches that major on 'church growth' are often driven communities with a tendency to get people in and then to use them, perhaps as fodder for empire building. Furthermore, playing the numbers game in a very focused way often does not actually result in much numerical growth.

The argument of this book is that quantitative growth is best not tackled directly – it will be a spin-off from qualitative growth. If we aim to improve the *quality* of church life in relevant ways, then the numbers will follow.

If we agree that the importance of growing numbers of adherents and attenders does not lie in the propping up of the institution of the Church, exactly why do we consider numbers so vital? There are four main reasons for this.

1. Increasing numbers is likely to be a sign of quality, of spiritual health, of good practices. The Church is getting something right, is making others want to join it, and we should rejoice over that.
2. The number of people involved in church life is the best indicator we have of the number of people with a living Christian faith who are part of the Body of Christ. We seek the joy in heaven and the joy in human hearts that comes from the Church's ministry of reconciliation of humans with God. Increasing the numbers of bums on seats is a worthy aim if it is an indicator of growing numbers of subjects of the kingdom of heaven.
3. The number involved in church life is a measure of the potential of the Church to do the work of the kingdom. The power of the Church to do good in the world is controlled and measured, in substantial part, by its size. A tiny Church might still be a pinch of salt in society, but a large Church has a greater chance of salting it thoroughly.
4. Perhaps the major reason why the Church of England has a hard time in

the public arena is the general perception of its decline. If it were generally known as a resurgent, growing Church then its representatives and what they stand for would be taken much more seriously by the media and the country.

So, a growing national Church indicates improving church health, successful evangelism, and greater kingdom-effectiveness.

Getting the balance right

So we are left with an apparent dilemma. Trying to increase the number of bums on seats as an end in itself can seriously distort the good news of Jesus Christ. But failure to pay attention to the issue is an even more serious threat to the well-being, even the very existence, of the Church. How do we find our way out of this impasse? The key is to pay attention to numbers within a larger and more holistic framework.

If I am overweight, there are several things I can do about it. An easy short-term solution would be to deny there is a problem, get rid of all the mirrors in the house, and continue with my existing lifestyle. Another response would be to despair of any solution: my metabolism is to blame, and there is nothing I can do about that. The result would be the same – I would continue to live as I did before. A third response would be to focus exclusively on the issue of weight. I could do this most comfortably by visiting a sauna and only weighing myself at the end of each visit. Sweating off a few pounds would bring my weight down. But it would not address the real issue – it would just make me feel good. Starving myself for a week or two would also bring my weight down in the short term – but the experts tell us that in the long term such shock tactics do no good. The best solution would be to adjust my regular diet and take more exercise every day – to make long-term changes to my lifestyle so that my weight is no longer a major issue. I would then just need to check my weight from time to time, whilst getting on with the things that really matter in life.

In other words, when a quantity issue (weight) threatens my quality of life (health, longevity, peace of mind, self-acceptance), the best way to address the quantity (and ultimately secondary) issue is to make some quality (lifestyle) changes. Then the quality issues can take centre stage because the quantity problem has been resolved. Similarly, the healthy response to the Church's quantity problem (lack of numbers) is to set it within a quality context. The quantity problem can be addressed by focusing on a quality solution. Put right the underlying quality factors, and the quantity will take care of itself. A frantic fortnight of evangelism once in a while will achieve very little – what is needed is a change of emphasis over a longer period of time.

This is the understanding at the heart of the 'Natural Church Development' movement in general, and the practice of 'Growing Healthy Churches'[1] in particular. If we work to raise the health and quality of the Church, paying attention to numbers within that broader framework, then we are more likely to see churches growing again than we are either by treating numbers as irrelevant or as an end in themselves. Moreover, this will enable us to deal with situations where churches are healthy but, for valid reasons like depopulation, are not seeing numerical growth. If the primary focus is on health not numbers, inappropriate judgements are less likely to be made.

The interplay between quality and quantity can be seen in the current focus of work in the Wakefield Diocese, which was mentioned earlier. Here the issue of numerical decline has been addressed head on, and solutions worked out, over a sustained period. Currently the diocese is working on the interweaving of four themes:

1. that the faith be taught
2. that congregations grow
3. that giving increases
4. that communities be served.

Two quality issues (teaching the faith and serving communities) and two quantity issues (giving and church attendance) are being worked out together. In doing so, the relationship between churchgoing, communicating the faith and serving communities is clearly established.

The senior staff of the diocese are currently paying their third visit in nine years to every parish in order to help churches address each of these themes. The local church decides the order in which the subjects will be tackled. The procedure is time-consuming for the seven senior staff involved, and it has achieved no instant turnaround. But the statistical evidence does suggest that nine years of this straightforward, holistic approach to the issues is bearing fruit in this 'missionary diocese'. We will look at this further in Chapter 4.

What is happening at diocesan level in a few places is also happening in many parishes across the country. It is worth remembering that, according to the English Church Census data, one in five Anglican churches grew their attendance by over 10 per cent between 1989 and 1998, in a period of general decline. It is likely that the morale, faith level and kingdom-effectiveness of these parishes is greater than most of the parishes that are experiencing numerical decline.

So we must conclude that there are indeed valid reasons for being wary of too narrow a focus on church attendance figures alone. But this is hardly the

Church of England's current danger. It is even less appropriate to pay no attention to, and do nothing about, declining church attendance. This is especially so when it is becoming evident that decline can be reversed. The best approach to church statistics is to hold the quality and quantity issues together in creative tension. In this way the Church can tackle the problem of decline before it is completely decimated by it.

3

Church growth – mission possible

'Consider the lilies of the field, how they grow; they toil not, neither do they spin.' (Matthew 6.28 AV)

Growth is not only possible, it is also the natural condition of the Church, and it is already widespread. Such optimism may seem inappropriate in the light of the trends we have already discussed and the paralysing reactions of denial, despair and inaction we have seen within the Church. Hope, however, does not arise *ex nihilo*. First, it springs from the fundamental belief that the Christian Church has a God-given growth dynamic at its core. Secondly, it comes from the fact that substantial pockets of growth already exist within the declining Church, they can be unearthed by a more detailed investigation of the facts, and they point the way to growth for the Church as a whole. When it comes to church decline, the devil has the headline but the Lord is in the detail.

The faithlessness of despair

After a century in which church attendance declined slowly, and some years of more rapid decline, it is easy to give way to despair. The pace of change in society gets ever faster. All institutions are in long-term irreversible retreat. We have tried everything already and it didn't work. The social climate is becoming ever more indifferent, even hostile, to the Christian faith. The Church has lost the respect it once had as a pillar of institutional England. Generations are growing up with no knowledge or experience of church, Bible or Jesus Christ. People might be interested in spirituality but they are losing interest in religion. In short, Jesus has become increasingly irrelevant to the modern world. He no longer meets their needs. How can the Church do anything other than shrink, and hang on by its fingernails if it can? It is the hapless victim of Jesus' irrelevance to contemporary culture.

Christians who believe this have swallowed the devil's big lie. Decline cannot be primarily the result of modern humanity moving on from Jesus, no longer in need of the Christian God. The Christian conviction is that God has made himself known in Christ and by the Holy Spirit for all people for all time. It is this conviction that compels us to find ways to make Christ known in every generation, to every human heart that is restless until it finds its rest in God; and so it will be to the end of time.

The labels we now give to succeeding generations – 'Generation X', 'Mosaics', etc. – certainly help us understand the frames of reference that shape the world views and life experience of different age groups, but there are dangers in this labelling. There is meaning in the idea of 'postmodern times', but danger in the concept of 'postmodern man', which can make the labelled seem like a human mutation, a new sub-species that will be impervious to the gospel. It loses sight of the fact that each unique individual is created in the image of God. 'Postmodern Man' is not a new missing link, its God-gene removed by evolution, whose novel skeleton will be found in the Thames Rift Valley in three million years' time. He is a figment of sociologists' imaginations. Real people born in recent times do indeed think in some interesting ways, but they are the same usual vast array of human individuals for whom Christ died. Our message that God can be known, in Christ and through the Spirit, is timeless in its relevance. Finding ways of communicating this faith afresh is the challenge to every age and Church, but such encounters with God are taking place in all generations all the time. If we thought otherwise, we would have lost our faith in God, humanity or both. Goodbye 'Postmodern Man', hello human beings!

Church growth is natural

The New Testament sees growth in the numbers following Christ as both natural and desirable. This is because the work of growing the kingdom is, at root, God's own job. He has created an organism whose natural tendency is to grow. Jesus explains this in the parable of the growing seed in Mark 4:

> 'This is what the kingdom of God is like. A man scatters seed on the ground. Night and day, whether he sleeps or gets up, the seed sprouts and grows, though he does not know how. All by itself the soil produces corn – first the stalk, then the ear, then the full grain in the ear. As soon as the grain is ripe, he puts the sickle to it, because the harvest has come.' (Mark 4.26-9 NIV)

Perhaps the Church needs to find some new types of sickles, or combine harvesters, that are more suited to today's harvest, but God ensures that a potential harvest is always around the corner for those who know where to look.

In 1 Corinthians 3 Paul likens the Church to a garden:

> I planted the seed, and Apollos watered it; but God made it grow. Thus it is not the gardeners with their planting and watering who count, but God, who makes it grow. Whether they plant or water, they work as a team, though each will get his own pay for his own labour. We are God's fellow-workers; and you are God's garden. (1 Corinthians 3.6-9 NEB)

So God's role is the central one – to create an organism that grows naturally – but the under-gardeners' work of planting and watering is essential to enable the growth to take place. If the climate changes, and the gardening methods fail to change with the climate, then the plants in the garden may get sickly. But once the under-gardeners adjust to the new conditions, the God-given impetus for growth will inevitably respond. It is God who makes the lilies of the field to grow, and it is God rather than ecclesiastical toil or public relations spin who ultimately makes the Church to grow. The task the leaders of the Church face today is to adjust the Church's gardening methods in response to change in the social climate, and to trust God for the harvest.

Let us change the metaphor from the horticultural to the more commonly used one of the building. When Jesus told Peter, 'On this rock I will build my church' (Matthew 16.18 NIV), he was promising to grow his Church on the foundation of a Church leader. Yes, there is only one cornerstone, but he allows individual Church leaders to be the key foundational building blocks of his churches. In the Great Commission he promises, as his side of the covenant he makes with his disciples, to be with them to the end of time. Their side is to make disciples of all nations. His intention is clearly to build and grow his Church in every time and place, but he chooses to place the success of his building project in human hands. Our responsibility is to be living rock alive to the times, rather than fossils from the past.

And so it is not an option to blame either the irrelevance of Jesus, or a new-found hardness of human hearts, for the shrinking of the Church. If the plant is in decline, better gardening will rescue it; if the climate is changing, different gardening methods will produce a new sort of garden. The shrinking Church is not the victim of the irrelevant Jesus, Jesus is the victim of the irrelevant Church. Those whom the Church is failing to reach are also its victims. Neither God's love nor human need have changed. But the shrinking Church is failing in its duty as matchmaker between the two. Decline is the result not of ineluctable historical processes but of the failure of the Church to adapt to changing and more challenging times.

Keeping up with the times

It is, however, true that the present pace of change, cultural complexity and range of new attitudes mean that the Church needs to be pretty nimble on its feet if it is to survive and prosper. We do not underestimate the strength of the new indifference, and sometimes hostility, to the Church and all it stands for. People are much less bothered than they used to be about marriage, about baptism, about sending their children to Sunday school, about going to church themselves. Duty, social conformity and respectability no longer motivate people to belong to churches, or to anything else for that matter. They go if they feel like it and if there is something in it for them. So, like every other organization in the modern world, the Church of England must work harder and behave smarter than it used to if it wishes to be relevant.

The task is not easy. And the Church of England has no great track record of being nimble on its feet. But it must be possible because the grower, the builder, the driving force behind the Church is Jesus Christ himself, and he will never desert us. Even if we lag a long way behind, he is the master of the quantum leap.

A dying institution?

There are three further objections to the view that the performance of the Church alone will decide whether it declines or grows. One is that God is not interested in the preservation of an institution that has outlived its usefulness. Rather than advocating a few easy reforms that will see the Church of England bounce back, some would argue that today's institution is an old and no longer effective wineskin. Revolution is required, not just reform. It may be desirable for the old form of Church to die so that something better can be resurrected from the ashes. The tension between the two responses of reform and revolution in the face of the decline of the Church will run through the remainder of the book. Suffice it to suggest at this point that neither reform nor revolution is a sufficient response by itself – both are needed in different aspects and areas of the Church's life.

The second objection is that, historically speaking, the growth of the Church is not inevitable. The churches written to in Revelation all died in the end. No individual plant in the garden lives forever. The Confessing Church in Nazi Germany grew in faithfulness and courage but not in numbers. Some individual parish churches seem never to grow numerically themselves but keep exporting their people to other churches. Some produce numbers of future clergy and other workers; some churches in urban priority areas see their people move up the ladder socially when their lives have been sorted out by their new faith.

The beneficiaries then are the middle-class churches in the new areas their people move on to as their earning potential and spending habits change.

Some churches have, of course, died as a result of persecution. Others have gone into decline because of faithlessness. Others have found it hard going in a hostile environment. We do not argue that it is the natural condition for every local church to be growing, simply that growth is the normative condition for the national Church in normal times if it keeps the faith and keeps up with the culture. After all, God is at work in the whole world, not just in the Church. The Church is not so much the franchise-owning dispenser of God to the community as the seeker after where God is already at work in the world, serving him where he is prompting his kingdom to come. If God's ceaseless activity is about renewal of life and growth of the kingdom, then so should be that of a Church that seeks and follows him.

Finally, some see the present time as so abnormal as to be unprecedented. Postmodernity is a bigger revolution than the Reformation, the Enlightenment, industrialization, or just about anything else in human history. But it is just possible that this case has been overstated. The times may not be quite as hostile to the Church as some imagine, for some denominations and many churches are growing well and healthily within our present society. Much of the solution to the problem of the decline of the Church still lies within the Church's own hands. But it needs to take its courage in its hands if it is to grow again.

Repentance

First we must face the facts of decline. Then we must acknowledge that our own failings, inaction and inadequacy have contributed to that decline. But in the Church we can cope with such things. Not for us the spin culture of the political world where no mistake or failing can ever be admitted. Christian culture is tailor-made for the creative use of past failure in building a better future: we believe in repentance, restoration, and new life. So first we must have the courage to make our confession. In Revelation Jesus points to the sins of the seven churches – loss of first love, sexual immorality, heresy, being lukewarm, being comfortable in wealth, appearing to be alive but actually being spiritually dead – and demands their repentance as the condition of their continued survival and spiritual prosperity: 'Those whom I love I rebuke and discipline. So be earnest, and repent. Here I am! I stand at the door and knock. If anyone hears my voice and opens the door, I will come in and eat with him, and he with me' (Revelation 3.19,20 NIV).

And so we come to a stupendously optimistic conclusion. If the decline of the Church is ultimately caused neither by the irrelevance of Jesus nor by the indifference of the community, but by the Church's failure to respond fast enough to an evolving, postmodern culture, to a changing spiritual climate, and to the promptings of the Holy Spirit, then that decline can be addressed by the repentance of the Church. For true repentance involves turning around and living in a new way in the future. A national denomination, diocese or parish which, out of repentance, grows a new relevance to the contemporary world may also grow in numbers and strength because the Spirit of Jesus has been released to do his work. We said earlier that Jesus is the master of the quantum leap. As we shall see in later chapters, many of the good practices and healthy ways of living that have been adopted by growing churches are not exactly rocket science. Even modest reforms can turn a 2 per cent per annum decline into 2 per cent per annum growth. All that the prodigal son had to do was to appear back on the edge of his father's estate. He did not even need his prepared speech. The father enthusiastically restored to him everything he once had, and more – but only because the son was prepared for a radically new station in life, as a servant rather than as one of the masters. In today's world, institutional authority no longer commands much of a following, but personal authenticity does. A Church that still wishes to parade as one of the masters is finished, but a servant Church may have a surprisingly bright future. We may feel that the Church is fast losing weight in a foreign land of spiritual famine. But the celebratory feast laid on by the Father may be just around the corner for a Church prepared to embrace major change.

4

Bringing growth out of decline

'But the hair on [Samson's] head began to grow again
after it had been shaved.' (Judges 16.22 NIV)

It may be that some readers have felt a measure of indignation at the
characterization of the Church of England as being paralysed by denial and
despair in the fact of decline. Many heroes in the Church have been fighting
the forces of decline for years. Indeed, the greatest tragedy of the modern
Church may be that the collective whole is such a poor reflection of the faithful
individuals who make it up. The organizational resistance to change, the legal
and bureaucratic tentacles, the financial mess, the crippling workloads, the
inability to locate levers of power for pursuing useful agendas, can eat away
at the souls of those most devoted to the Church's true business. And yet
many local churches have found a spiritual vitality and relevance amidst all
this that has made them beacons of hope. If their spiritual vitality and relevant
good practices could be spread through the whole Church then national growth
would be assured. This is entirely possible because, as Samson found, spiritual
vitality has a strange way of returning to God's people even when it has
apparently been shaved away.

It is now time to take a more detailed look at what statistics tell us about
these signs of hope for the Church in a period of overall decline.

Pockets of growth

One key feature of the data from the 1989 English Church Census and 1998
English Church Survey was that 1,888 out of 8,681 churches of all
denominations, 22 per cent, grew their attendance by at least 10 per cent
between the two years. The proportion of growing Anglican churches was 20
per cent. In fact, 7 per cent of the sample of Anglican churches grew their
attendance in the period between the surveys by at least 60 per cent. In a
period of apparent general decline, quite large numbers of Anglican churches
were growing strongly. These churches live in the same society as declining
churches. They are spread over all church traditions, sizes, and locations. The

evidence suggests that they are growing not because they happen to be in favourable places, or by some other process of chance or luck, but because they have found a spiritual vitality and adopted some good practices that are available to all.

Reliable data, authoritative findings?

Many of the statistics used in this book come from the attendance returns of parishes to their own dioceses. This may be the first time that such attendance analysis has been reported in a book concerned with the growth of the Church of England. Some conclusions already seem pretty certain, others are perhaps more interim or speculative. Conclusions are deliberately not hedged around with proper but confusing academic statistical explanations, justifications and cautions – common-sense clarity has been the aim. There is also much ground still to cover, and new discoveries to be made

Findings from survey data are also reported. Following the publication of the results of the 1998 English Church Attendance Survey, and Peter Brierley's book *The Tide is Running Out*, Springboard, the Archbishops' Initiative in Evangelism, commissioned Christian Research to analyse further the database that had been built up. The fruits of this analysis are scattered throughout this book. It was possible to compare the attendance growth and decline history of the 8,681 churches of all denominations that had responded both to the 1998 survey and to the 1989 census.

There are always two potential problems with survey results: was the sample size large enough, and was it random enough? The study includes data from 3,127 Church of England sources, usually incumbents, reporting a congregation count in October of the year in question together with a profile of the church. This amounted to 37 per cent of benefices and 24 per cent of parishes, so the sample was large, but was it random? It is, of course, possible that certain types of incumbents (busy ones with large or growing churches?) generally failed to fill in their forms. (This possibility is mentioned because your author fell into precisely this category in both 1989 and 1998!) Such possible distortions cannot be quantified directly. However, the geographical spread of the sample was not statistically different from the population of Anglican churches, and nor was the percentage of Anglican churches in the whole. These facts suggest that the sample was reasonably representative. Randomness problems, moreover, are limited by the fact that we are here dealing only with comparisons between the two surveys rather than trying to establish features of the population such as average congregation size. Results are only reported as significant if they were found to be so at the most stringent possible 99.9 per cent level. Finally, many of the findings from the survey are supported by independent data from parochial returns. For example, the finding that smaller churches are more likely to grow than big ones is confirmed by the returns from a number of individual dioceses. So is the finding that churches offering specialist youth provision are more likely to have growing congregations. We may therefore place a reasonable degree of reliance on the findings of the survey and consider the most clear-cut results to be operationally useful.

However, the randomness question means that we would be unwise to consider matters finally proven and closed. The fact that it has been possible to extract so many operationally useful implications from the data available does not mean that the Church can afford to skimp on future research.

Transfer growth or real growth?

It could, of course, be argued that the churches that are growing, scattered as they are around the country, are the more attractive and go-ahead outfits. Their growth may therefore be due to people transferring from other, less attractive, shrinking churches. In fact, it is not unknown in church committees for Anglicans to complain about the activities of these more 'successful' churches. Their adoption of attractive good practices is seen as letting the side down, for all they are doing is stealing people from parishes that cannot match their magnetism. Better to do the other clergy a favour, become 'one of us', and offer the same poor-quality product as everyone else. That way, no one else need feel threatened.

In fact, research into where people attending newly planted congregations come from shows that only 16 per cent have transferred from other churches.[1] Some 20 per cent were members of the original planting team, and 63 per cent were new or re-committed churchgoers. The significance of this finding is that newly planted churches are the fastest growing group in the country (see Chapter 12). It also bears out the general feeling of leaders of growing churches that most, though by no means all, of their growth is real rather than transfer growth.

The fact that there are large variations in growth and decline performance between regions and areas of the country also demonstrates that transfer is not the main reason for the growth of some churches. People may travel between London and Manchester to watch a football match, but few will do so to attend a church service. Total Anglican church attendance is estimated by the surveys to have fallen nationally by 23 per cent between 1989 and 1998. This is rather more than the figure of 16 per cent suggested by the official Church statistics. This may be either because churches have told slightly different stories to the surveys than to their dioceses, or because there is some bias in the survey samples, or because the October Sunday count genuinely had a somewhat greater fall than the official statistics' Usual Sunday Attendance averaged through the year. However, the regional variations in the two sets of figures are similar. According to the surveys, attendance in the north-west fell 36 per cent in the period, while in Greater London it actually grew by 3 per cent. A similar variation is apparent from published diocesan attendance figures. But we do not normally imagine that Bolton is the beating heart of the postmodern revolution, while Brent is stuck in a 1950s time warp. Rather, we would expect the capital to be leading the way in church decline if this were caused by cutting-edge changes in society. London can hardly have been left out of the cultural change experienced by the rest of the country. So the difference must have something to do with the ways in which churches have been adapting and responding to cultural change. Or, perhaps, cultural change in London is ahead of the rest of the country, and has now become, in some way, favourable to church attendance. We don't yet know.

Variations between dioceses

It may be that the ecclesiastical unit or level that holds the key to turning around the decline of the Church of England is the diocese. Tables 4.1 and 4.2 show the wide variation in attendance trends between different dioceses. From 1989 to 1999, for example, London Diocese added 12 per cent to its adult attendance and 4 per cent to its children, while Durham lost 28 per cent of its adults and 42 per cent of its children. There are three possible areas of explanation for these huge differences.

Firstly, there are two purely statistical possibilities. One is chance. Nationally, 20 per cent of Anglican parishes grew their attendance in the period, 15 per cent stayed about the same and 65 per cent saw their attendance decline. If all parishes were allocated randomly to different dioceses we would expect some random variation in diocesan attendance trends. However, the numbers of parishes involved, hundreds per diocese, means that the deviation from the national average in each diocese will be low. The difference between the attendance decline in a diocese and nationally will be very small if random variation is the sole cause of differences between dioceses.

The other possible statistical explanation is changes in the way the statistics are provided or in the environment in which they are provided. But the definition and question remained the same nationally throughout the period until 2000, and were basically the same for each diocese. If a diocese moved from one parish share allocation mechanism to another which took either more

Table 4.1 Percentage change in the uSa of adults, 1989–99: diocesan league table

1	London	+12	22=	Sheffield	−14
2	Coventry	−2	22=	Wakefield	−14
3	Canterbury	−3	24=	Gloucester	−15
4	Derby	−4	24=	Portsmouth	−15
5	Oxford	−7	24=	Ripon	−15
6=	Bradford	−8	27=	Exeter	−16
6=	Guildford	−8	27=	Norwich	−16
6=	Peterborough	−8	27=	Southwell	−16
9=	Chester	−10	30=	Birmingham	−17
9=	Southwark	−10	30=	Hereford	17
11=	Salisbury	−11	30=	Rochester	−17
11=	Sodor & Man	−11	33=	Liverpool	−18
13=	Ely	−12	33=	Newcastle	−18
13=	Leicester	−12	33=	Worcester	−18
13=	St Eds & Ips	−12	36=	Blackburn	−21
13=	Truro	−12	36=	Bristol	−21
13=	Winchester	−12	36=	Manchester	−21
18=	Chelmsford	−13	36=	York	−21
18=	Chichester	−13	40	Bath & Wells	−22
18=	Lichfield	−13	41=	Carlisle	−23
18=	St Albans	−13	41=	Lincoln	−23
			43	Durham	−28

Source: Official Church of England statistics.

or less account of uSa figures then one might imagine this could have a significant effect on reported attendance figures. However, there were actually very few such changes during the period, and the variations among children, which never count towards parish share, were actually greater than among adults.

The second possible area of explanation is that the external environment of dioceses differs and so causes the variations in their trends. Clearly this is likely to be at least part of the explanation. There appears to be, for example, a tendency for dioceses from the south-east and the Midlands to be nearer the top of the league tables, and dioceses from the north and south-west to be nearer the bottom. This is illustrated in Maps 1 and 2. But if regionality were the main explanation, it is hard to see, for example, why Bradford should be near the top of the league and Rochester near the bottom; or why Coventry should be so far ahead of its neighbours like Lichfield, Birmingham or Gloucester; or why one half of the capital (London Diocese) should show a 12 per cent growth in adult attendance and the other half (Southwark) a 10 per cent fall. And why should Manchester lose only one child in seven whereas Carlisle managed to lose almost six in ten?

Similarly, if external environment were the main explanation of trend differences we would expect the trends in each diocese to be fairly stable.

Table 4.2 Percentage change in the uSa of children, 1989–99: diocesan league table

1	London	+4	23=	Salisbury	−31
2	Sodor & Man	0	23=	Winchester	−31
3	Southwark	−3	25=	Bath & Wells	−33
4	Canterbury	−6	25=	Chester	−33
5	Coventry	−12	25=	Ely	−33
6	Manchester	−16	28=	Sheffield	−34
7	Peterborough	−19	28=	Southwell	−34
8	Guildford	−20	28=	Wakefield	−34
9	Chelmsford	−22	31=	Hereford	−35
10=	Oxford	−23	31=	Worcester	−35
10=	St Eds & Ips	−23	33=	Gloucester	−36
12	Ripon	−26	33=	Lincoln	−36
13=	Bradford	−27	33=	Liverpool	−36
13=	Derby	−27	36=	Birmingham	−38
13=	Leicester	−27	36=	York	−38
13=	St Albans	−27	38=	Blackburn	−39
17	Portsmouth	−28	38=	Newcastle	−39
18=	Bristol	−29	40=	Durham	−42
18=	Rochester	−29	40=	Norwich	−42
18=	Lichfield	−29	42	Truro	−48
21=	Chichester	−30	43	Carlisle	−58
21=	Exeter	−30			

Source: Official Church of England statistics.

External social and economic environments do not change rapidly. But, over the decade, some dioceses seemed to race up the league table and others to race down. York and Wakefield, neighbouring northern dioceses with similar towns and cities, both lost 7 per cent of adult attendance from 1989 to 1994. York lost a further 15 per cent from 1994 to 1999 and fell from 30th to 39th in the league table, whereas Wakefield lost only a further 7 per cent and rose to 10th. Bristol rose from bottom in 1989–94 to 15th in 1994–9. Oxford dropped from 2nd to 27th.

Population change must have an impact on changing geographical church attendance patterns. The population of Durham grew by 1.8 per cent between 1989 and 1998 whereas the population of Greater London grew by 6.1 per cent (*Religious Trends 2002/3*, Table 12). So a small proportion of the different attendance trends can be accounted for in this way, but no more than that.

This leaves lots of room for the third possible explanation – that the large variation in attendance performance between dioceses is actually connected with the policies, personnel, ethos, culture, spiritual health, financial resources, or corporate performance of the dioceses themselves. This is not unlikely. Management performance, personnel, style, ability and resources are perhaps

Map 1 Percentage change in the uSa of adults by diocese, 1989–99

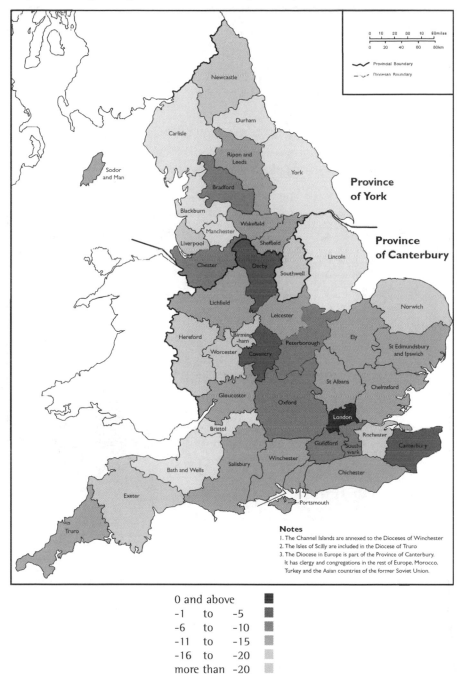

0 and above

-1   to   -5

-6   to   -10

-11   to   -15

-16   to   -20

more than   -20

Source: *Church Statistics* 1989 and 1999, copyright © The Archbishops' Council.

Map 2 Percentage change in the uSa of children (under 16s) by diocese, 1989–99

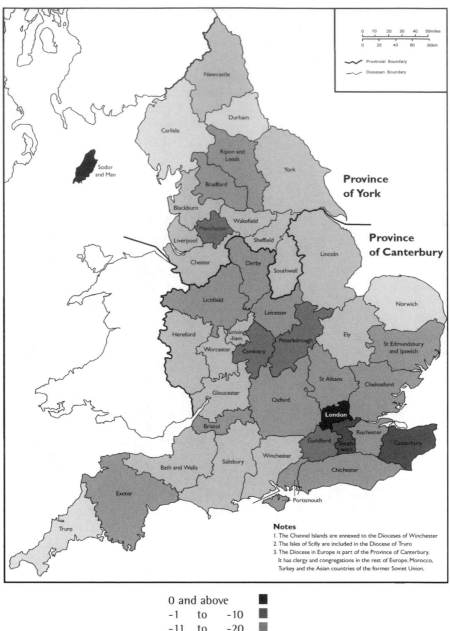

Notes
1. The Channel Islands are annexed to the Dioceses of Winchester
2. The Isles of Scilly are included in the Diocese of Truro
3. The Diocese in Europe is part of the Province of Canterbury.
   It has clergy and congregations in the rest of Europe, Morocco,
   Turkey and the Asian countries of the former Soviet Union.

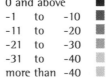

0 and above	■
-1 to -10	■
-11 to -20	■
-21 to -30	■
-31 to -40	■
more than -40	■

Source: *Church Statistics* 1989 and 1999, copyright © The Archbishops' Council.

the main determinants of the relative success of companies that are in the same line of business. It is widely believed that leadership is the single most important factor in determining the effectiveness of local churches, and perhaps the same is true of dioceses. Those who know the Church of England well recognize that there are significant differences between dioceses in the way they operate, their culture and organization, the types of people central to them, their church traditions, and their alertness to the modern world. In fact, it is sometimes said that there is not one Church of England but 44. So it would not be surprising to find that the history of leadership in a diocese is a significant determinant of relative attendance performance.

Further evidence for the powerful impact of the Church's own characteristics on its growth and decline is provided by comparing denominations. In these comparisons there is no hint that differences might be caused by regional or local socio-economic factors. Figure 1.5 on page 14 compares some of the denominational adult attendance trends estimated in the handbook *Religious Trends 2001*, published by Christian Research. One of the most striking features of these figures is the contrast between the Methodist and Baptist denominations. Attendance at Methodist churches fell by 21 per cent, but at Baptist churches it rose by 13 per cent. In the same period, the Methodists lost nearly half their children and the Baptists gained in numbers. The Baptists and the Methodists do not live in two different countries. They appear to have similar sorts of buildings in similar places up and down the land and do similar sorts of things. Yet one denomination is growing and the other is fast disappearing. They are clearly performing very differently in the same environment. It is not the culture of the country that is determining their different attendance trends, it is the culture of the denomination. The Baptists saw their numbers decline in the 1980s, and their national leadership took steps to reverse the trend by restructuring the denomination for mission and by adopting proactive policies on church planting, process evangelism, and other pieces of modern good practice.

The huge differences in attendance trends between parishes, regions, dioceses and denominations confirm our argument that the internal features of the Church are at least as important as the external features of society in determining growth and decline. This also accords with contemporary church theory. The Gospel and Culture movement accepts that Western culture is a problem to the Church, but thinks the solution lies in the Church finding the right way to address the culture, not in waiting for the culture to change to suit the Church. Books like Philip King's *Leadership Explosion* (Hodder, 1987) argue that the key to the healthy life, growth and mission of the Church is high-quality enabling leadership. It is not just leadership ability but also leadership style that is important – it is thought that effective leaders today work through teams and through bringing out the gifts and ministries of others. Christian Schwarz, in his *Natural Church Development Handbook* (BCGA, 1998), reports worldwide research that shows a strong correlation between a church's quality characteristics and its growth rate. Wherever they are in the world, healthy churches are more likely to grow numerically than unhealthy churches.

Clergy numbers and decline

We have just seen that leadership is a key factor in the growth or decline of the Church. The life and ministry of the Church of England has always revolved around its parish priests, But during the 1990s the number of full-time stipendiary clergy fell from 11,076 to 9,412, a fall of 15 per cent. Could the numbers attending churches be declining because the number of pastors and leaders is falling? Could the churches that have lost their priests be the ones that have declined the most?

The short answer to this question is 'probably not'. One reason for this is that the churches that have lost their clergy have tended to be the smaller ones. We will see in Chapter 11 that most of the decline in attendance has happened in the larger churches, which, by and large, have kept their vicars. It is precisely those churches that are most likely to have lost their own stipendiary priests (that is, the smallest ones) that have been most successful in maintaining their attendance levels. The other reason is that, as the numbers of stipendiary clergy have declined, so the numbers of unpaid ministers, non-stipendiaries and Readers, and the numbers of other paid staff such as youth workers and administrators, have grown. The mix of types of authorized ministers may be changing, but the overall numbers are not going down.

The number of stipendiary clergy in the Church of England is forecast to continue to fall in the first decade of the twenty-first century, but only by between 0.5 per cent and 0.75 per cent per annum, and there will be compensating increases in the numbers of non-stipendiary clergy and of Readers. We conclude, therefore, that falling numbers of clergy or ministers will not lead to an inevitable decline in attendance in the future. Past attendance decline is not strongly correlated with falling clergy numbers, and overall ministerial numbers are not forecast to fall. What will matter much more is the effectiveness with which the clergy and other ministers are deployed and the culture of the Church in which they minister.

Recent examples of upturn

So far, the statistical evidence cited has yielded comparisons between the experience of different groups of churches at a particular point in time. Some groups of churches seem to be thriving and others to be dying. But is there any evidence of Anglican churches or dioceses turning themselves round from decline to growth through new policies or initiatives? Doubtless many individual parishes have done this. Table 4.3 shows the adult attendance figures at 14 parishes in the York Diocese where there was decline from 1989 to 1994 and then growth from 1994 to 1999. This is especially significant given the fact that the overall attendance trend in the diocese from 1994 to 1999 was steeply downwards. These 14 parishes are just a few examples of the hundreds, maybe thousands, of ordinary churches up and down the land that have reversed their decline trends.

Table 4.3 Examples of parish churches reversing adult attendance decline, 1989–99

| | Attendance figures | | |
Parish	1989	1994	1999
A	373	283	327
B	252	200	223
C	243	100	151
D	234	110	160
E	111	88	97
F	100	80	90
G	96	62	65
H	90	75	86
I	55	40	45
J	53	30	40
K	53	32	40
L	40	32	35
M	30	15	20
N	21	10	16

Source: Diocesan attendance returns.

Another example from York Diocese is the experience of some of its largest churches. Research on parish attendance returns over a period of years (which could well be a useful prototype for similar research in other dioceses) uncovered the fact that almost all the decline in attendance was concentrated in a relatively small number of larger churches. The smallest churches were in fact growing significantly even in an era of overall decline. The large churches (at first the definition was an average adult attendance of at least 150, but this was later reduced to 125 as decline continued) were invited by the diocese to attend a series of day conferences over several years to compare notes and agree first the reasons for their decline and second what steps could be taken to reverse it. Some of the large churches joined in, others did not. Almost all were in decline at that time. A list of reasons for decline and steps to halt it was drawn up (many churches have been influenced by these). According to the latest attendance data available, for 1999 and 2000, the churches that took part in the exercise have collectively halted their decline, and have even started to grow. Those that did not take part have seen their decline accelerate. The turnaround began in 1999, when the 16 churches that participated (and for which there is reliable data) grew their collective adult attendance by 1 per cent. The nine churches that did not take part in the exercise lost 9 per cent of their adult attendance in that year. Prior to the 'larger churches' exercise both groups had had similar downward trends. By 2000 a 'control group' was no longer available because more churches had attended the conferences. Once again, the 34 churches for which there is good data for both 1999 and 2000 were found to have grown their collective attendance, this time by 5 per cent. The very simple steps taken to help the churches eliminate their decline (see Chapter 11) seem to have worked. Indeed, the turnaround in the attendance figures for the larger churches in the diocese in 2000 was enough to halt attendance decline in the diocese as a whole.

In Chapter 2 it was mentioned that since the arrival of a new bishop in the Wakefield Diocese in 1992, there has been an attempt to reverse decline by the adoption of a more missionary mode of being, as exemplified in the title 'The Missionary Diocese of Wakefield'. How have things worked out? Figure 4.1 shows that the last year of decline in uSa of adults was 1998, although it is likely that there have been modest falls in the numbers of children since. In fact, it is likely that the majority of the churches in the diocese have recently been growing because, as elsewhere, the smaller churches are doing much better than the large ones. The growth of three small churches and the decline of one large one can easily cancel each other out. This achievement

Figure 4.1 Adult uSa in the Diocese of Wakefield, 1990–2000

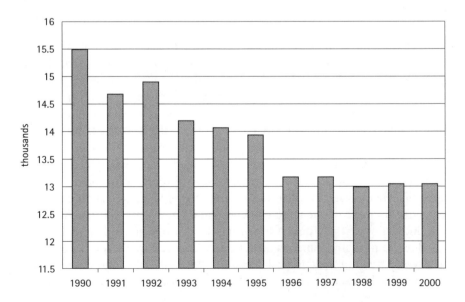

Figure 4.2 Adult attendance decline in northern dioceses, 1996–9

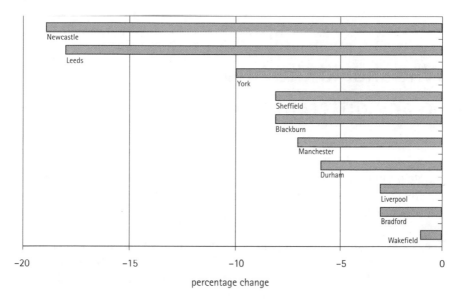

is in contrast to Wakefield's neighbouring northern urban dioceses, as Figure 4.2 shows. The conclusion we can draw from this is that, although the new approach has not yet kick-started significant growth, decline in adult attendance does seem to have been halted, at least for a while.

So we have seen examples from individual parishes, a group of similar-sized churches and a whole diocese where action taken to halt or reverse decline is bearing fruit. It is possible to buck the trend and bring growth out of decline.

5

Why should the future
be any different?

> He brought his people out like a flock; he led them like sheep through
> the desert. Thus he brought them to the border of his holy land.
> (Psalm 78.52,54 NIV)

The last two chapters have argued both theologically and statistically that the
future growth of the Church is a natural and realistic possibility. But many
questions still rattle around in a Church that has got used to decline. This
chapter deals with five of the most common of these doubts about the future
prospects for growth.

The Decade of Evangelism

We now know that the 1990s – the 'Decade of Evangelism' – turned out to
be a decade of decline. We tried to stem the tide, but it only rushed out faster.
For every ten children in the churches in 1990, there were only seven in 2000.
So why should the future be any different?

But perhaps the 1990s were not actually a 'decade of evangelism' after all.
Yes, a policy objective was set – to engage in successful evangelism that would
result in the incorporation of new believers into the people of God, and the
advance of the kingdom through the strengthening of the Church. An
evangelism adviser or missioner was appointed, usually at a fairly low level in
the pecking order, in each diocese. However, typically, once they had declared
their policy objective and appointed their specialist, dioceses did little more
than issue some vague exhortations. Thought-out strategies and implemented
policies for achieving the objective were few and far between. In other words,
simply calling the 1990s the Decade of Evangelism did not turn them into a
decade of evangelism. The Government does not meet its inflation target by
wishful thinking, or even by appointing a new Governor to the Bank of England,
but by implementing a set of coherent economic policies. Dioceses that did
not focus and co-ordinate their activities and policies around the evangelism

objective should not be surprised it wasn't met. And in case you are thinking that it is easy to be wise after the event, the above is a summary of an article by your author which appeared in the *Church Times* of January 1992.

However, the Decade of Evangelism did give rise to many benefits, most of them long term. Evangelism is now respectable again. It has gained widespread acceptance as a central activity of the Church. We have embraced Emil Brunner's truth that the Church exists by mission as a fire exists by burning. Our understanding of the nature of evangelism has broadened. It is no longer restricted to verbal proclamation, the work of specialists and para-Church organizations. It has become accepted that evangelism is the whole process by which the Church attracts and incorporates new believers into the people of Jesus Christ. It is not a bolt-on activity for enthusiasts, it is the very stuff of the everyday living of normal churches. Some churches have begun to restructure their regular programmes and budgets with evangelism in mind, but the fruits of this are likely to be fairly long term. We have learnt, for example, that in today's world it takes people, on average, two to four years to move from their first attendance at church to a full acceptance of the Christian faith. As people today tend to believe only after they have begun to belong, then helping them belong is the best route to helping them believe. This is why we now understand evangelism to be the work of the whole Church, because everyone has a part to play in helping newcomers to feel they belong. And this is also why we now see evangelism and conversion as a process rather than an event, and a process that needs the local church at its heart. Springboard, for example, the Archbishops' initiative in evangelism, has a broader approach than simply offering missions and evangelists: it also offers help to parishes and dioceses in their attempts to organize their lives around the objective of incorporating people into the life and faith of the Christian Church.

In truth, the main storyline of the Church of England in the 1990s did not turn out to be evangelism, which swiftly dropped down the list of priorities. This was partly because the Church was also going through what did turn out to be the principal story of the decade – the ordination of women. This watershed experience may well have had a deleterious impact on attendances at first. Following the decision in 1992 to ordain women to the priesthood, around 400 stipendiary clergy left the Church of England under the measure allowing them compensation. This was about 4 per cent of the whole. Numbers of lay members also left the Church, mostly for Rome. Yet other clergy and parishes were preoccupied with their own response and decision, a preoccupation that often lasted for several years. The main years of resignations and disruptions were 1993–7. Figure 5.1 shows that these were also the peak years for attendance decline. This is surely no coincidence.

Figure 5.1 Annual loss of adult Sunday attendance in the Church of England (three-year moving average), 1991–9

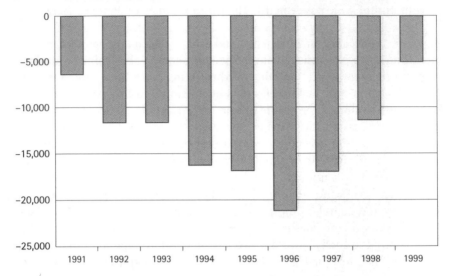

However, by 2000 there were 1,140 full-time women diocesan clergy, nearly three times the number of men who left because of their arrival. There is beginning to be some evidence from diocesan surveys that women incumbents and priests-in-charge are at least as likely, and possibly more likely, to lead growing churches as are men. We need more evidence over a greater number of years before this can be firmly established, but initial indications are promising. In one diocese, for example, ten parishes with women incumbents added a total of 20 per cent to their adult attendance from 1998 to 2000, compared with a slight fall overall. In another diocese over the same period, 16 women saw a total fall in adult attendance in their parishes of 4 per cent compared to a diocesan average of 6 per cent.

The conclusion, therefore, is that the beneficial impact on church attendance of the Decade of Evangelism was never going to be large, initially because it did not quickly become the core agenda of the Church, because what impact it did have was swamped in mid-decade by the fallout from the ordination of women, and because the pay-off from the resultant culture shift is long term. However, decline was slowing down at the end of the decade. In the longer term, and for the first decade of the new century, both the lessons learnt from the Decade of Evangelism and the new growth dynamic brought by women incumbents auger well for the growth of the Church.

Church traditions

Some traditions have been doing better than others. If 'adopting good practices for growth' is a euphemism for becoming charismatic-evangelicals, many Anglicans will have a problem. 'We can't behave like they behave nor believe exactly what they believe. Real hope only comes from the possibility of growth within every tradition.'

It is widely thought that evangelical-charismatic churches have been doing better than other sorts of churches, and it is certainly true that evangelical congregations are on average about 50 per cent bigger than non-evangelical ones. Some evangelicals may therefore be tempted to think that decline happens only to other sorts of Christians, and so doesn't concern them: 'Churches like our own that preach the Bible are doing okay.' All that other churches need to do is copy the evangelical-charismatic churches and growth will be assured.

Is this true? Are only certain sorts of churches able to grow in today's climate?

There is a sense in which all Anglicans need to review the way they do things, their traditions, and their inherited modes of thinking and worshipping. It was Friedrich Nietzsche who said: 'Many are stubborn in pursuit of the path they have chosen, few in pursuit of the goal.' Our church tradition is only the path we have chosen, offering the love of God in Jesus is our goal. We are right to be stubborn in pursuit of our goal, but wrong to cling to the path we follow to achieve it. Paths that worked well ten years ago may need to be modified today. And we ourselves change. So no Christian should put the style of their worship, their ministry or their church above the love of God. Church tradition is a means, not the end. If Anglicans are to focus more clearly on the objective of evangelism then they may all need to review their pathways of church tradition and modify them if necessary.

However, this is in no way to suggest that all should gravitate towards some manufactured 'best practice' new church tradition for the postmodern world. Postmodernism is all about diversity, about there being no single right way. We will together reach more people in our varied culture by being varied ourselves. We must encourage each other in our diversity – let a thousand flowers bloom.

Church tradition is not the issue it once was. This is partly because Anglicans of different traditions have grown towards each other in recent decades, and often learnt from each other. Evangelicals have embraced aspects of Catholic spirituality, while many non-charismatics have learnt to enjoy the warmth of charismatic styles of worship. Evangelism and church growth are also less divisive issues than they used to be. Evangelism often majored on the exposition of theology. Even quite fine theological differences therefore got in the way very easily. For good or ill, evangelicals have moved away from this. Perhaps the liberation theologians' complaint that Westerners were too interested in orthodoxy (right Christian belief) and too unconcerned with orthopraxis (right Christian behaviour) hit home. It is now becoming generally accepted that the most likely starting point for evangelism is not an exposition on the nature of sin and the need for the cross, but an expression of love from the Christian community to those it meets. This has a much less divisive impact upon the Church. And so it is that the good practices and signs of health that seem to be associated with evangelism and growth in the Church today are not restricted to one church tradition. As we shall see in later chapters, they can be adopted with integrity by all types of church.

It should therefore come as no surprise that the differences in growth and decline between church traditions also appear to be narrowing. Figure 5.2 is derived from the results of the 1989 and 1998 English Church Surveys. The percentage of evangelical churches that were static or growing is not vastly greater than those of other traditions. However, substantial proportions of churches of all traditions grew or stayed static in the period. Growth is possible for all. This finding is reinforced by more detailed investigations in dioceses. For example, a study of the growing parishes in Durham diocese conducted by Springboard found that they were of all types of churchmanship. The recovery of larger churches in York Diocese that we saw in Chapter 4 applies across church traditions and parish types. In fact the whole process in York was undertaken by a team unaware of the church tradition of many of the

Figure 5.2 Percentage of Anglican churches of different traditions with static or growing attendance, 1989–98

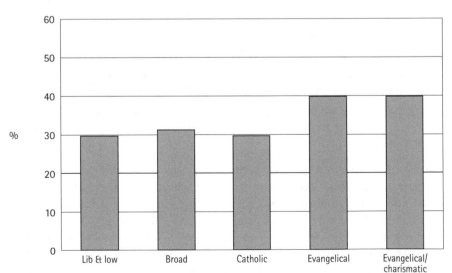

parishes. It was not an issue that mattered particularly. Wakefield Diocese worked out recently that of its 12 most significantly growing churches, 4 were Anglo-Catholic, 4 open or moderate catholic, 2 charismatic-evangelical, 1 evangelical, and 1 central. In both Durham and Wakefield the growing churches were in every sort of neighbourhood, from urban priority area and town centre to plush suburb and rural communities. Wakefield wonders if the strong showing of its Anglo-Catholic parishes in the late 1990s is due to a recovery of confidence following the period of uncertainty after the 1992 vote on the ordination of women to the priesthood. And so we conclude that growth is possible for every type of church in every type of place. This is both an encouragement and a challenge to us all.

Reform, revolution, or renewal?

Those who research trends in society in relation to the Church are increasingly suggesting that our inherited mode of being Church has had its day. Only radical change can give the Church a future. How can a Church that has failed to respond rapidly in the past do so in the future? How can tinkering with good practice within a semi-inherited mode of being church turn around a decline that has been going on for 100 years? Surely something much more drastic is required – and something much less likely to happen!

In sixteenth-century Europe, the great battle that took place in the Church was between the advocates of three parties – reaction, reform, and revolution. Ironically, history tells us that all that the revolutionaries led by Luther achieved was a Reformation. Those, led by Erasmus, who tried to reform the Church while remaining good Catholics apparently surrendered their moderate label to their revolutionary enemies. The same three options tug at the Church of England today. This book certainly contains some polemic against reaction, but is it for reform or revolution? Those like Michael Moynagh and John Drane, who chart societal changes for the Church, are now saying that the Church as we have inherited it is probably doomed.[1] Society is moving away from traditional Church so fast that there is little point in clinging on to what used to be. Rather, the Church needs urgently to re-invent itself in radical new modes with some 'out of the pew' thinking. From such a perspective, implementing good practices and health checks for the Church as it is can seem like taking blotting paper to dry up the sea. Death and resurrection is a more realistic model than reform and renewal.

However, the first imperative for Church growth is not to attack the ocean of secularism with the Church blotting paper – it is simply to stop the leaks from the Church bucket. The evidence and arguments marshalled in this book suggest that even a modest amount of reform can plug the most obvious leaks and so achieve some surprising growth. There is still a growth dynamic in semi-traditional church so long as it is done well. Despite all the fancy talk, human beings have not changed their essence, and neither has God. We must deal with the Church today as we find it, and encourage it with manageable ideas for reform. There is no point in presenting the Church of England with an agenda it is incapable of delivering. The message of this chapter is that decline is not inevitable for the Church as we know it, because reform is already turning it round in certain places.

The revolutionaries do, however, have a case. For every one who has heard of Erasmus, a hundred have heard of Luther. The Church of England has had its reformers these last 100 years, and it is still declining. Revolutionaries like the house church pioneers did rather well. A whole new strand of the Christian faith, Pentecostalism, with its revolution of authority derived from the present work of the Holy Spirit rather than either the Bible or the tradition of the Church, arose during the century of the traditional Church's decline. In most of the world, and in most of Church history, attendance has grown not by tinkering with existing congregations but by planting new ones, often radically different ones. So perhaps the Church of England today needs both reform and revolution, both reformers and revolutionaries. It needs ordinary parish churches to change with the times, to attend to their health and practices in order to grow, and it needs a wide range of new, experimental ways of being church to meet the challenges of the twenty-first century without being weighed down by inherited baggage. It also needs its prophets and revolutionaries to be brought in from the edge onto centre stage where they can influence and be resourced.

Traditionally, the Church of England has been expert at marginalizing and neutering its prophets and revolutionaries. It is often said that Jesus would never have got through a clergy selection conference – he was clearly not safe and would have offended the selectors. The clergy selection process is designed to weed out such uncomfortable people, hierarchies have traditionally been full of 'safe' appointments, and the PCC–synodical structure prevents radical departures almost by its very nature. To bring those on the cutting edge for the future into the heart of the Church of today is to import risk into the system. The demise of the Nine O'Clock Service in Sheffield demonstrates that. But true leadership is about taking risks, about hearing in the authentic prophetic voice the voice of God. Individual church, diocesan and national leaders have it in their power to affirm, encourage and make central the holy radicalism that is breaking out in the Church as a response to the challenge of the times: approaches to church planting, teenage worship, moving into cells, setting up non-geographical parishes, or having new concepts of what church is. Each of these brings new hope for the future, but only if the mainstream Church allows and embraces the progress of the radical from the edge to the centre of the stage.

Talk of 'reform' and 'revolution' can sound simply organizational in character. How fast and how far should the Church reorganise itself in order to reverse its numerical decline? I have suggested above that the Church should pursue both agendas at once. But there is, of course, another dimension to changing the Church to meet the challenges of the day. The Church cannot only be reformed by its leaders, it can also be renewed by God. Where does renewal fit into this debate about reform and revolution? The answer is that only a Church seeking renewal from the grace of God's Holy Spirit has the heart and hears the guidance for successful, God-breathed change. But only a Church that reforms or revolutionizes itself in response to the Spirit's promptings is able to channel and enable renewal to work its way through the life of the body of Christ. This book does not ignore the need for God-given spiritual renewal, rather it presupposes both the desire for renewal in the heart of the Church and the gift of renewal in the mind of God.

This presupposition is entirely realistic. Signs of the quickening activity of God in his Church are all around us, from the extraordinary growth of process evangelism courses, to the explosion in the numbers of those with a vocation to full-time Christian youth work, to the proliferation of new congregations and ways of being church, and to the growth of movements of personal renewal within the overall life of the Church. We are just beginning to appreciate the contribution of women incumbents to the growth of the Church. Since the start of the Decade of Evangelism there has been a sea change in the mood of the Church as a whole – there is a much more universal desire for evangelism, for change in the inner life and outer structures of the Church, for a new and different path from that of the dull acceptance and management of decline. The debate about reform or revolution is a debate between those for whom spiritual renewal is already a way of life. The debate about good practices, tactics and strategy arises from the hand of God already being on the Church for change, and that is why change is capable of delivering the church growth goods.

The small and the weak

'Growth may happen elsewhere, in churches with money, talented people, clergy resources, Christians keen to adopt exciting new good practices. But how can it happen in this poor, weak church with so few resources?'

This is the question that is asked by smaller congregations, often in villages or in urban priority areas. The implication is that large, strong churches, usually in the suburbs, have the resources to plan strategy and to implement it, and the capacity to adjust to the modern world. But everyone in our church is over 60, and half of them never leave the village. Average attendance is only 15, and the tower is about to fall down. In ten years, half the congregation will have come to live in the graveyard. Our church will be lucky to survive, let alone grow.

Chapter 11 deals in detail with the issues of church size. It is sufficient here to note that there is overwhelming statistical evidence to demonstrate that, in recent years, attendance at small churches has, on average, been rising. On one level the reason is easy to see: if a congregation of 20 is joined by just one new couple, it has grown by 10 per cent. A congregation of 200 needs to find 20 new people to achieve the same level of growth. The smaller the congregation, the better the chance that it has been increasing, and will do so in the future. Churches do not need sophisticated resources in order to grow. They need high-quality relationships. Smaller fellowships are better able to provide these in a natural way. One key problem the Church of England has with decline is that it is happening mainly in the strong churches, the ones that finance the others to help keep them going. In the letter to the seven churches of Asia in Revelation, it is those churches that were poor and weak that seemed the healthiest and the ones Jesus commended most strongly. The outwardly successful came in for some hard words. Far from lamenting their weakness, small churches should rejoice in the advantages their size gives them while they can, for, if they keep on growing, they will one day hit the problems that beset the large churches!

The culture of the Church

Finally, some of the pessimism about the future growth of the Church of England stems not from doubt about the existence of possible answers to the problem of decline but about the ability and readiness of the Church to adopt them. How can we stop the people in our Church preferring a comfortable death to an uncomfortable change? How can we expect such a sluggish institution where nobody has any real levers of power, and *everyone* feels frustrated, suddenly to become dynamic and focused?

It will be apparent to every reader that this book finds many aspects of the culture of the Church to be problematic for its growth. Yet there are hopeful aspects too. The status and independence of parishes and incumbents allows great freedom of action. The Church of England is used to variety, and is by its very nature a broad and tolerant Church. This is a key characteristic in a society that needs its Church to offer a variety of both tried and experimental routes into the heart of God. It is part of Anglican culture that the Church, from its bishops downwards, is plugged right into the heart of local and national life. The leadership of the Church is traditionally intelligent and thoughtful. The Church possesses the ability to put two and two together – the change in society and the decline of the Church – and make the necessary four – how to grow the Church and so serve society afresh.

More than this, the culture of the Church of England *is* changing, as we will see in Chapter 15. Many individual parishes are waking up to the needs and demands of the times. Evangelism has become an acceptable concept across the board in the Church. A study such as this one of how statistical and management data can inform the life of the Church is (hopefully!) culturally far more acceptable to the Church today than it would have been even a few years ago. Aspects of the culture that are still inimical to growth are 'named and shamed' in the chapters of this book precisely as a contribution to changing the culture for the better. As soon as we become determined to change the culture, that change has begun, even if the outward structures remain the same. If sufficient numbers of Anglicans decide that their priority is to share the faith and grow the Church through its own health and witness, then half the battle is already won.

There are already numerous examples of churches and church life in tune with the culture of the age that are growing and flourishing. We may need to take account of the traditional culture of the Church, but this no more precludes future growth than the colour of the sky stops us flying. Yet, having taken a look at the Church, we must now wrestle with the tremendous changes in society that are happening all around us, and do some grappling with what it may mean to be church in the twenty-first century. This should give us a realistic context for the detailed exploration of the means of growth that seem to be working today that occupies the remainder of the book.

6

The Church after Christendom

> Foxes have holes and birds of the air have nests, but the Son of Man has nowhere to lay his head. (Luke 9.58 NIV)

So far we have considered the Church's own contribution to its attendance decline – giving free reign to the forces of decline due to paralysis brought on either by denial *of* the facts or despair *at* the facts. But the role of the Church in contributing to its own decline is only half the picture. We now look at the changing nature of the culture in which the Church is set, especially at changing incipient belief, or folk religion, and the apparent move out of the Christendom era which began with the conversion of Constantine and has continued (with some gaps) until recent times. By Christendom I mean society organized around an alliance of Church and state, where the Christian faith is the official glue, the guiding principle of its laws and culture. In English Christendom, the established Church and its teachings formed an integral part of the nation's authority structure. Now we seem to be moving into a new era where Christian values and beliefs no longer underpin those of society as a whole.

The tip of the iceberg?

It seems ironic that, as the West pushes its Christian religion more and more towards the margins of its society, radical Muslims are pushing their religion towards the centre – with Muslim law as the law of the land, and Muslim clerics as its leading politicians. This is becoming a titanic clash between two cultures, between two vastly different world views. But, despite President Bush's unfortunate use of the word 'crusade' soon after 11 September 2001, it is hard to see it as a clash between two religions. Unlike in the Middle Ages, in the era of the Crusades, Christendom is not the combatant – rather, it is Western materialism that is the real antithesis and enemy of radical Islam. The possibility that the Church of England's clerics might so radicalize the masses that they take over the governance of the country at the barrel of a gun, and impose Old Testament law, is hardly the most pressing political danger of the day. So just what is the place of the Church in our society today, and how is it likely to change in the future?

It may be that church attendance figures are the tip of the iceberg of a Christian culture. If that is a valid analogy, then the global warming of secularization will not only reduce the hidden Christian background to our culture but will also, almost certainly, reduce the visible part of the iceberg. On the other hand, global warming does some funny things. Due to the unpredictable vagaries of the ocean currents, the icebergs in some parts of the world may actually get bigger.

Christianity as the framework of our culture

A useful fourfold framework for understanding the impact of Christianity on our culture, and of the culture on the experience and expression of the Christian faith, is the following:

- *Institutional Christianity* covers patterns of involvement in church life, acts of worship, and corporate expressions of religion.

- *Intellectual Christianity* deals with the way that Christianity informs and shapes the way people think about life, the world and themselves. The moral framework within which people see the world and handle their own decision-making is an expression of this. It also includes the shaping of customs, such as the use of Sunday, and the shaping of laws such as those to do with marriage and divorce.

- *Functional Christianity* is about the role of the faith in civic society, such as Remembrance services, as well as its role in education and welfare. Clearly, the Christian faith has had a major impact in all these areas. When it first came to these islands, through the Celtic saints and through Saint Augustine, the focus of mission was to the kings and lords of the land. The established Church is the inheritor of this approach, which is seen most clearly at events such as state coronations and funerals. Schools and hospitals were largely founded as conscious expressions of Christian compassion and service. Although the state has taken over much of these areas, the recent development of the hospice movement, which has Christian roots, and the resurgence of Church schools, are evidence of the Church's continuing engagement with national life.

- *Diffused Christianity* covers what is more frequently called 'folk religion', or the innate background of religious views and instincts abroad in our culture today. It is about the shaping of people's religious instincts by the dominant religious culture around.[1]

Gathered church v. parish church

The fourfold framework outlined above underlines the point that attendance figures by no means tell the whole story. There is more to Christianity than going to church. Bishops in the House of Lords, church members being school governors, and clergy doing school assemblies will do little to boost church attendance, for they are not intended to. They are an expression of the Church's engagement with and service to the whole community.

This raises an issue that has always divided Christians. There are those who see the local church as a community of gathered believers, and those who understand it as a servant of the local community. Is it the task of a church to attend to its own well-being or to that of its parish? Interestingly, the word 'parish' originally meant 'resident alien' – a people who lived a different life within the existing community. For centuries, Christians have argued about whether the church should be a gathered community of faith or an organism with no real membership boundaries committed to the care of all. The Baptist Church could be seen as a classic example of the former, the Anglican Church of the latter.

However, perhaps this debate has now run its full course and needs to be laid to rest. What has happened, as much by default as design, is that each side has recognized the strength of the practice and argument of the other, and has adjusted its own practice accordingly. Today, there are few 'gathered' churches that do not have a clear sense of calling to be involved in and to serve the communities around the church. Equally, even Anglican churches with a strong sense of their civic role have a sense of coming together to be nourished in the faith and to function as a loving community of believers. Differences are really about balance. An exclusive emphasis on either 'gathered' or 'parish' is seen as odd or unhealthy. And so we have reached the point where we can say that a church that lives for itself, dies by itself. But equally unlikely to survive is a church that neglects to nurture the faith of its members and the inner life of its community. This is made very clear by the 'good practice for growth' findings reported in the chapters that follow. Healthy churches are working at both sides of the equation at once. Only part of the Church's attention should be on its own attendance figures, but if the Church does not pay them proper attention then it will become too weak to be the servant to the community God calls it to be. Attendance, then, is a barometer that measures how well the Church is maintaining its potential for its core tasks. There is one other way in which attendance figures can give an indication of the real strength of the Church. The Church of England, more than most, still attracts the attention of the media and the population, for it is not just a gathered church quietly going about its own private business. It is still supposed to be the official religious expression of the country. Every decline statistic is seized on by a media that seems hostile to all institutions, including the Church of England, and anxious to announce and speed up the demise of Christendom. Every piece of statistical decline is another nail in the coffin of the Church whose parish is England. Never mind that the reality Anglicans experience is not as bad as that painted by the media – those outside the

Church do not necessarily know that. They may believe what they read in the papers and see on the TV. The image many people now have of the Church as incompetent, dying, irrelevant and corrupt may be unfair, but it does not encourage them to start attending or belonging. News of past decline can become fuel for future decline.

Therefore, if the Church of England wants to be taken seriously again in the media, and so perhaps across the country, it must reverse its numerical decline. Then there is a chance that the stories will change. To begin with, they will fall into the 'man bites dog' category: in a world where dogs usually bite men, this is news. The success of Alpha is such a story – in a world where the Church is shrinking and irrelevant, especially to the young, here are thousands of young adults having their lives turned upside down by the Church of England. It may not take many such favourable statistics of attendance trends for the fashion in Church reporting to change, and for a benevolent spiral between image and substance to replace the present vicious one. If the Church of England grows as a gathered church, it will increase in respect and influence in the parish that is the country as a whole. Truly, it is not 'gathered church' or 'church for the nation', it is both or neither.

Folk religion – goal or pathway?

The primary issue that folk religion, or diffused Christianity, raises for our central focus is whether going to church matters. How important is the gathered church? Is it belief in God, or membership of the Church, that matters most? What is the relationship between the two? Is diffusing Christianity in watered-down form around the community the priority, or is concentrating it within the tightness of the gathered congregation that matters? Is a lot of diluted sulphuric acid, or a little bit of concentrated sulphuric acid, the more potent force?

Grace Davie has coined the phrase about a shift to 'believing without belonging'.[2] Her central thesis is that church attendance has declined much faster than changes in belief – though she recognizes that residual belief is more vague and less obviously shaped by a Christian understanding of the nature of God and redemption. This holding up of belief in our culture is widely attested by many sources.[3] The 2001 Census result that 72% of the population still calls itself 'Christian' adds substance to this view. This contradiction of the view that, in the postmodern world, absence of religious faith is normative may be welcomed by evangelists trying to make connections. But it must be likely that folk religion will become ever more weakly diluted Christianity if the decades of decline roll on.

Robin Gill challenges belief in the robustness of folk religion by introducing a third factor along with belonging and believing, namely 'behaving'. As a result of detailed analysis of attitudes and patterns of behaviour, he establishes a strong connection between belonging, believing and behaving. It is clear to many practitioners and observers that the normal sequence of events in a person's journey of faith today is first belonging, then believing, then behaving. Occasionally it can be belonging – behaving – believing. For most people, the first step in engagement with the Christian faith is some connection to or involvement with the life of a local church – belonging. Their involvement may stop at that point, or it may lead on to changes in what they believe and how they behave.

What does seem clear, even working within Grace Davie's understanding, is that distance from participation in the life of the church does lead – even if only after a long period – to the erosion of a distinctive Christian conviction or behaviour. My basic contention is that, with no gathered church, the wider influence of the Christian faith on the attitudes, beliefs and behaviour of people is bound to fall.

But what of the churchgoers? Are we right to assume that going to church does enrich and change lives? Some Anglicans seem to have lost confidence in the value of church attendance for those who come. The Churches' Information for Mission recently conducted a large-scale Church Life Survey in Britain comparable to those that have been informing the life of the Church in Australia for a number of years. The first report on this, *Faith in Life*, was published in November 2001. Over 100,000 churchgoers in around 2,000 churches of many denominations, including 700 Anglicans, filled in substantial questionnaires.

The results demonstrate the importance and impact of church attendance on the lives of those who go. For example, a third of all respondents said that they had a strong and stable sense of belonging to their local church, and a further half said it was both strong and growing. A sense of belonging to a community is something many people in our society long for and never find. Four out of five said that the preaching they hear is usually very helpful to their daily lives. Three out of four said that the activities of their local church were helpful to them in their daily lives. Two out of three said that they always or usually experience the presence of God in church worship. So much for 'Nearer to God in a garden than anywhere else on earth'! Four in five said that they had grown in their faith during the last year, and two-thirds of them said this was through their local church. Three in five experience a growth in understanding and in joy when they come to church. Seven out of ten pray, meditate or read their Bibles at home during the week. Four out of five have invited people to church events in the past. One in five are currently involved in evangelistic activity of one sort or another within their church. One in three are active in serving their community through their local church, and another one in three are active in serving their community in other ways. Nearly one in four hold positions of responsibility in the voluntary world outside the church, and are active in lobbying for good causes. These levels of involvement are way in excess of those of the general population.

The evidence of the Church Life Survey is that church meets the spiritual and social needs of ordinary churchgoers, and empowers their social action, to a level far in excess of what weary or jaundiced professionals sometimes imagine. And the heart of it is their worship. The single factor most appreciated by church-goers from a wide range of denominations was the receiving of communion. This was the most valued aspect of church for 18 per cent of respondents, with preaching coming second with 12 per cent. Different sorts of worship, traditional and modern, together were the most important aspect for a further 20 per cent.

The testimony of ordinary Christians is that it is church attendance that creates, grows and empowers their Christian faith, witness and service. If our aim is to make Christian disciples, folk religion may be a way in, but going to church is what matters.

The end of Christendom?

Sociologists and historians alike ask the question 'How "Christian" is the UK?', and their conclusions vary. Anton Wessels, in *Was Europe Ever Christian?*, questions whether Christianity ever had more than a superficial impact on European culture. He therefore questions the concerns of those who fear that the UK is losing its Christian roots – he argues that they hardly existed in the first place.[4]

The more usual understanding of the impact of the faith on the wider culture is that there has been a steady, creeping secularization of society stemming from the Enlightenment and from the Industrial Revolution, which brought about the shift from settled rural living to a more fluid and impersonal urban life. On this understanding, there has been a long, slow, steady erosion of background Christian understanding that has affected both personal identity and social cohesion. This shift began in the early 1800s and has continued through to today, when one of the last vestiges of a 'Christian culture', namely an established Church, is now questioned both inside and outside the Church.

A third, more radical, view is that espoused by Callum Brown, not least in *The Death of Christian Britain*, who sets out two major arguments. He begins by challenging the whole thesis of a slow secularization of culture, arguing rather that from 1800 to 1950 the shifts in culture and drop in levels of church attendance and belief in God were really rather modest and slight. He suggests that the 'secularizing' theory stemmed from anxious clergy in the early nineteenth century who feared a drift from the Church, and tended to interpret all statistics as evidence of that. This emphasis was adopted by later sociologists of religion, who too readily assumed that the religious spokesmen of the day must have been right.

Brown then sets out his alternative thesis: that in the 1960s there was a profound and terminal shift of culture away from its Christian roots, imagery and self-understanding. Christianity as a focus that shapes our culture died quickly and recently, but it is already dead (hence the title of his book). It would seem that Cardinal Cormac Murphy O'Connor, the leader of Britain's Roman Catholics, would agree. In September 2001, in a widely reported speech, he said: 'Christianity, as a sort of backdrop to people's lives and moral decisions – and to the government and social life of the country – has now almost been vanquished.' This was doubtless not meant as an admission of final defeat and surrender, but it was interpreted as such.

And yet it is always tempting to see in the failure of the contemporary Church to be central to the formation of social, economic and public affairs some sort of degradation from a previous golden age of Christendom when the Church's authority over social order was somehow acknowledged. In his book *Christianity and Social Order*, William Temple reminds us of some of the ebb and flow of history.[5] Elizabeth I's archbishop, Grindal, attempted to prevent usury, though not too successfully. Archbishop Laud tried to use the Star Chamber to stop enclosures on behalf of the landless poor, but he did not die in his bed. 'After the Restoration, the Church of England ceased to claim moral control in the field of business. Then there was a rapid retreat upon the central citadel of religion, and during most of the eighteenth century theology and the direct relation of the soul to God were alone regarded as the Church's concern', says Temple.[6] In the nineteenth century the Church again claimed moral authority to support the abolition of the slave trade and the passing of Factory Acts. But in 1926, a group of bishops attempted to bring the political parties together to end the great coal strike. Stanley Baldwin, then Prime Minister, asked how the bishops would like it if he referred the revision of the Athanasian Creed to the Iron and Steel Federation. 'And this was acclaimed as a legitimate score', adds Temple.[7]

So perhaps the truth of the matter is much more complex than any theory of the steady or sudden erosion of 'Christendom', from whatever date. The Church has always had a hard time of it in the public arena, and history teaches us that what has ebbed may flow again one day. For example, the number of marriages had been going down for 8 years, and the number of divorces had been going up for 22, but in 2000 more people got married and fewer got divorced than in 1999. The Office of National Statistics now expects the number of marriages to keep on rising for the next ten years.

From these different perspectives, we may pick out three threads. One is that there is a clear erosion of any meaningful 'Christendom culture', if it ever existed, in our contemporary society, though this does not mean it is necessarily permanent. The second is that the influence of the Christian faith and Church seems surprisingly resilient. If the rot set in at the Enlightenment, or in 1800, or even in 1960, the Church is taking an inordinate amount of time to die. Finally, history rarely proceeds in a straight line and it is unwise to forecast the future by extrapolating recent trends.

The erosion of Christendom is not all bad news

It may be that many who left the Church in the post-war decades attended primarily for social rather than religious reasons. As those social reasons have evaporated and alternative ways of spending Sundays have emerged, the churches have increasingly been left only with those who have a living faith. Those with long memories sometimes comment that the Church of England has never been in better fettle, not only in terms of practical things like the giving of the people and the state of the buildings, but also in spiritual things like the amount of genuine prayer coming from the hearts of congregations and the numbers of people involved in spiritual leadership. If it is true that the spiritual temperature of the churches has been rising because it is only the committed who go anymore, then surely there will come a time when this new authenticity will attract a new numerical growth.

Until now, the Church of England in particular has largely assumed that a background understanding and acceptance of the broad tenets of the Christian faith were part of our heritage. We can clearly do so less and less. However, this does not necessarily mean that the level of faith commitment within our now rather smaller churches is lower than it used to be. On the contrary, it may be that the gulf between churchgoers and the others is widening from both directions at once: society is losing its Christian basis at the same time as the Church is becoming a tighter community of committed believers.

So, although the decline of the Christendom background has profound implications for the Church in this country, it should not threaten its existence, or even erode its size or vitality. After all, the Church existed and expanded before Christendom, and in the periods when Christendom loosened its grip, so it should be well able to function afterwards, though in a much changed form. 'Change and decay in all around I see' – change, yes, decay, not necessarily. After all, those denominations least associated with Christendom

63

as I have defined it – the Baptists, the Pentecostalists, the new churches – are the ones with the best recent record of attendance growth. Were the Church of England finally to decouple from Christendom and become more like the others, its attendance levels might be unaffected, or they might even improve. Around the world, the most rapidly growing churches are often those in countries with little Christian background. Nepal is the only officially Hindu country in the world, and the Christian Church there is less than 50 years old. Where once we had 'Christendom', Nepal has 'Hindudom'. The dominant culture is hostile to the Church and sometimes persecutes it. Yet Nepal has one of the fastest-growing national Churches in the world. Its success is based not on its authority as the official religious voice of the land, but on its authenticity as a weak and humble embodiment of the self-sacrificial kingdom of heaven. In fact in Nepal it is 'Hindudom' that is under threat of decline, from Western materialism, not the Church. Clearly, the Christian Church has the ability to thrive in a counter-cultural form.

Nearer to home, the Diocese of London is the one diocese in the Church of England that has seen consistent attendance and adherence growth in recent years. Yet in London the decline in the numbers of people asking clergy for infant baptisms, weddings and funerals has proceeded as far as anywhere in the country. In 2000, London Diocese performed only 2.9 per cent of the Church of England's baptisms, 2.8 per cent of its weddings, and 2.9 per cent of its funerals, yet the diocese contained 7.1 per cent of England's population. The residual 'Christian culture' or 'folk religion' background looks to be as withered away in London as anywhere in the country. Yet it is the one place where the Church of England is experiencing substantial growth.

Perhaps these two factors are connected the opposite way round from the traditional theory that the Church is built by the pastoral contacts of the occasional offices, for they are enormously time-consuming. This in no way demeans the importance of the occasional offices as a service to the nation, it simply suggests that there may be a net advantage to the church growth side of the equation in clergy being freed from them. London clergy on average in 2000 performed 6 infant baptisms, 4 weddings and 12 funerals each. The average for the Church of England during the year was 12 baptisms, 7 weddings and 24 funerals. So London clergy had only half the burden of occasional offices of the national average. Perhaps this freed them up to spend more time on church development. In Durham Diocese, on the other hand, where adult attendance decline has been as rapid as anywhere in the country, the clergy performed 18 baptisms, 7 weddings and 35 funerals each. This makes a total of 60 occasional offices in the year compared with the London clergy's 22, or a difference of almost one more occasional office per working week – which may equate to between half a day and a day's work. The average funeral requires a number of organizational phone calls, a visit to the next of kin, some preparation time, the service in church, the ride to the crematorium, the service at the crematorium, an appearance at the funeral 'wake', and a later pastoral visit to the next of kin. This is a very large slice of the 'discretionary' time parish clergy have at their disposal once the necessary weekly tasks have been performed. Far from the church attendance tip of the Christendom iceberg melting away as underlying residual Christianity disappears, this evidence suggests it might have a new chance to grow through the clergy and their churches having more time, energy and focus available for building the gathered community of faith.

An extreme example of this is a certain city church in an almost 100 per cent Muslim parish. This church has a distinctive culture and attracts a large and growing eclectic congregation. Its parish makes almost no demands on its clergy. They spend their whole time, energy and thought processes ministering to, leading and growing their own gathered congregation. It could, of course, be argued that this church has lost its proper missionary and pastoral vocation to its own parish, but, from the purely church growth point of view, the fact that its parish has left Christendom completely behind has become a very helpful thing. The church has grown as a relational community in a postmodern world, with many young adults in its congregation drawn to the church by the presence of 'people like me'. Perhaps one day this church will have the energy and vision to re-engage with its own parish in a new, mission-minded way.

The loss of Christendom, and the decline in the use society wishes to make of the Church of England for family and for state occasions, does not, therefore, inevitably imply that the Church itself will continue to decline. Its position in a post-Christendom, postmodern world might be different, but there will be gains as well as losses. We might have to get used to operating from the margins, rather than the centre, of society – but, as someone has remarked, that is no bad place to be, since the margins 'are where all the interesting things get written, not least because there is space to do so'.

So should the Church of England cling to the trappings, the responsibilities and the vestiges of its Christendom privileges – establishment, prestigious buildings, palaces for bishops, presence in Parliament, civic positions, clergy as registrars, canon law – and attempt to hold back the secularizing tide that threatens to sweep it away from such things? Or is it better to walk with dignity into the margins, still strong as a gathered community, before we are humiliatingly pushed? Should the Church accept, even embrace, being freed from palace and power in order to rediscover the servant ministry of Jesus Christ who had nowhere to lay his head? To put the question a final way, and in order that I might use the longest word I know, how antidisestablish-mentarianistically inclined should we be? This debate will doubtless mature in the Church of England over the next few years.

Living at a time of transition

We need to be aware of one final point about the 'death of Christendom'. For the foreseeable future, the Church will have to work in both a Christendom and a post-Christendom context. Whichever we may prefer, a mix and muddle between the two will be the reality of our experience. There are still many ways in which Christendom and folk religion are alive and well in the UK today. The resurgence of the observance of two minutes' silence on Remembrance Day, for example, is a striking reminder that the tide of folk religion is quite capable of running both ways. The Archbishop of York was credited, through his views on the inappropriateness of political campaigning in foot-and-mouth country, with having the 2001 general election postponed. Not many archbishops have managed that particular trick in recent centuries. We would be ill advised to talk down Christendom so far that we assume it has already disappeared.

So we are left with the major question of how the Church should give expression to its life in the changing and fragmenting culture that surrounds it. This is why the wider perspective of this chapter is so vital. If all around were staying broadly the same, then the task of the Church in addressing decline might simply be a matter of implementing the 'best practices' that are the subject of the rest of this book. As it is, we must set our analysis within the context of the major changes that are affecting the Church's place and role in society, and thereby re-imagine the Church to make it relevant for the new century that has just begun.

A threefold task for the Church

The profound changes taking place in society today call for a courageous reworking of the life of the Church on three fronts:

1. We must re-think – and then re-live – the very nature of Christian faith. Alexander Schmemann, in a relatively obscure work about liturgical theology, makes the fascinating observation that 'in order to evangelise the Empire, the Church had to turn itself into a religion'.[8] That immediately raises the question of what the Church was before it was a religion. The short answer must be along the lines of 'a way of life'. Indeed, that was the earliest title for the disciples of Christ. Before being called Christians, they were called simply 'followers of the Way'.

Since the Christendom context that Western society is moving out of has existed for well over 1,000 years, that reworking of the nature of Church and religion will not come easily. Nor will it come just as a result of rethinking. It may well come as various fringe groups explore the faith from a fresh aspect and then find it connects in ways not hitherto dreamed of. The monastic movement was not designed as a way of converting the Roman empire, or of keeping the flag of learning and of the historic faith flying through the Dark Ages, or anything as grand as that. It came into being as groups of people came together to resist the blandness of faith into which the Church had lapsed. It then became a vital part of the renewal of the faith in its day.

In our day it looks as if the exploration of the faith from the perspective of spirituality, and the development of a sense of belonging, are likely to connect with the felt needs of society. Furthermore, that is likely to happen when the faith is courageously followed by people willing to reshape their lives in the light of their encounter with God in Christ. This can already be seen in the way that centres of spirituality are playing an increasing role at a time of general Church decline: Taizé, Iona, Walsingham, Spring Harvest and Toronto have become sources of spiritual renewal for many. Movements such as Cursillo, Focolare and, indeed, Alpha are in the same stream, acting as revitalizing agents of the faith of many. The burgeoning of small 'faith communities' is also part of this process. One researcher in this area started making a list of the names of such communities in the UK. She called a halt to the exercise when the list numbered 3,000. Many of the participants of such groups may never show up, or not very often, on counts of church attenders. Part of the future work of statistical research into the size and changing nature of the Church must focus on ways of assessing the size and trend of such contemporary expressions of the faith.

2. *We must discern a new role for the Church in society today.* Christendom probably came as something of a surprise to the Church at the time – it was coping with martyrdom one minute and high office the next. However, the Church quickly adapted to its newfound authority and responsibility, and to a totally new role in society, shaping laws rather than suffering under them. Now it looks as though the Church will need to learn to function more from the margins than from the centre, from the bottom rather than the top, from a place of weakness instead of strength. It will be an invigorating experience to follow more closely Christ the Servant rather than Christ the King. We have had 1,000 years or more to model the kingly aspect of Christ – perhaps a good dose of servanthood is just what the Church needs. There are many things a marginalized, apparently weak Church can do that an established, apparently strong one cannot. It may not be a major speaker but it can be a good listener. It may not be the exclusive preserve of the privileged, but it can be inclusive for society's marginalized. It may not be part of the dominant culture but it can speak prophetically to it. It may lack authority but it can radiate authenticity.

3. We must re-imagine the Church. Robert Warren has developed a framework for a new way of seeing church, in which he envisions the twin circles of *worship community* and *mission* being held together and energized by *spirituality* (or faith).[9] Since he first developed this framework, it has become clear that two particular things are needed for this to happen. One is the renewal and awakening of the spirituality that lies at the heart of the life of the Church and within each follower of Christ. We need to be helped to see that the faith is more about following the Way of Christ than it is about being a religious person. The other is to find ways in which this spirituality can be expressed through worship, relationships and mission. I will return to this in the final chapter of this book.

We are already coming to see church as being essentially an engaging faith community rather than a religious institution. Even as the Church of England adapts to the new *Common Worship*, it knows that worship is not primarily about texts but about encounter. This is not to put 'texts' and 'encounter with God' in opposition to one another: it is to be clear that encounter is the primary element of worship, and texts are secondary. Encounter is the goal, texts have their role in achieving that goal.

Only worship, whether personal or corporate, that connects the individual with the reality and presence of the God revealed in Christ is truly Christian worship. This is already being discovered in retreat houses, in the practice of meditation, and in simple acts of worship in informal groups as well as in officially recognized church services. It may be at those sorts of margins of normal church life that worship will be renewed. And the new life that emerges will eventually touch what happens in church on Sundays. Equally, though, the church of the future may find that worship is not primarily experienced in, or seen as essentially being about, what happens in a consecrated building on one particular day of the week. The inner spiritual vitality of the faith may already be bursting the banks of organized religion.

So it may be that the new millennium in which the Church finds itself will also be a significantly new setting and context for the conduct of its life and ministry. We have mentioned three areas in which the Church is being challenged to think and live differently in response to its contemporary setting. It needs to address its own self-understanding of what Christianity is about – a way of life rather than an organized religion. It needs to recognize and act on its contemporary vocation to be the servant of society rather than one of its masters. It needs to discover how to give expression to its own incarnation as a life-giving community energized by faith in Christ, rather than simply as a safe religious organization.

Some of this newness is, and will be, expressed in new ways by new groups and structures. Church leaders need to encourage and facilitate as many encounters on the edge of the life of the Church as possible. But alongside these new ways of being church there needs to be a reform or reworking of existing structures to give visible expression to the challenges presented above. The Church needs both to live better the life it is living now, and at the same time to seek out the radical new forms of being that might match it to the challenges of the future. It is to this twin response, of living better in the now and transforming for the future, that we now turn as we examine the range of good practices that are already bearing fruit in the contemporary Church.

7

Using figures

'If a blind man leads a blind man, both will fall into a pit.'
(Matthew 15.14 NIV)

Beyond collecting facts

Church people have long been good at collecting facts but poor at facing them. Churchwardens and clergy faithfully record the number of communicants and of children and adults attending services week by week in the service registers. Once a year they fill in a complicated form for the diocese. The diocese collates the information it receives from the parishes and sends it off to the Church's statisticians in London. The figures are used for allocating resources between dioceses, and financial share between parishes.

The Church of England has not, however, been in the habit of studying its own facts and figures to see what it can learn about itself. Parishes have been unaware of their own history of growth, change or decline because they have never consulted the records they themselves dutifully create. Many diocesan leaders have not known what is happening in their own dioceses because they did not think to look at the data their diocesan offices had spent so much time and money acquiring. Dioceses usually know some of the national trends in a general way. But one diocese, for example, was blissfully unaware that it had lost one in eight of its children in one year. They had spent over a thousand man-hours in the parishes and the diocesan office counting the children and collating the results, but not half a millisecond looking at the answers. The data the Church collects on children is not even used for parish share divisions within dioceses or to allocate resources between them. It has usually been completely ignored. And the result of this is that no focused, informed attention has been paid either to the reasons for the loss of children from our churches or to the remedies. If the directors of a business never looked at the facts and figures its staff painstakingly prepared for it on things like sales, turnover and profitability, the business would almost certainly fail. In today's competitive market place for people's time and spirituality, so will the Church. We can argue that the Church is not a business. But what is more important – the spiritual future of the nation's children or the sale of baked beans?

New perspectives

However, things are starting to change. There is a growing understanding of the importance of research and analysis for informing diocesan agendas. The more aware that parishes, dioceses and the national Church become of their own trends and patterns, the more they will be able to address the issues the facts and figures reveal. For example, increasing numbers of dioceses are realizing that there is a particular problem of decline in their larger churches (see Chapter 11), and so are setting up programmes to help these churches grow again.

A church trapped in the fog of its own ignorance about itself stands as much chance as a blind man in a minefield. A church that knows itself can find the way to break out. As Jesus said, 'You will know the truth, and the truth will set you free' (John 8.32 NIV). And so it is that churches that dare actually to look at the facts, and work to address the issues that arise, fare better than those unwilling to do so. Parishes should take care to keep good records, and to improve their record keeping if it is inadequate. Does someone actually count the congregation, or just put down a wild guess? Are the columns for adults and children filled in separately? Are the old service registers readily available? Do we know in this parish what the trends are for baptisms, confirmations, weddings and funerals? Is the giving per head going up or down after allowing for inflation?

What parishes can do

A good database is a parish's eyes. Suppose that overall membership and attendance appear to be in decline. Someone with a ministry of discouragement in your church declares: 'I can remember in Canon Ball's time when we still had the Prayer Book and there were 200 every Sunday at Matins.' A look through the old service registers reveals that there were indeed 200 at Matins, once, in October 1978 when the bishop came for a special service. The old-timer is suffering from selective memory syndrome. Or you have a hunch that the 8 a.m. Communion service is at the heart of the decline because there were only six there last week. However, the registers reveal that the congregation only averaged nine five years ago, and twelve 20 years ago. The main decline must be elsewhere. Then you discover that, whereas the number of adults at the main service has hardly dropped at all, the number of children has halved in the last three years. You have found where the church bucket is leaking, and you can start to think about how you can improve what you offer to children and their parents.

One church recognized that its existing congregations were all in decline, and that it would be difficult to turn them around (see Figure 7.1). The church

Figure 7.1 St Mary's: adult attendance at different services, 1989–92

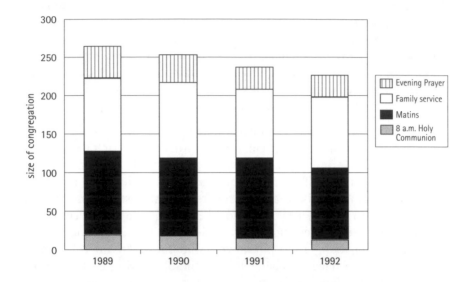

decided to allow the congregations to close down when they dropped to an unsustainable level, and to plant new congregations to replace them. During the 1990s, the Sunday evening service stopped, and the 8 a.m. service was reduced to once a month. In their place were begun a new Eucharist-based

Figure 7.2 Average total attendance at St Mary's, 1993–2001 (October counts)

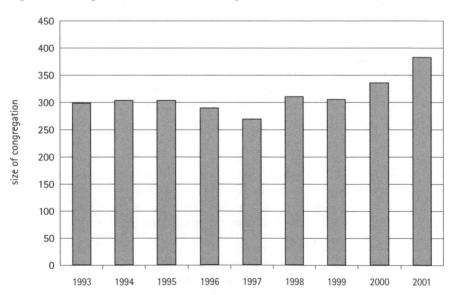

Sunday morning service, a youth service and a Tuesday evening service. Figure 7.2 shows how total attendance was sustained and grew even though the average large church in the same diocese lost a third of its attendance in the same period. In this church, the attendance figures were used both to help decide a policy for church growth and to monitor its effectiveness.

Another church discovered that the sudden increase in attendance that followed the arrival of a new vicar gradually dropped off over the following six years (see Figure 7.3). Most of this decline was in the largest of its four congregations. In 1996, empowered by a legacy, the church made two new staff appointments, a children's co-ordinator and an Alpha co-ordinator. Attendance recovered, with increases recorded in 1997, 1998 and 1999. By 2000 and 2001, however, the two staff members had moved on and the new growth ceased. Statistical analysis shows the church leadership that a new initiative is now required if growth is to be resumed and that alternatives need to be debated.

Survey data can be very useful for uncovering trends common to several parishes. One diocese conducted a survey of all of its larger churches, many of which were in decline. Two key findings emerged. Firstly, as Table 7.1 shows, declining attendance appeared to be concentrated on just two service times – early Communion and Sunday evenings. There was as much growth as decline at main Sunday morning services. The growth points were midweek services and newly planted congregations. Such findings not only pinpoint just where the Church of England is losing ground and gaining it but also provide useful

Figure 7.3 Total attendance at Christ, 1990–2001 Church (October counts)

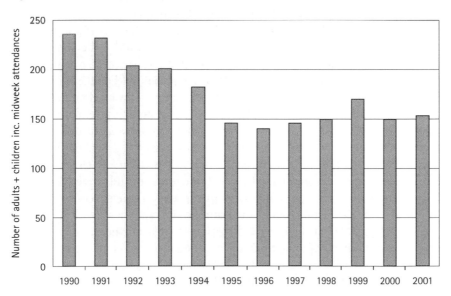

Table 7.1 The relationship between numbers attending and type of service in larger churches in one diocese

Service	No. of churches showing significant growth	No. of churches showing significant decline
Early Communion	3	8
Main morning	20	16
Sunday evening	8*	18
Midweek	6	1
Congregation plant	4	0

*Four of the eight churches with Sunday evening growth reported that it was due to a revised, contemporary service style.

pointers to parishes considering changes to their service patterns. The second key finding was that parishes that had made changes to their service styles and patterns were keeping their people much better than those that had made no changes. Between the electoral roll re-signing years of 1996 and 2002, the 15 churches that had made no changes since 1996 lost 22 per cent of their collective electoral rolls. The 26 churches that had each made at least one change added 1 per cent to their collective electoral rolls.

What deaneries can do

It is often helpful to conduct an exercise across a deanery, or to compare notes with other, similar, churches. One reason for this is that not every church has someone with the skills or aptitude for collecting statistics and arranging them in an operationally useful way, but there is almost bound to be someone in the deanery with the skills for the task. If not, then it is always possible to find someone to act as a consultant. Another reason is that there are some things churches can do well together, but struggle to do by themselves. For example, a deanery-wide investigation reveals that church attendance in the deanery has fallen by 15 per cent in the last five years. Main Sunday morning services have held up quite well, but there has been rapid decline in almost every church on Sunday evenings. Each church is reluctant to close down its Sunday evening service because of the half-dozen who still come. The clergy all agree that there may be scope for starting new midweek services, but no one church has the resources and the courage to start one in addition to the existing services. The deanery agrees to close several of the Sunday evening services and to encourage the remnant congregations to combine at the four remaining venues. They also agree to start two new 'deanery' midweek services at two of the churches and to 'market' them across the deanery.

What dioceses can do

Dioceses send out finance and attendance forms to every parish each autumn. The current forms ask for both Usual Sunday Attendance (uSa) figures on ordinary Sundays through the year when nothing special is happening, and a count of those attending all services on Sundays and midweek during four weeks in October. These figures give each diocese essential information about where growth and decline are happening. Suppose the total attendance figure is down on last year. Is the decline mainly in the towns or the villages? Is it in the large churches or the small? Is it in the suburbs or the urban priority areas? Is it in certain deaneries or everywhere? Is it connected with one church tradition or all? Is it in just a few churches with pastoral or conflict problems? Or, looked at positively, which of our churches have been growing in recent years and what can the rest of the diocese learn from them? A diocese can identify its growing churches and get them together to work out what they have in common, and what lessons can be passed on.

It is still true that some diocesan leaders and officials fail to conduct even the most simple analysis. This cannot be because they are incapable of reading figures, for the same diocesan leaders will probably be quite familiar with the parish share data. They know exactly which parishes and deaneries have failed to pay their share in full, and they are taking action to put the problem right. If such effort and expertise can be used to help secure the diocese's own income, why can it not be used to help grow the body of Christ? In any case, the two sets of data are inter-related. There is bound to be a relationship between the size of parish share a church can pay and the number of worshippers, and givers, it has. Dioceses serious about increasing the amounts of share payments would do well to pay attention not only to the giving levels of church members but also to the number of church members there are to do the giving. And there is also now a connection between the size of the parishes and the financial health of the diocese. Until recently, diocesan income came primarily from the centre. Now it comes from the parishes. A vicious circle can easily develop which goes something like this: Declining attendance makes parish share arrears more likely. These result both in higher parish share bills for all parishes the next year, and in reductions in the number of parochial clergy being paid. The remaining congregations divert more time and effort to fund-raising. Some have their priests taken away. Interregnums become longer. The net result is a further drop in attendance, and further parish share arrears.

Unless we join up our financial and church growth thinking by examining all the data, the vicious cycle of decline may be unchecked. So dioceses that are serious about reversing attendance decline have their attendance data at their fingertips and know how to use it. The key person in a diocese for informing its mission may well be the financial secretary or stewardship officer – whoever has charge of the database. This official should be tasked with ensuring that a usable set of updated management data is available to diocesan staff, together with an analysis of the key trends. This key office holder supplies the tools with the help of which the senior staff can forge a vision for the diocese. If the diocesan office does not have the capacity to analyse the trends, then someone numerate from within the diocese, or a consultant, could be employed. If the office does not have the capacity to key in the returns within a short time span, then a sub-contractor could be given the job of keeping the records up to date.

We have already looked at one example of the usefulness of attendance analysis – identifying the large churches as the heart of the decline problem in York Diocese. In this instance, the attendance data was analysed to find the root of the problem. The data can also be used to check the efficacy of a particular policy. For example, one diocese began to appoint and support rural clergy who would have a greater commitment to the spiritual health and numerical strength of their congregations. Attendance data showed that this was matched by a turnaround in rural church attendance. The most rural of its deaneries increased attendance by 6 per cent from 1997 to 2000 in a period of declining attendance elsewhere. The data suggests that the policy works.

A helpful approach to the use of statistics to inform parish, deanery or diocesan strategy is to think in terms of *description*, *decision* and *evaluation*: first *describe* past trends and the present situation, then *decide* on courses of action based on the information available, and finally *evaluate* the results. Honesty about success and failure will lead to informed future action.

A further service a diocese can easily offer its deaneries is to circulate to area or rural deans each year the attendance figures for their parishes. In dioceses where deaneries are allocated a financial share, and it is their job to divide it between the parishes, such data may already be sent to financial advisers for parish share division purposes. Deanery chapters and synods could be asked to discuss the attendance trends, their causes, and their implications for the life and policies of the deanery and its parishes. Perhaps each deanery could be asked to make a short report to the bishop each year following these discussions.

What the central authorities can do

There is some work on attendance data that only the central authorities can do or commission. For example, only they can compare the situation in different parts of the country. Sometimes larger sample sizes are needed – samples that only a national database can supply. For instance, are the non-geographical, counter-culture, 'on the edge'-style congregations growing or not? Are the very large churches, of which there may only be one or two in each diocese, growing or declining? What are their common characteristics? Only the centre can undertake comparisons between dioceses. What good practice do dioceses with growing church attendance have that can be shared with those in decline? Finally, the centre can employ researchers to discover and analyse trends and their causes in greater detail than is possible with parish or diocesan resources. It is then important that findings are shared with and taken up by dioceses and parishes. It would be suicidal of the church to leave basic research and development work for growth to be done in parallel 44 times over by 44 separate dioceses. Such a national function must involve both diagnosis – in what situations and with what policies are growth and decline happening around the country – and prescription – what can be done about halting decline and promoting growth?

A big step forward in this area was taken by General Synod in summer 2000 when it adopted the report *Statistics: A Tool for Mission* from the Statistics Review Group chaired by the Bishop of Wakefield. For the first time it was acknowledged that statistics could be used by the Church of England for mission purposes as well as for resource allocation. The Statistics Unit of the Archbishops' Council has now been renamed Research and Statistics. There is a new vision here for using the Church's database to inform the mission and growth of the Church. Unfortunately, both the people and the financial resources of the unit have been cut in the economies forced upon the Archbishops' Council by the very cycle of decline that research could have shown how to reverse. In a time of financial stringency and numerical decline it is easy to cut uncommitted expenditure such as future research budgets. However, it is for just such times that research is most needed. To decide both that statistical information and research is needed for mission, and that failure of mission means information and research cannot be afforded, is both short-sighted and foolish. Ways round need to be found.

One particular problem with the information system of the Church of England is its slowness. Parishes are asked to record their attendances in October of each year, on forms which are often not sent out until after that date. The forms don't need to be returned until the following April or May, that is, at the same time as the financial form, which has to wait for parish accounts to be audited and approved by annual church meetings. There is no reason for this apart from history, but the result is that it is harder to get parishes to return their attendance data as no sense of urgency is conveyed. Response rates in some dioceses can be quite low by the deadline date. Dioceses begin to add up the attendance returns in May, and start to send their raw data and, perhaps, their adding up, to the Research and Statistics Unit over the summer. However, because diocesan practices vary, the unit has to make its own additions. It takes some months to do the counting, and then there is a further delay while the results are checked with the dioceses before they are finally published. *Analysis* of the data has recently been speeded up thanks to the efforts of the Research and Statistics Department at Church House. The 1999 figures were not released until summer 2001, but the 2001 figures were released in December 2002. What needs to happen now is that the *collection* of the statistics is speeded up to match. The Church of England cannot respond appropriately to its own management data when it only appears when out of date. If Marks & Spencer had had the Anglican system of data collection they would only have learned about the downturn in sales in 1999 sometime in 2001. They would probably have gone out of business in the meantime. In fact, they knew about their sales downturn instantly, and quickly had policies in place to reverse the trend. By 2001 they were beginning to turn things around.

Is it possible to provide up-to-date statistics for mission purposes? There is no reason why dioceses should not send out the October count forms in advance and ask for them back at the beginning of November. Outside contractors could punch in the data within a matter of weeks, and it could easily be available internally quite early the following year. It could then be analysed centrally for trends and lessons, and a report be made available by the Archbishops' Council to every parish and diocese by March. In such a way, and with only a modest input of resources, important information could be made available to parishes, deaneries and dioceses while it is still relevant.

The Church of England is making progress in facing the facts about itself and acting upon them, at parish, deanery and diocesan level as well as in the Church nationally. However, there is still a long way to go before the Church learns to use the data it already has to release the great potential for growth through self-knowledge that lies latent within it.

Practical actions for a parish church

1. Find someone to conduct a statistical analysis of past attendance figures. What have been the growth and shrinkage points? With what were past changes in attendance associated?

2. Study the results of this analysis to help you determine future strategy. If decline has been principally among a certain age group or in a certain church service, what can be done about it?

3. Evaluate past actions. If there have been significant changes (e.g. closing or starting a particular service), what impact did these have on total attendance?

4. Analyse the attendance records of the children's groups. At what ages are you losing your children? How many children and young people are in each school year? If all the children were to stay in the church, how many could there be in a youth group in five years' time? What provision could be made for this?

5. Ask the diocese to supply you with your deanery's attendance records for the past five years and ask a deanery working group to draw conclusions from the data.

6. Keep your electoral roll up to date each year by working hard to include newcomers and to remove those who no longer attend. You will then have up-to-date information on membership or belonging as well as attendance.

7. Ask someone in your church to become familiar with national trends and lessons through reading articles and books like this one.

8. Ask your diocese to circulate an analysis of significant trends in all its numeric data in order to help each parish understand its wider context.

Chapter 8

Nurturing faith

'Go and make disciples of all nations ... teaching them to obey everything I have commanded you. And surely I am with you always, to the very end of the age.' (Matthew 28.19,20 NIV)

From event to journey

In the Great Commission Jesus did not command the Church to win converts but to make disciples. In the period up to the 1980s when many people already knew, and even subscribed to, the basics of the faith, one-off evangelistic events were a viable means of bringing them back to Church membership and so to growing discipleship. Billy Graham's 'Mission England' in the 1980s was on a scale unlikely to be repeated today, with perhaps 30,000 people a night in a football stadium. In the year following Billy's weeklong visit to Sheffield in 1984, adult attendance in that diocese rose nearly 10% – from 14,300 to 15,400. Today, however, fewer people have the inclination to attend large-scale evangelistic events, partly because they no longer associate their spiritual yearnings with the Christian Church and they have· no prior knowlege of or interest in its teachings. Today, the most well known evangelist, J John, typically aims his major events at three to four thousand people a night.

It seems that, in order to make disciples today, the Church must invest time and effort in a long and careful process of induction or nurture. Evangelism has moved from being a one-off call to repentance at the foot of the cross to a journey alongside those who are making their way into Christian discipleship. However, this will never exclude 'event-evangelists' from the process. J John is careful to ensure that his 'Ten' missions are part of a lengthy process. Local churches must undergo a long period of preparation before his visit, and be ready with the follow up. His series of meetings spread over ten weeks (going through the Ten Commandments) encourages enquirers to return week after week, as to an Alpha Course.

The journey into faith today typically starts with friendship and personal invitation, continues with exposure to church life, teaching and worship, and is completed when the new disciple acts in conformity with Christian ethics and doctrine. In other words, it starts with belonging, moves on to believing and finally to behaving, often over a period of two to five years. Only the local church can provide the continuity to do the accompanying along the journey, and so process evangelism groups within the life of the local church are commonly seen as the core of evangelism strategy today. But society is changing: one day, perhaps sooner then we imagine, today's cherished courses will seem terribly old-fashioned, and something new will be required.

The Alpha factor

We said in an earlier context that conventional wisdom is not always sound wisdom. Similarly, being fashionable does not necessarily mean that something works. Those who despair about the decline of the Church may believe that no form of evangelism can be successful in today's disinterested world. We need to test this theory against some statistical evidence.

There are many evangelism and nurture courses on the market today, but the most widely used by far is Alpha. Each year, *Alpha News* prints full lists of those churches that are using Alpha. Springboard engaged Christian Research to identify which of the 8,681 churches whose attendance figures for 1989 and 1998 were known from the Church Census data were running Alpha courses in each year from 1995. Some 1,866 'Alpha' churches were identified, and 6,815 others. Comparisons between the two groups are shown in Figure 8.1.

These figures show that there was no significant difference in growth and decline performance between non-Alpha churches and those that have run Alpha courses for just one or two years. In both cases just 21 per cent of the churches showed significant attendance growth. This is not surprising as many churches begin their process evangelism life with groups consisting mainly of existing church members. Also, most groups are of modest size and only have the capacity to add small numbers to the worshipping community each time. However, once Alpha groups have existed for at least three years the difference becomes statistically significant, and the significance increases each year. Alpha is a comparatively recent phenomenon, so the evidence for its impact over a long period is limited, but the evidence suggests that, by adding small numbers to the worshipping community with each successive course, Alpha produces a steadily accumulating growth dynamic. The difference between the percentage of churches shrinking and growing in non-Alpha churches during the period was (67–21) = 46. For regular (3–5 years) Alpha churches it was

Figure 8.1 The effect of Alpha on church attendance, 1989–98

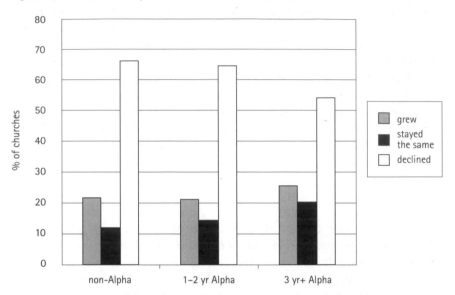

(54–26) = 28. Two-thirds of non-Alpha churches experienced shrinking attendance but only half of Alpha churches. It seems that Alpha is associated with a major slowdown in the rate of decline, but did not in the late 1990s by itself turn overall decline into growth.

There are, however, three reasons for supposing that the impact of Alpha may be rather greater than suggested by these figures. The first is that for the first half of the period 1989–98, Alpha did not exist. The difference it has made only applies to the last year or two of the period under review. A similar comparison between, say, 1995 and 2005 would be expected to show a bigger difference. The second reason is that some of the non-Alpha churches in the sample will have been using other process evangelism courses like Emmaus, Credo, Just Looking or Good News Down the Street. Evidence from diocesan surveys suggests that these are all equally likely to feed new people into the worshipping community. Alpha is not so much the most effective as the most widely used. If we were able to remove these churches from the non-Alpha sample then, presumably, we would find the gap between the non-process evangelism churches and those using one course or another would be greater than indicated in the table. Thirdly, the research showed that larger churches are much more likely to be using Alpha than small ones. We have already seen that large churches fared much less well than small ones in the 1990s, and were far more likely to be in decline. If we were to compare Alpha churches with non-Alpha churches in a similar size group, the difference would again be greater.

Further statistical evidence for the impact of Alpha on church growth has come from the Baptist Union. Their Department for Research and Training in Mission surveyed all 2,122 Baptist Union churches and found that 848 of them, or 40 per cent, were running Alpha courses. This 40 per cent between them conducted 60 per cent of all baptisms, and 51 per cent of the Alpha churches had recorded an increase in attendance at worship compared with 31 per cent of non-Alpha churches. The widespread take-up and impact of Alpha is clearly one of the reasons why attendance at Baptist churches nationally has been increasing in recent years.

Process evangelism courses, moreover, appear to attract a younger age group. According to Christian Research, 22,000 people under the age of 34 attended Alpha courses nationally in the autumn of 2001. Over three-quarters of those attending Alpha courses at Holy Trinity Brompton, the home of Alpha, are under the age of 35. The 23–28 age group is the one most attracted by these courses. We shall see in Chapter 13 that churches that are able to attract a wide age range are far more likely to grow than those lacking younger adults. The fact that Alpha seems to attract younger adults makes it doubly good news for future church growth.

Despite this evidence, however, it could still be argued that churches with the resources and the inclination to put on Alpha courses are likely to be those with the vigour and spiritual dynamic to grow anyway. Perhaps, rather than finding that Alpha churches grow, we have found that growing churches are likely to be doing Alpha. But Alpha is used by many different types of church, not just by the most obviously dynamic. The research shows that factors that are normally thought to correlate with church vigour – church tradition, location, denomination, age structure of the congregation, provision for youth worship, for example – do not correlate significantly with the hosting of Alpha courses. In any case, it is hard to see how being the sort of church that might do process evangelism (but doesn't actually) can be a plus point for growth. The evidence is everywhere – people join process evangelism courses, find faith, and engage with worshipping communities, which, as a consequence, get larger than they would otherwise have been.

Encouraging process evangelism

So churches that invest time and effort on a long-term basis in the renewal and articulation of the faith of church members, and in the sharing of that faith with enquirers to help them into discipleship, are more likely to grow than those that do not. Every church in the land can decide to adopt process evangelism as part of its long-term strategy, to structure its daily life around such courses, and to select the course which best meets the needs of its local situation.

For such a strategy to work, it is essential that church members develop their friendships in the community and encourage new and fringe church members, so that the pool of people who would appreciate the chance to join a course does not dry up. Most people will only attend if they are invited or encouraged personally by someone they trust. People whose lives have been changed by attending a course are the most likely people to invite others to subsequent courses. The growth in Alpha courses in recent years shows that there are indeed many people in the community who are seeking spiritually and are happy to explore the Christian faith in this sort of way. Table 8.1 shows that,

Table 8.1 The soul of Britain, 1987 and 2000

	1987	2000
The percentage of people:		
Seeing a pattern of events such that 'it was meant to be'	29%	55%
Having awareness of the presence of God	27%	38%
Having awareness of answers to prayer	25%	37%
Having awareness of sacred presence in nature	16%	29%
Having awareness of the presence of the dead	18%	25%
Having awareness of an evil presence	12%	25%
Cumulative total (at least one mentioned)	48%	76%

Source: Professor David Hay, Nottingham University, for the BBC series *Soul of Britain*.

although the 1990s were a time of declining religious observance, they were also a time of heightened spiritual awareness and need. Courses designed to help people explore their spiritual journey in a Christian context seem to be in tune with the age. They enable the Church to make contact with many people as they explore their spiritual experiences and longings, and try to find out if a Christian faith can make sense of them and satisfy them.

So how do we do it?

Some churches may see the point of process evangelism, but feel too small or inadequate to sustain a course by themselves. Other churches may feel they lack the leadership necessary to deliver such a course successfully. Such churches need not feel disenfranchised. They can join with others and seek the help and resources of the Alpha network or para-church groups, other local churches, a deanery or a diocese. Each deanery could consider how all its churches could best work together to deliver process evangelism throughout the deanery. Each diocese could have a policy of encouraging blanket coverage, such that in every deanery and parish there would be a route for enquirers into a relevant and appropriate process evangelism course. London Diocese, for example, has an ambition to develop a process evangelism course in every parish by 2004.

The sheer scale of Alpha's success, together with its charismatic flavour, can be a problem. People may not be aware of the other courses that exist, or of the range of choice available. Churches which have trouble subscribing to the particular churchmanship and theology of Alpha may need help from a different structure. Dioceses therefore need not only to encourage, but also to make sure that potential course leaders are aware of the full range of courses available. They can provide training for these leaders, and finance where necessary for training and course expenses. They can also spread some of the good news stories that emerge from these courses through diocesan newsletters and mailing lists. By promoting all courses equally, a diocese can demonstrate that process evangelism need be a threat to neither churchmanship nor theology. Rather, it is an integral part of good practice for the whole of today's Church.

It is undoubtedly true that the rise of process evangelism has been a major result of the Decade of Evangelism. It has already had an impact on church life in terms of both the renewal of the faith and the growth of the Church. However, there is still plenty of scope for more growth as the practice continues in those churches that have adopted it and spreads to others. Existing courses will outlive their usefulness and new ones will need to be prepared, with both new material and new formats. The job for the Church of England in the next few years is something it is normally quite good at – to take what began as a fringe idea, recognize its God-given potency for sharing the faith and the growth of the Church, and make it thoroughly and respectably mainstream in the life of every parish.

Practical action for a parish church

1. Look at the alternative courses on the market and decide which one to use on a long-term basis.
2. Choose and train a small group to run and lead the course. Send someone to a training event.
3. Personally invite potential members of the first course – people on the fringe of church life or friends and neighbours of church members.
4. Consider joining with another church to create a more viable course.
5. Work hard at developing and maintaining contacts with potential members of future courses.
6. Make it a priority to offer a process evangelism group at least once a year.
7. Keep contact at the end of the course, help each member to a next step, and monitor the impact on church life over the years.

9

Welcoming all

'And other sheep I have, which are not of this fold: them also
I must bring, and they shall hear my voice.' (John 10.16 AV)

Narrow church cultures

A parish church should be open and welcoming to everyone in the community.
Yet many churches seem only to attract one type of person – perhaps one age
group or one social class or one musical sub-culture group. The stronger and
more well-defined the tradition and style of a parish church, the more likely
it is to become a congregation of the like-minded. Churches also develop their
own brand of worship culture, and this can easily exclude certain personality
types. Introverted contemplatives may not feel at home in a noisy charismatic
service, nor exuberant worshippers at Matins. Most churches think that they
are a welcoming church, but many churches only successfully welcome 'people
like us'. Newcomers will often know within half a second of entering a church
building whether they have a chance of joining this congregation – if there
are insufficient 'people like me' then the newcomer will not be sticking around.

There are also two dynamics at work that tend to narrow down further the
band of the population with a chance of relating to a particular church. Firstly,
quite naturally, a church will put on the type of service that the majority of
its members want. The average age of Anglicans has increased in recent years,
and many churches have few people under the age of 60. If your church is
full of grannies, then you put on granny services. The problem is that, if you
only put on granny services, your church will only ever be full of grannies.
What is right for those who attend today might not be the best vehicle for
attracting others and ensuring a long-term future. Imagine if this same church
switched to putting on only youth services. The grannies would soon melt
away, and before long the only people around would be teenagers.

The second dynamic is that of tradition. Many of our larger churches grew on
the backs of their own particular fine traditions, of whatever sort – a musical
tradition or a preaching tradition or a particular style of worship. This worked
when society was more homogeneous than it is today. Enough people could

be found to cohere around a particular tradition and form a large church. Today, this is no longer the case. Society is fragmenting fast, the number of sub-cultures is multiplying, and yet at the same time many people seem isolated and alone, and don't seem to belong to a sub-culture at all. In this environment, churches that try to hang on to their fine tradition from the past are likely to be shrinking today.

Anglicanism must be multi-cultural

It comes as no surprise that the evidence suggests that churches that engage with a variety of cultures are more likely to grow today than those dominated by just one culture or type of person. This is, after all, what the Church of England is supposed to be about – making itself available to the whole nation rather than retreating into a small, sub-cultural ghetto based around a particular prayer book, liturgy, type of music or preacher. It is also what the gospel imperative is about – to go and make disciples of all, not just of a few who happen to be like us. Jesus was an inveterate crosser of boundaries – between fishermen and tax collectors, freedom fighters and lawyers, Jews and Samaritans, rich and poor, young and old, men and women. The history of Christian mission is that of the progressive crossing of boundaries. The Mar Thomas Church in Kerala State in South India survived in a fossilized state for centuries by keeping to itself and not troubling the Hindu culture around it. It abandoned the mission imperative of the Great Commission, and suffered spiritual atrophy as a result. The Christian gospel only came to the rest of the subcontinent when missionaries, with all their faults, started crossing boundaries in the nineteenth century. Similarly, the local church today needs to engage with the cultures around it if it is not to retreat into its own private, shrinking little world, abrogating the responsibility given it by Christ to reach all people with the gospel.

Some of the evidence that churches that engage with a variety of cultures are more likely to grow comes from ethnicity data. The 1989 and 1998 Church Census forms asked ethnicity questions. Just as a barium meal is easier to track as it passes through the body than is ordinary food, so those from different ethnic groups are easier to track through the body of Christ than are other social groupings. Figure 9.1 summarizes the findings – only 20 per cent of all-white churches grew in the period, but 23 per cent of those with a 1–24 per cent ethnic mix, and 27 per cent of those with at least a 25 per cent ethnic mix. The richer the mix, the more likely a church is to grow and the less likely it is to shrink. The most significant difference between the ethnically mixed and the all-white churches was in the percentage of those experiencing major decline. Some 18 per cent of all-white churches lost at least 60 per cent of

Figure 9.1 The impact of ethnic mix on church attendance, 1989–98

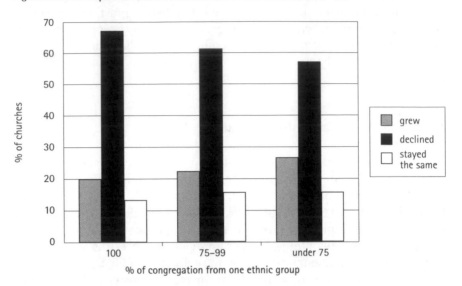

their attendance between 1989 and 1998, but only 7 per cent of ethnically mixed churches declined as much. The reason for this difference may in part be due to the extra spiritual energy that some ethnic groups bring, but it is also the consequence of churches successfully opening themselves up to 'people who are not like us'.

Other evidence comes from those churches that make worship provision for young people. The data in Chapter 10 shows that churches that offer specialist youth worship alongside their adult services are twice as likely to grow – two in five churches with youth worship provision grew their attendance in the period, compared with less than one in five of those without youth provision. Other evidence comes from age profiles, as we shall see in Chapter 13. Only 20 per cent of churches with no one over 45, and 13 per cent of those with no one under 45, grew in the 1990s. But 42 per cent of those with a good mix of ages were growing. Once again it proves the point, that churches that contain a wide range of different sorts of people are more likely to be flourishing today than those that do not.

Building a coalition

So, how can churches build healthy coalitions of different sorts of people in contemporary culture? How can churches best encourage new and different people into participation, decision-making and leadership? How can churches themselves become multicultural so as to serve, reflect and grow in the multicultural society in which they are set?

Once again, the starting point for many churches is to take a look at themselves and their parish in order to assemble some facts and figures. Which groupings in our area are poorly represented in the life of the church? What can be done to engage with such groups of people? Who in the church has the gifts, the vision and the vocation to lead such an engagement? What resources and attitudes will they need from the whole church to back them up? Most churches lack the resources to engage with every local group at once. It is much more sensible to work out through prayer and practical research which the one or two priority groups should be. Then a congregation can find out from their 'missing groups' how they view the church and the Christian faith. They can go looking for people who will change and enrich the culture of the church. They can start a project or group or worship service focused on the groups in question, aiming to use the gifts of the people from that group to run the activity.

Unity or choice

We are immediately faced with a strategic issue. On the one hand, Christians are supposed to be 'all one in Christ Jesus' (Galatians 3.28 NIV), with no distinction between different groups of people. The love of God embraces all, and all should be included. The gospel imperative demands reconciliation not just with God but with each other as a sign and foretaste of the kingdom. However, it seems that expecting people to jump through cultural hoops in order to belong to the worshipping community is to put a stumbling block in their way. Unless we offer a diversity of culture in nurture, fellowship and worship we cannot offer belonging to a diversity of people types within our local situations. Large congregations have been in decline in recent years, mainly because of relational problems. The need of people to find community within their church life is more easily met within smaller fellowships where everyone can know everyone else. So on the one hand we want to reach out to and embrace a diversity of peoples and cultures in one big, happy church family, but on the other hand we need to offer the experience of worship and community to different people from different cultures in ways they can relate to.

Many churches deal with this dilemma by offering worship that includes both traditional and modern elements, both classical and popular music, both a formal and an informal approach. Sometimes, by the grace of God, as a sign of the counter-cultural nature of the kingdom, such services work well. The joy of relationships across the boundaries outweighs what many people would see as a compromise, as the watering down of worship to its lowest common denominator. But in too many churches the reality has been one of division and dissatisfaction, where services designed to express unity have resulted in conflict. Relationships between the choir and the music group have varied from sullen acceptance to open sabotage. Vicars have been told week in and week out both that the worship was too traditional and that it was too modern. Two or more power groups in the church have fought for control of the worship agenda, and those who have lost the battle have left. For the sake of the growth of the kingdom and the future of the Church, is there a better way to welcome all and grow in unity?

The multi-congregation model

One solution to this dilemma is the multi-congregation model of church. Any church that holds more than one service a week can let each service develop in its own distinctive style, and begin new ones as new groups are reached. The parish mentioned in Chapter 7, with its Prayer Book Matins congregation, its family worship congregation, its modern Eucharist congregation, its youth congregation and its Tuesday evening congregation is one such church. Each service is conducted entirely in the appointed style without the need for compromise and without posing threats to other members of the church. No congregation is expected to grow beyond what seems to be its natural maximum size (usually today around 100), for new growth will come through new planting. Such a church is able to offer its parish, if not tailor-made worship and spirituality solutions, at least a wide range of off-the-peg models to suit most tastes. Unity comes through a shared vision and purpose, strong leadership that affirms every style of worship and of being church as equally valued and honoured, mingling in the organizational and group fellowship life of the church, a single PCC and authority structure, and taking part in occasional joint 'celebration' level services.

The cell model

Another way of being church that can help to celebrate diversity while maintaining unity is the cell model. Cells can take a wide variety of forms, and enable many different people to find a place of belonging, mutual pastoral support, and Christian service within a single worshipping community. (The case for the cell church model being increasingly appropriate to the times is made at greater length in Chapter 11, in the context of how large churches can capture the relational advantages of the small, and so grow in new ways.)

Both the multi-congregation and the cell model require much committed and energetic leadership to enable them to function well. A vicar with six or ten congregations needs to work with a strong team of Readers, assistant clergy, and other leaders. Cells require high-quality leadership to work well. If there are, on average, six people in a cell then one church member in six must be a cell leader. It may even be that part of the strength of such a model is that leadership is perforce multiplied and shared. No longer is one man or woman in control of every detail of everyone's worship and pastoral care: everyone is enabled to offer their own talents and leadership to God in the varied worshipping and fellowship life of the church. Structures that require a lot of leadership are liable to grow new leaders. Not least, they can give opportunities to young adults to assume leadership positions in local churches. This is how future leaders, including future clergy, are best discovered and developed – 'He who is faithful in a very little is faithful also in much' (Luke 16.10 RSV). The multiplication of leadership responsibilities also increases commitment and participation levels as more people feel valued and needed. As long as responsibility is evenly spread, no one need be overburdened or burnt out by such a system, rather the capacity and ministry of many can be developed and nurtured through the daily life of the church.

How can small churches welcome all?

However, there will always be churches that are too small or too weak to adopt either of the above models. A village church with 20 members which shares a single minister with six other churches is unlikely to be able to put on more than one service a week. In towns and cities, the Church caters for cultural variety through the different types of church it has to offer, plus a tacit acceptance that people will shop around to find the church that suits them best. But some churches have grown too weak to make any impact at all, others have closed, and in other places the variety needed for today's world does not exist because the lottery of patronage has dictated a local preponderance of one type of church only. For these situations, deaneries and dioceses need to play a more proactive role than they have done in the past. A deanery can ask the question 'What groups are not being engaged with by the churches in this area?' just as well as a single church can ask it of itself. Churches working ecumenically or deanery wide can take initiatives together. For example, a group of churches that have each lost their Sunday school could begin a new joint worship club for children, pooling their leadership and financial resources and reaching right outside the existing worshipping communities for the children. A rural dean could chart the worship events on offer in the deanery, identify the gaps, and work on a deanery-wide strategy for filling them. This could be done with a completely new venture, or by persuading parish A to reach out to one missing group in the town and parish B to another. Churches in a rural area with no young people worshipping in them could together employ a deanery youth worker with a deanery youth minibus, and turn one little-used village church into a deanery youth centre.

Can anything good come out of a deanery?

Actions, such as those above, that deaneries can take are scattered throughout the practical sections of this book. But many Anglicans' experience of deaneries is that they are an artificial, inappropriate and barely functional bureaucratic imposition. 'What have the deaneries ever done for us?' is a not uncommon cry. Deanery synods are commonly composed of '33 Anglicans with nothing better to do all waiting to go home'. However, this is not the case everywhere, and in some areas deaneries fulfil a useful function. One major reason why deaneries have such a bad name is that parishes used to have very little concept of or interest in working collaboratively with one another. Many good practices for the future growth of the Church now demand such working together, as we have seen. Maybe the deanery's hour has come. It will still be the case, however, that many deaneries will not be the natural unit for some co-operative ventures. In that case, a smaller unit of naturally relating churches, either all Anglican or a mix of denominations, is what is needed. The word 'deanery' can then be read as shorthand for any such grouping of churches at the local level.

The role of the diocese

A diocese has a broader perspective again from which to assess which groups the churches of an area are failing to reach. For example, one diocese has noticed that there is a large evangelical church with a strong youth ministry in every town in the diocese except one. Very few young people in this town relate to any Anglican church. The diocese is looking for ways of making provision for young people in the town in question – perhaps with a directly employed youth minister, or by encouraging the churches to work together, or by appointing someone in one of the parishes who will make young people a priority.

Hearts matter more than structures

We are called by God to be church in a way that enables a welcome to be given to all, but so often the mechanics and realities of church life make this hard to achieve. However, there are ways in which individual churches and churches working together can achieve this objective. Some of these, such as the multi-congregation model, are organizational and technical solutions to the problem of mixing fellowship-welcome to all with tailor-made provision for all. But, as in the whole of church life, it is the attitude of the heart that matters most. Unless the people of a church genuinely wish to welcome all, and are prepared to take the consequences to their own comfort that such a welcome will inevitably bring, any attempt by its leaders to open up the church to all will fail. Or, to put it another way: if the hearts of the people are open to the world outside the church, then all manner and condition of human beings will be drawn to Jesus Christ through the church.

Practical actions for a parish church

1. Do a survey of your church members to build up a picture of your church community with regard to things like age and ethnic mixes.

2. Find out about your local area and compare the types of people in the church with those outside it.

3. Identify one initiative that will bring the church into contact with a 'missing group'. Appoint a team to run the initiative.

4. If your congregation is divided between two camps with different ideas about worship, have two different Sunday morning services instead of one compromise one.

5. Decide to adopt a multi-congregation model and start by planting one new one. Bring in outside help from the Church Army's Sheffield Centre.

6. Join together with other churches to reach out to a missing group.

7. Appoint a deanery youth worker and give him or her a minibus and a church building to use as a base.

8. Ask the diocese to provide some seed-corn funding for these initiatives.

10

Taking risks

'If anyone causes one of these little ones who believe in me to sin,
it would be better for him to have a large millstone hung around
his neck and to be drowned in the depths of the sea.'
(Matthew 18.6 NIV)

The C of E has slow reactions but it takes risks eventually

The Church of England has never been famous as an impulsive, quick-thinking
risk taker. Stephen Neill describes a classic period in its history thus:

> The Church of England had become inflexible and immobile. In 1750
> England had been in the main a country of villages, and its great
> centres of population were all south of the Trent. By 1850, with a
> greatly increased population, it had become a country of teeming
> towns, and the centre of gravity of the population was in the north.
> But the Church was still trying to meet the problems of the modern
> world with the creaking machinery of the Middle Ages.[1]

Neill then goes on to describe the Victorian era of church building, which got
under way long after the cities had begun to grow, and which he describes as
'too little too late' because the Church had already alienated the urban working
classes by its neglect of them. However, it was, by any standards, a radical
move on the part of the Church to put up so many new buildings in so short
a space of time – perhaps the most visibly radical and financially risky thing
the Church of England has ever done.

It is, perhaps, reassuring to remind ourselves that the social change of the
early nineteenth century was probably every bit as great an upheaval as that
of the onset of postmodernism, and that the Church of England lagged behind
at least as far then as it does now. But by the end of the century a lot of
catching up had been achieved through radical action, and we now look back
on the period as something of a golden age in the life of the Church and its
influence on society. So can the Church of England regain lost ground again

through imaginative risk-taking initiatives, or is it already so far behind that any response will inevitably be 'too little, too late'?

Holy desperation

Not everyone has responded to the decline of the Church with either denial or despair. Some of those who have devoted their energies to the renewal of the Church in recent decades have seen the Church change and, in part, be renewed. But the pace and scale of this movement has not kept up with rapid social change. The Church still often feels 'inflexible and immobile'. In its inherited or traditional form, the Church has continued to lose ground and become ever more irrelevant despite these people's best efforts. It seems as though new waves of renewal have brought momentary hope, only to be dashed when the exceptional wave has receded to reveal that the tide has kept on going out underneath it. These disappointed hopes have led not to despair but to a sort of holy desperation. This desperation drives those who despair of the ability of the Church to rise to the challenge of the times with a new radicalism. For the despairing there is no hope, for the desperate there is still the possibility of radical risk taking, of creating new wineskins for some new wine.

Can dioceses deliver?

The argument between the reformers and the revolutionaries, between those who see new life and growth in semi-traditional church and those who see only death without radical new forms of church, was mentioned in Chapter 5. The conclusion there was that the model of renewal and revival in the wake of attainable reforms still has the capacity to turn around the church, if not to convert England. However, the model of exile and restoration, or death and resurrection, which is far less comfortable, also needs to be embraced. In many situations, the death of the existing church building or congregation may be a necessary ground-clearing exercise to make way for the resurrection of missionary activity and worshipping community in a new form. If a diocese fails to re-energize its life sufficiently to survive as a viable unit in the face of financial crisis and numerical decline then its death as an organizational unit may need to be welcomed. The Baptist Union appears to be dismantling its version of dioceses in order to create more mission-minded organizational units, and it is possible that the Church of England will need to do the same. However, the existing structures will continue in business for the moment, and it is clear that they are capable of at least limited reform for growth because they are already doing this. However, part of that reform must involve the institutional Church moving, as in the mid-nineteenth century, from being a barrier to radical change to being an agent of it.

Taking risks 'on the edge'

A church takes risks when it closes down some of its old activities or services. It risks going into decline, and it risks internal conflict with those who do not wish to let go of old forms. A church equally takes risks when it starts new ventures, tries things out, is willing to have a go, to make mistakes and learn from them. Such churches, evidence suggests, are more likely to grow in today's fast-changing world than those that are cautious, dubious about new ventures and fear failure. The church in Chapter 7 that took the risk of closing services down and opening new ones up saw its total congregation rise instead of fall. Chapter 12 will demonstrate the immense growth potential of newly planted congregations. Chapter 11 will show that larger churches are liable to decline unless they take quite significant action to improve their structures of welcome and fellowship. One key area where innovative risk taking in response to holy desperation is already taking place across the country relates to the place of children and young people within church life. Reactions have indeed been slow – Sunday schools have been shrinking for 100 years – but radical changes in the way children's ministry is conducted are now giving significant glimpses of hope for the future. It is to this key area of risk taking that we now turn.

Do Sunday schools have a future?

Figure 10.1 shows the trend in the number of children (under-16s) attending Church of England Sunday services and their associated children's groups from 1910 to the end of the twentieth century. During the 1990s the number fell by 28 per cent, double the decline rate among adults. But child attendance decline also leads on to a decline among young adults, and builds in a 'demographic' decline for decades to come. Figure 1.4 (see page 13) includes a projection up to the year 2030 on the assumption that future attendance decline will run at the same percentage rate as in the 1990s. Such a projection may or may not turn out to be accurate, but in a way this hardly seems relevant. The main loss has already been sustained. For every 100 children who were in Sunday school in 1930 (and who are now in their seventies and eighties), there are only 9 today. If any of the traditional ministries of the Church of England have declined to the point of almost complete failure, it is Sunday schools. If the model of death and resurrection applies anywhere in church life, it is here.

Figure 10.1 Usual Sunday Attendance of children (under 16) in the Church of England, 1910–2000

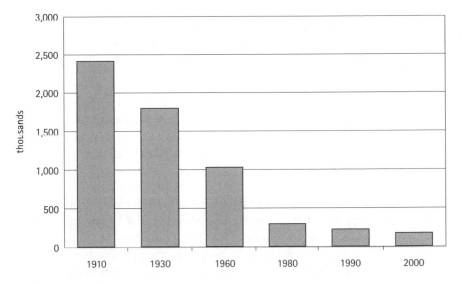

The only children left in most churches are those of church members who are brought by their parents. Many of these children come unwillingly. Fewer and fewer parents see any way in which the Church is relevant to their children's upbringing, although some may attend in order to get their children into the Church school. It is increasingly difficult to find Sunday school teachers or youth leaders for the few children that remain because churches have fewer people in their twenties and thirties to be the leaders, and because many feel that they do not have the time and energy in today's pressurized world. Many are also keen not to miss out on the adult act of worship each week by leaving with the children just before the sermon. The complications of the Children Act have put some churches and individuals off children's work. There is a continuing increase in alternative Sunday activities for children, including those arranged by schools and sports clubs. For children whose parents have separated, Sunday is often 'Dad's Day', perhaps spent away from the child's own home neighbourhood. The way in which children learn, and the culture within which young people live their lives, continues to change and to involve ever more sophisticated entertainment and educational gadgetry. It is difficult for many churches (where colouring in is still a major activity) to match the experience and expectations of children today. The fact that children in church form an increasingly small minority both of their own peer group and of church members means they often feel isolated there. They do not fit the culture, their church is not full of 'people like me', and, in truth, the life and worship of the church is not suited or geared to 'people like me'. In many churches there may still be some children, but hardly any teenagers, and so there is little provision for them. The children therefore absorb the expectation that they will leave once they have 'grown out of it'. It is no wonder that most church children take the first opportunity they can to leave, usually around the time of starting secondary school. We cannot expect traditional Sunday schools to be the powerhouse of the growth of the kingdom in the lives of children at the start of the twenty-first century.

However, this is no reason for giving up either on Sunday children's groups or on children. In many churches it is still vital to make proper provision for children on Sunday mornings, both for their own sakes and to enable their parents to come. There may be no point in a church extending a welcome to families coming for baptism if those families can't attend each week without major traumas because there is no crèche facility. Well-run Sunday children's groups are still the main way in which children are nurtured in the faith in Anglican churches. But if these are to be a church's first choice, the quality must be high, resources must be poured into the leadership of them, and there must be an attractive structure for the children to progress through. Children in churches with Sunday schools but no youth fellowship already know that they are expected to leave when they reach the age of about twelve. How would older folk feel if there were no fellowship groups for them to belong to once they retired? A church will get what it expects. However good the crèche, the Climbers or the Pathfinders groups, a church will have failed its children, and will lose them, unless it can deliver belonging and peer group all the way through to adulthood.

Some churches are finding ways of delivering this to today's young people, sometimes through making traditional methods work well, but at other times through the adoption of more radical change. The rest of this chapter will look at five recent risk-taking developments in the Church's approach to children and young people that together have the potential to bring about a revolution in provision and a reversal of decline. Each one has its own risks and costs, but together their impact on the future not only of the Church but of the nation could be profound.

1. Churches working together

The Sunday school model involves churches working in isolation from each other, except that they might buy in teaching resources from a national agency such as CPAS. But in places where the numbers of children in each church are small, and leadership resources are limited, working together looks a better option. Figure 10.2 shows child attendance totals for the deaneries of the East Riding Archdeaconry of York Diocese in 1998 and 1999. With rapid decline

Figure 10.2 Percentage change in the uSa of children in East Riding deaneries, 1998–9

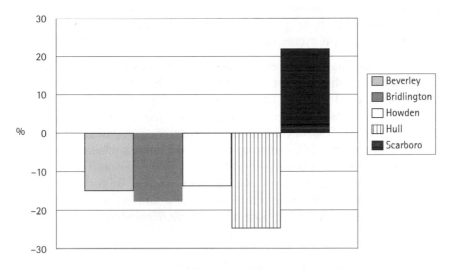

all around it, one deanery showed a substantial increase. That increase was partly due to the fact that the churches came together to form a joint group for all their children of secondary school age, called Scarborough Rock. This was able to offer high-quality worship, teaching and social events to a large group of young people, who responded to it enthusiastically. The local churches are also combining to provide a Christian dry bar and a Christian schools worker for the local secondary schools. It seems that working together to produce one high-quality joint provision is better than working in isolation, offering small-scale provision to just a few children at a time.

2. Moving away from Sunday

In the late 1970s, the Crusaders' Union (an organization that runs Bible classes all over the country) began to notice a new phenomenon. Most of its groups met on Sunday afternoons, and they were beginning to decline in numbers. But a few groups, usually for local, practical reasons rather than due to any special policy, were meeting on week-night evenings, and these were growing in numbers quite well. Groups were therefore encouraged to switch their meetings from Sundays to week-nights, and now most Crusader groups meet during the week, and numbers attending overall have risen.

Churches that make a similar change to their provision for children today sometimes have similar success. One advantage of such a change is that week-night meetings are much more likely to attract children whose parents do not come to church. It is also easier to find leaders for them because the activity does not clash with Sunday worship. In today's mobile society, both leaders and children are likely to go away for weekend or Sunday outings, but not for many week-night evenings.

One format that has shown remarkable results recently is Kidz Klub, which is now being established by churches in a number of towns and cities. One urban priority area (UPA) parish in Liverpool currently has 350 children belonging to its Kidz Klub, which meets in different age groups for worship and for entertainment on Thursday evenings. The children themselves take a part in leading the worship, for example by leading the prayers. Children are visited regularly in their homes by members of the leadership team and given puzzles, worksheets and memory verses as preparation for the following Thursday.[2] Church has been re-created for children at a time and in a way that they can access and enjoy, and the response has been overwhelming.

3. Professional youth and children's workers

The advertisement columns of the Church press in recent years have borne testimony to the increase in the number of paid church youth and children's worker posts available. A number of factors have led to the professionalization of this ministry. One is the more stringent and professional approach required of churches by the Children Act and by child protection policy. Another is the decline in the number of young adults in churches able to act as role models and leaders for young people. Then there is the failure of existing provision and the desire to improve it. And finally there is the age of the clergy. In the late nineteenth century, the Church of England ordained about 750 young men a year, usually between the ages of 23 and 25. For most of the twentieth century it was common for the curate to lead the youth work. But by the end of the century the number of stipendiary curates had dropped by two-thirds, and most were in their thirties or forties when they were ordained. More than half the stipendiary clergy in the Church of England are now aged over 50, and many feel that they are no longer able to take an effective lead in work with children and young people.

If demand for professional youth workers has risen, so has the supply. The Centre for Youth Ministry (CYM) was established in four major training colleges (three of them Anglican) in Cambridge, Oxford, Nottingham and Bristol in 1998–9. Large numbers of young adults (usually aged 19–25) are being trained alongside ordinands in three-year courses leading to validated university degree level qualifications in church youth work. CYM students study by distance learning, living most of the time where their placement post is located, and attending teaching at the college for two or three days a fortnight. The first students graduated in 2001, so a large new trained and professional workforce for youth and children's work is just starting to be available to the churches, particularly the Church of England. This huge response to the crisis with children and young people seems bound to have an impact on the national statistics providing that the churches actually employ the graduates as they come on stream.

A church youth and children's worker is not supposed to do all the work by him- or herself, but to raise, train and lead a team to do it. The core purpose of this ministry in many churches is to maintain and grow the faith and worship of church children as they develop into adulthood, to help them into active discipleship, and to enable them to evangelize their friends. In churches that have few children at the moment, the main purpose is to begin with children and young people without existing church connections. PCCs need not be put off the idea of employing a youth or children's worker by a glance at the annual accounts. Large and medium-sized churches with more prosperous members can often raise the finance through a special appeal to parents and concerned church members – 'You spend £5 a week on music lessons for your child, could you spend £5 a week on their Christian upbringing?' Smaller churches can each make a contribution towards the cost of a joint post. UPA parishes can apply to a range of grant-making bodies that are interested in making provision for youth work. No church and no child need be excluded. National and diocesan funds could be invested in such projects. One diocese has a start-up fund to help parishes get going with youth work initiatives. Dioceses might also employ a few young people's evangelists, church planters and pastors themselves for projects that are not parish-based.

Funding is widely available for youth work from grant-making bodies, but finding such bodies and making the right sorts of applications often requires some specialist expertise. Perhaps the diocese could assist parishes in this by employing an expert in this field. Some parishes, especially UPAs, have developed their own expertise in this art, but for most the prospect is daunting. It is likely that such a specialist would bring far more money into a diocese during a year than it would cost to employ them.

Research into the impact of professional workers on church youth and children's ministry is overdue. People are being trained, and resources are being deployed, because many in the Church believe this to be a way of turning the tide. Anecdotal evidence is encouraging, but systematic national statistical evidence is needed to shed light on what practices seem to be successful. Some evidence from St Albans Diocese, however, is encouraging, as shown by Figure 10.3. Out of 15 parishes with a professional youth and children's worker, only 6 had a net loss of Sunday attendance among under-16s between 1995 and 1999. Collectively, this group slightly increased their numbers of young people.

Figure 10.3 Usual Sunday Attendance of children at large churches with and without a professional youth and children's worker, Diocese of St Albans, 1995 and 1999

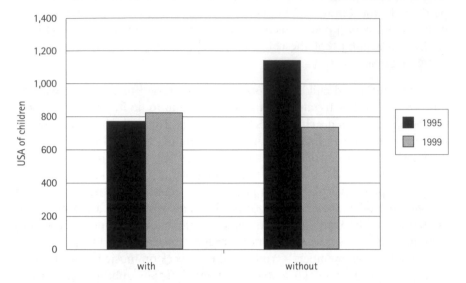

A comparable 'control' group of 15 churches which had similarly large numbers of children in 1995, chosen randomly from other parishes in the diocese, collectively lost over a third of their attendance in the same period. All but one of this group suffered a decline in their numbers of children and young people. It would seem that employing professional workers did not lead to significant numerical growth, but it did halt the decline, which in itself is a significant achievement.

Coventry Diocese aims to employ at least one full-time youth and children's worker per deanery. The number of workers in the diocese rose from 5 in 1996 to 30 in 2001. Coventry is one diocese where child church attendance has not been declining rapidly. From 1996 to 1999 it remained about the same, whereas nationally attendance declined by 8 per cent. Although further work on this needs to be done, the figures do suggest that employing professional, specialist staff members is a good practice that at least halts the decline in the numbers of children and young people in the churches. And one would imagine that it also gives them a better quality of Christian learning and experience.

4. Worship geared specifically to the young

Imagine that you are a quiet-living pensioner, getting a little frail, who loves the Book of Common Prayer. In your church you are the only member aged over 25, and everyone else arrives by motorbike. Services are accompanied by strobe lighting, the pews have been replaced by a dance floor, and the organ by a rock band. It is the only time in the week that you are able to leave your hearing aid at home. The rest of the congregation talk to each other in a language that may be English, but not as you would understand it. The sermon is all about 'relationships'. You would move to another church, but in your area they are all the same. How long before you stay at home on Sundays?

This situation in reverse is exactly that faced by young people and younger adults in many Anglican churches today. It is abundantly clear that church is not designed for them and so they cease to belong. It is not that their generations lack religious instincts – it is that the Church fails to offer them what is needed to nurture and release those instincts. Churches may respond by saying that they would make provision for worship in styles that young adults and young people could relate to if they had any, but they don't so there is no point. But which comes first, the chicken or the egg? Do churches fail to provide worship for young adults and teenagers because they have none, or do they have no young adults and teenagers because they make no provision for them?

It is still true that the most common time in life for people to come to faith is in their teens. This is when world views and fundamental attitudes are formed and harden. Teenagers respond as readily as ever to a well-presented, relevant and appropriate Christian invitation. Evangelistic organizations working with children and young people are still able to elicit mass initial response when they present the love of God in Christ. Their problems begin when they bring youngsters into contact with local churches.

In those places where there is good practice, however, the seed sown does have a chance of being nourished and growing. In other places, perhaps the good practice for the future will be to plant a new youth church at the end of every youth mission, in fact for that planting to be the aim of the mission. This might best be done by one or a group of the local churches in co-operation with the evangelistic agency. For an integral part of all good practice is the provision of worship, fellowship and nurture that is specifically within the culture of new enquirers and believers. The cultural gap between middle-aged and elderly worshippers and young ones is often too great to bridge on a regular basis. Many older people would love to have young people worship with them, but only on their own terms. Not many are willing to give up their liturgy, formality, music and sermon for the sake of the next generation. And perhaps they should not be expected to do so. The multi-congregation model of parish church set out in Chapter 9 sets us free from the 'theology' that all Christians should worship together in the same style in order to express and develop unity. Just as Kidz Klub demonstrates that specialist children's worship can be very effective in bringing children back to church life, so specialist youth services demonstrate the way to bring back young people.

The statistical evidence for this comes from the 1989 and 1998 attendance surveys used before in this book. Of the 8,681 churches of all denominations surveyed in both years, 1,379 (16 per cent) offered youth worship in one form or another by 1998. The exact form of provision is not always clear, but it involved a service aimed primarily at young people, even if only on a monthly basis. Figure 10.4 shows the results. Seven out of ten churches without a youth service suffered overall attendance decline in the period, but less than one in two churches with a youth service. Churches providing for young people in worship were twice as likely to grow as those not doing so. The difference between the two groups in such a large sample size is gigantic. This indicates that adult, as well as child, attendance at churches making provision for young people was affected. Many parents are attracted to churches that can hold their children. The morale of a whole church rises when it can feel the vibrancy and enthusiasm that young people and young adults bring. It begins to feel that things are possible and that God is at work. An extended family without children is a dull place indeed. Children ignite a family with new joy. A church's policy towards children and young people is not peripheral to its policy for restoring adult attendance, it is central to it.

Figure 10.4 Growth and decline in churches with and without a youth service, 1989–98

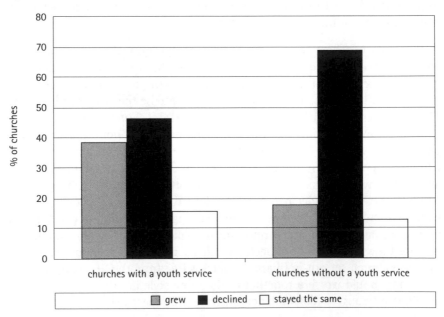

It could, of course, be argued that attractive, successful, growing churches are also likely then to be able to cater for young people. The correlation proves no cause and effect. However, it is hard to see how a church that is just the right sort to put on a youth service, but doesn't, would attract and hold young people in its worshipping life. Time and again we see the same thing happening – where young people and young adults have control of their own worshipping agenda they stay in the church and bring their friends. Where they feel excluded from the decision-making and worshipping processes, they leave.

Chapter 1 identified the three main places where the Church of England's attendance bucket is leaking – certain dioceses, younger people, and larger churches. Without doubt the most important and most universal of these leaks is the younger people. We have concluded here that more often than not the Church needs to make new buckets if it is to hold on to its young people. Individual churches, groups of churches working together, and dioceses may need to concentrate on the planting and staffing of many more youth and young adult congregations as the core of their response to the absence of young people in our churches. Sometimes this may mean planting a new, independent 'church', perhaps a city-wide fellowship based on a secular venue like a nightclub, financed and overseen directly by a diocese. But often it will mean simply planting a new congregation within an existing church structure, perhaps under a 'Churches Together' or deanery umbrella, or as part of one local church. In this way the younger congregation will be just as integral a part of the church as the older congregation at Wednesday communion or Sunday Evensong.

5. Church schools

The previous four initiatives have come largely from the bottom up. The recent initiative to pay more attention to Church schools has come largely from the top down. The Government has expressed a willingness to develop more faith-based, and especially Anglican, secondary schools. Bishops, on the whole, are responding enthusiastically. Perhaps, not only with new schools but also with existing ones, the Church can make renewed efforts to ensure that the Christian faith and Christian values are transmitted to children through Anglican schools. This may in part make up for the decline in the churches' direct influence on children.

This approach has its limitations. Research by Professor Leslie Francis suggests that children in existing Church of England schools receive on average no more explicit Christian teaching than pupils in county schools, and exhibit no different religious attitudes.[3] If the aim of opening more Anglican secondary schools is to win the allegiance of the pupils to the Church and its beliefs and values, it may be a naïve one. Moreover, it is not necessarily true that Christian teachers can have a bigger influence on children when they teach in Church schools than when they teach elsewhere. The new secondary schools will carry with them a financial commitment the Church of England might barely be able to afford in the present climate. There is no evidence to suggest that children who attend Church of England schools are more likely to attend church as adults. The growth of faith-based schools is seen by some as stoking up trouble for the future, as witnessed by the recent riots in Oldham between 'Muslims' and 'Christians' with effectively segregated schooling, and the trouble in Belfast over children walking to a Catholic school through a Protestant area. Others mutter darkly that the meaning and origin of the word 'Taliban' is 'student at a faith-based school' – although it has to be said that the thought of the Church of England breeding militant fanaticism through indoctrination at school is a novel one.

However, there must be scope for local churches to develop closer links with their Church schools as well as with others. In some areas, Christian schools workers have been appointed to go into schools, take assemblies, run Christian clubs at lunchtime, and help deliver the RE curriculum. Often these workers are equally welcome at Church and non-Church schools. This is not just because of personal sympathy on the part of the head teachers but also because these workers can help schools meet their statutory obligations in the area of religious education and worship provision. Church-based youth and children's workers can also find entry into schools, and so make contact with large numbers of children who do not normally go to church. The Diocese of Manchester has the highest concentration of Church schools in the country. It is also one of the few dioceses in the Church of England where the decline in child attendance has been slower than that in adult attendance. From 1989 to 1999 the diocese lost 21 per cent of its adult attendance but only 16 per cent of its children. It came 36th in the league tables for adults and 6th for children (see Tables 4.1 and 4.2 on pages 37 and 38). Many people in the diocese believe this is due to the large number of Church schools and the strong links that exist between them and the churches.

Taken together, the five initiatives we have looked at in this chapter have the capacity to move the Church of England a long way on from its traditional mode of ministry to children, the Sunday school. They form a radical new agenda that the church, in uncoordinated bits and pieces around the country, is starting to pursue. It may be early days yet, and the good practice in a few places may need to be adopted and adapted in many before the national numbers turn around. The introduction of October counts of children in the worshipping life of the church midweek as well as on Sundays should help us to measure the growing impact and to look for the first turning of the tide. The Church of England lost the urban working classes through lack of provision for them in the early nineteenth century, then began a partial recovery through the mass church-building programmes of the mid-century. Perhaps – just perhaps – we are now at the start of a similar historic turning point with young people. Having lost them in the latter part of the twentieth century, the Church has the chance to begin a partial recovery in the early twenty-first century through a massive new programme of youth provision using the elements outlined above. Here is a project worthy of the best attention and the resources of the whole Church.

Practical actions for a parish church

1. Review your Sunday morning children's groups and the youth fellowship, if you have one. Are there ways of making them more effective? Don't forget to ask the children and young people themselves.

2. Talk to other churches about the possibility of working together, pooling leadership, resources and children.

3. Visit a number of other churches to find out how they do children's work.

4. Ask the Diocesan Youth Officer to visit your church, talk to your young people, and suggest a future strategy.

5. Experiment with a mid-week teaching/worship/fun group for children or young people. To get help, contact the Crusaders' Union development worker for your area, or someone involved with Kidz Klub.

6. Ask the PCC to consider employing a youth and children's worker.

7. Talk to CYM about being a placement church for one of their students.

8. Seek advice on starting a monthly youth service even if, to begin with, numbers will be small.

9. Find out if local schools would welcome the involvement of a Christian schools worker with assemblies or lunchtime clubs.

11

Acting small – whatever your size

They could not get him to Jesus because of the crowd. (Mark 2.4 NIV)

Larger churches

As already mentioned, research into church attendance decline has yielded one surprising and hugely important finding: decline is a particular problem for larger churches. I take a larger Anglican church to be those with a total weekly attendance of at least 150 people, though congregations are bigger in the south than the north. The average Church of England congregation today is 50 adults and 10 children. Since most larger churches are in towns and suburbs, that is where decline is concentrated. Smaller congregations in villages and UPAs have held up comparatively well. In fact the average very small church (about 25 or less) grew in size during the 1990s. For example, total attendance at the 70 churches in York diocese with an adult attendance of under 10 in 1988 grew 41 per cent by 1994 and only one closed down. Such results explain why, in an era of general decline, so few tiny congregations have actually closed down. They have in fact been quietly growing. But decline has been surprisingly fast in the churches normally considered strong and successful. These are also the churches that, through the parish share mechanism, subsidize the smaller churches. So the whole Church of England is threatened by the decline of the strong. In fact one of the most likely consequences of the decline of the large churches is the withdrawal of paid ministry from the smaller churches because they will no longer have someone else to subsidize them. When St Peter the Great sneezes, St James the Less catches a cold.

The evidence for this surprising finding is now overwhelming. It is important to note that this relates primarily to the larger churches in the 100 to 300 or 400 adult attendance size bracket. The much smaller number of very large churches seems as a group to be holding its own. This chapter first reviews the nature of this evidence, then considers the reasons for the special difficulties that larger churches face today, and finally looks at how parishes, dioceses and denominations can reverse the decline of the larger church. We know that this reversal is possible because it is already happening in some places.

How size relates to decline

Figure 11.1 shows what the 1989 Church Census and 1998 Church Survey found about the relationship between size and decline in the churches. The 8,681 churches of all denominations that replied to both surveys were divided into categories by their total congregation size in 1989. The result was a steady and smooth transition from the very largest churches, only 10 per cent of which grew in the period, to the very smallest, 59 per cent of which grew. Only changes greater than plus or minus 10 per cent were considered as growth or decline – anything less was considered steady. It is clear that, across the country and across different denominations, small churches are more likely to grow and large churches are more likely to shrink or be steady. Christian Schwarz, in the research that led to his insights on 'natural' church development,[1] found that this phenomenon was repeated all over the world, and that smaller churches were also healthier than larger ones. He concluded that the large churches' comparative ill health helped generate their poor growth performance.

Small churches

Before we think about ways in which our large churches might turn around their numerical decline, it is worth considering possible reasons why the very

Figure 11.1 Church growth and decline in all denominations, 1989–98 (grouped by size of church in 1989)

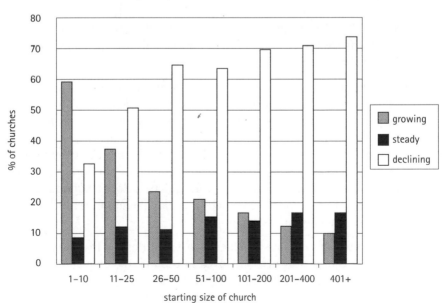

starting size of church

small churches in England have been doing so well. The diocesan data reported below reinforces the results of the national surveys we have just mentioned, so there can be no doubt that the tiny churches have been increasing their attendance on average in recent years. This is important both because there are a lot of very small churches in the Church of England (York Diocese in 1988 had 202 churches with an adult attendance of less than 20) and because they may have something to teach the others.

First, there is the matter of location. As we have already seen, almost all the tiny churches are to be found in village or rural communities. Perhaps here the church is still seen as being at the centre of the community. Other facilities (the village pub, the village shop, the village post office, the village school) may be in danger of being withdrawn, or may actually have closed down. But there is no outside agency that can impose closure on the church. The village will rally round to keep it going, with money for the tower appeal, and perhaps with attendance on Sundays. In other words, in the countryside people will support the institution even if their own personal faith is uncertain. This support will not wither away with postmodernity because the inhabitants will fight to preserve their communities – aided and abetted by people from the towns migrating to the countryside in search of just such an experience of community.

Secondly, small churches have probably had to learn to live and work without their own resident, paid clergyperson. Where a vicar has four, six, twelve or sixteen churches to look after, each set of wardens and office holders has to learn greater independence. Worldwide, it is a fact that churches without full-time paid ministry are growing faster than those with it. Along with taking more responsibility for practical matters, members of small churches may also develop the attitude that it is down to them to find new members, because the professional clergy 'are never here'.

Thirdly, the numbers involved in tiny churches are often no more than the average home group, or cell, or choir in a larger church. It has long been recognized that members of large churches need a small-group structure in order to find fellowship and belonging. But this comes naturally in a church that is so small it doesn't need to divide up. Belonging, loyalty and commitment levels are likely to be high. Most people will have a job of one sort or another. If someone leaves, they will be missed, and will still be a close neighbour unless they move away from the village completely. It may therefore be much harder to leave a small church than a large one.

Finally, there is the simple statistical fact that it is quite easy to grow a church of ten by 10 per cent just by getting 'Joyce's husband' to come along as well. This does not make the comparison with large churches unfair, for it is just as easy to lose 10 per cent of the congregation by upsetting 'Joyce's husband', or through his untimely death. But it drives home the point that, in the modern world, a church that is organized into very small units is more likely to be able to withstand the forces of decline, and even to find a new dynamic for growth.

Large churches around the dioceses

The figures for various English dioceses reflect the international and inter-denominational situation. For example, church attendance grew in Sheffield Diocese in the 1980s, but Figure 11.2 shows that this growth was concentrated in the smaller churches, where attendance increased 30 per cent. In the larger churches there was hardly any growth at all. There was also a particular size of church, with a congregation of between 140 and 210, where most of the churches were in decline. So the small and medium churches, and one or two giants, were growing, but run-of-the-mill larger churches were not.

York: a case study

Whereas there was a pattern of overall growth in Sheffield in the 1980s, there was a situation of overall decline in York in the 1990s. Between 1988 and 1994 the 38 churches with a usual Sunday attendance of between 150 and 399 were collectively in decline, but the rest of the diocese was not. This is shown in Table 11.1. If those 38 churches had not been in decline then overall attendance in a diocese of 477 churches would actually have risen.

Figure 11.2 Adult attendance growth in the Diocese of Sheffield, 1982–8 (grouped by size of church in 1982)

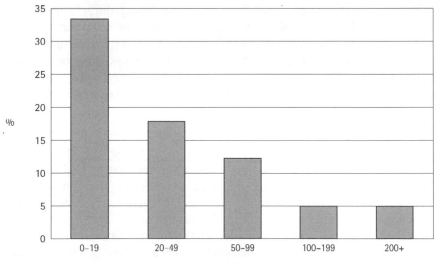

starting size of church

Table 11.1 Adult attendance in the Diocese of York, 1988–94

Average attendance	Category	Attendance 1988	Attendance 1994	Change	% change	No. of churches	No. that grew	No. that shrank	No. that stayed the same
0–9	Miniscule	486	685	+199	+41	70	48	16	6
10–19	Micro	1,840	2,000	+160	+9	132	64	47	21
20–34	Midget	2,181	2,216	+35	+2	89	38	43	8
35–49	Modest	1,731	1,678	−53	−3	43	12	29	2
50–74	Middling	2,871	2,676	−195	−7	48	13	32	3
75–99	Medium	2,050	2,082	+32	+2	24	10	14	0
100–149	Meaty	3,842	3,825	−17	0	32	13	16	3
150–249	Major	5,662	5,090	−572	−10	30	8	21	1
250–399	Massive	2,508	2,134	−374	−15	8	3	5	0
400+	Monumental	400	482	+82	+20	1	1	0	0*
Total		23,571	22,868	−703	−3	477	210	223	44

*We should not read anything into the experience of just one parish. However, there is some general evidence to suggest that a few churches in the 'monumental' category (400+) are able to break out into new territory and continue growing.

These figures proved to be very helpful indeed. It is obviously much more realistic to offer useful help to 38 churches than it is to 477. From the mid-1990s a message began to go round York Diocese: 'If we can turn the large churches round we can turn the diocese around.' Accordingly, the diocesan evangelist arranged a series of annual day conferences for the leadership teams of the larger churches in the diocese. The general plan was threefold. The first aim was to show the churches that they were not alone – their decline was part of a general trend. This had the effect of taking away burdens of guilt and strategies of denial from church leaders. 'I thought it was just me, now I realize we are all in the same boat. We were not addressing the problem; now that we have owned up to it, and pooled our experiences and ideas with other churches, I feel that we can.' The second aim was to think about the reasons for the decline in attendance, and the third was to come up with a list of anti-decline strategies. In this way, churches were empowered to tackle the problem themselves.

Not every large church took part in the exercise, so those that did not became a control group for the purposes of statistical analysis. The difference in performance between this group and those churches that had taken part in the exercise soon started to become clear. In 1999, for the first time, the churches that had attended conferences recorded collective, modest adult attendance growth of just 1 per cent. The control group, on the other hand, collectively lost 9 per cent of their adult attendance in the same year. Prior to the start of the project, both groups had very similar trends. By the year 2000, however, it was no longer possible to make this comparison, because almost every large church in the diocese had joined in, encouraged by the archbishop making a personal invitation to the 2000 conference and speaking at it himself. Some of the churches were also taking part in a consultancy exercise, whereby someone from outside the parish visited it a couple of times a year to discuss how anti-decline strategies were working out.

In 2000, the large churches together grew their attendance by about 5 per cent, so the momentum was building. Moreover, the forecast made in the mid-1990s came true: the large churches had been turned around, and so the whole diocese had turned around. Figure 11.3 shows clearly how the large churches, which had been dragging the total down, have now started to pull it up. For the first time after many years of decline, total adult attendance in the Diocese of York rose slightly in 2000. Statistically, this was almost entirely due to the turn around in the attendance figures of the large churches.

It is, of course, impossible to prove that this exercise to inform, motivate and empower the large churches through conferences and consultancies was the main reason for the turnaround, but if it was not, it is a big coincidence. The anecdotal evidence suggests that it was indeed influential. If that is the case, the result is rather startling, because what was done was really rather modest. In fact the people involved have been somewhat surprised at their apparent success. It may be that simply helping churches face the facts of decline, helping them see they were not alone, and answers were available, was enough to provoke them into effective action. Decline was not inevitable. The diocesan bucket was leaking, the leak was found, and it was plugged, at least for the moment.

Figure 11.3 Diocese of York: annual percentage change in attendance at the larger churches and in the diocese as a whole, 1996–2000

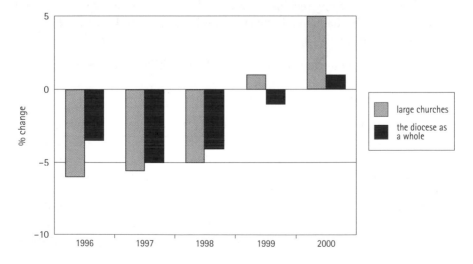

Other dioceses

But is the decline of the large churches a problem common to all dioceses? Lichfield Diocese discovered that, whereas in 1986 they had 25 churches with a Usual Sunday Attendance of adults of at least 200, by 1999 this had dropped to 6. Two-thirds of their larger churches (150+) were in clear decline. Figure 11.4 expresses the contrast between church types in another way: it shows

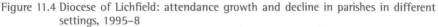

Figure 11.4 Diocese of Lichfield: attendance growth and decline in parishes in different settings, 1995–8

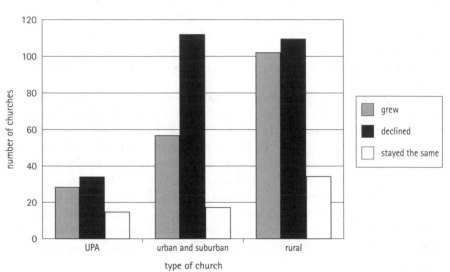

that urban and suburban non-UPA parishes were the ones most likely to be in decline. This category included almost all the larger churches. Sixty per cent of urban and suburban churches were in decline, but only 44 per cent of rural or UPA churches.

In late 1999 an initial consultation was held in Lichfield Diocese for churches with an adult Sunday attendance of at least 100, and was developed with further conferences led by a team from Springboard in 2002.

Figure 11.5 shows the situation in Guildford Diocese for the period 1997–9. The same pattern across the size spectrum emerges here, though the percentages are somewhat smaller owing to the shorter time frame. Once again, it is interesting to note that the very largest churches seem to be able to buck the trend that affects those in the 150–250 or so size bracket. Figure 11.6 shows the situation in St Albans Diocese for the period 1991–9. More than 60 per cent of the total attendance decline happened in the 32 parishes that had at least 200 adults attending in 1991. If these large churches had remained stable

Figure 11.5 Diocese of Guildford: percentage change in adult attendance, 1997–9 (grouped by size of church in 1997)

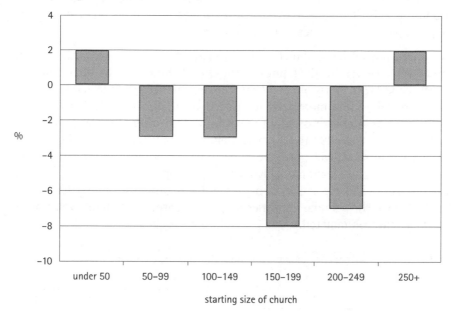

Figure 11.6 Diocese of St Albans: change in adult uSa, 1991–9 (grouped by size of church in 1991)

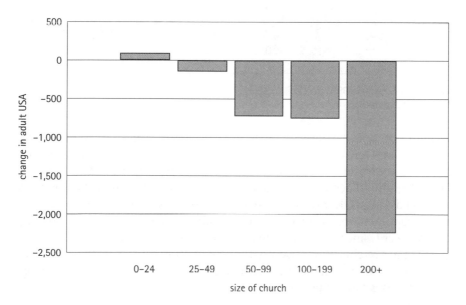

then the drop in total attendance in the diocese would have been under 6 per cent instead of over 14 per cent. It is also worth pointing out that, in both Guildford and St Albans, the smallest churches were growing. This pattern appears to be repeated across many dioceses.

Naturally, not all large churches have exactly the same experience as each other. Table 11.2 shows the figures for the largest churches in St Albans Diocese in 1991 and 1999. Thirty out of 32 churches experienced decline in attendance, but some felt it in a more dramatic way than others. Imagine, for example, the impact on a church of going down from 223 to 99 attendance, or from 506 to 297, or from 294 to 170, in just eight years. It is likely that the burden of the parish share will not have gone down in proportion, and the same buildings and staff team probably have to be supported by far fewer people. Maintenance will have become a bigger problem, and mission may have been pushed down the agenda. Ministries may have ceased, and morale will almost certainly have plummeted.

Table 11.2 Adult attendance at the 32 largest churches in St Albans Diocese, 1991 and 1999

1991	1999	1991	1999	1991	1999
238	175	257	277	509	481
235	223	397	566	215	140
294	170	250	200	275	180
210	130	225	160	300	207
330	220	520	304	285	208
310	194	820	609	204	164
300	255	220	183	388	273
254	177	226	155	240	169
220	170	216	90	250	200
223	99	205	135	506	297
306	211	250	197		

Total: 1991: 9,678; 1999: 7,219 (–25.4%)
Source: Diocesan attendance returns.

Coventry Diocese, however, appears to be a partial exception to the general trend. Figure 11.7 shows the same pattern of growth for the smallest churches, but in Coventry in 1997–2000 the large churches declined at a rate little faster than the diocesan total. Table 4.2 (see page 38) showed that between 1989 and 1999 Coventry's attendance fell by less than any other diocese apart from London. In 2000, Coventry's adult attendance actually grew by 3.3 per cent, meaning that there were therefore slightly more adults worshipping in church in Coventry Diocese in 2000 than there were in 1989. Somehow, Coventry's large churches managed to avoid the decline that most other dioceses have experienced.

Figure 11.7 Diocese of Coventry: percentage change in adult attendance, 1997–2000 (grouped by size of church in 1997)

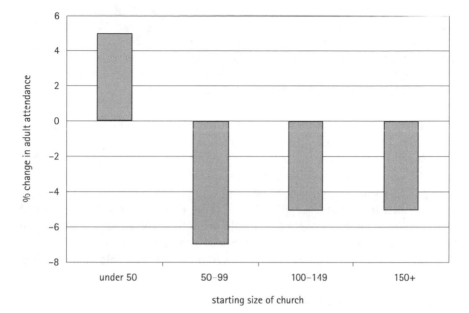

The conclusion from all this evidence is that decline has indeed been led by the larger churches in most dioceses. Any diocese interested in reversing its own decline should therefore take a look at its own figures and start a process of helping the large churches to work together on their common problem. The experience of York Diocese suggests that there is no quick fix, but that addressing the issue over a period of several years has the potential to turn decline around.

The fact that large churches do not inevitably decline, and can be turned around, means we do not need to despair about them or to suggest that the future simply lies with the small. Would that every church were large and growing! The correct conclusion is that, though all is not well with larger churches, appropriate help can enable them to turn things around. The lists of common causes and common remedies offered below form part of the help that churches need.

Large churches: reasons for decline

1. The health of the church

Christian Schwarz suggests that small churches grow because they are healthier than large churches. What does he mean by 'health' in this context? One sign seems to be that members of small churches attend worship more regularly and more frequently. The average membership of growing churches in his worldwide sample of 1,000 was 297, and their average worship attendance was 202, or 68 per cent of the membership. The average membership of declining churches was much bigger – 636 – but only 235 of them (37 per cent) were in church each week. Large, declining churches appear to suffer from a relative lack of regular Sunday commitment on the part of their members. Smaller churches are more tightly knit communities whose members have a greater sense of obligation to each other.

The survey also measured a number of quality factors in church life, and the large churches came out worse in nearly all of them. For example, 46 per cent of people in the smallest size category were integrated into a small group, but only 12 per cent in churches of the largest size category were part of a small group. In the smaller churches, 31 per cent of members had a role in the church that seemed to match their gifts, but in large churches only 17 per cent of members were similarly blessed. It would seem that, on average, members of large churches across the globe come less often, are less involved in the fellowship life of the church, and are less happy with their role in church life.

2. Attending and belonging

Members of large churches appear more likely to have a modern consumer attitude to their church than do members of small churches. People may still have a residual loyalty to the corner shop, but none to the supermarket. Not many of us think, 'I must shop at Tesco's today, they are relying on me, they'll miss me if I don't turn up, and I would feel terrible if their sales dipped because of me.' Also, churchgoers today are more likely to aspire to 'belong to a fellowship' than to 'attend a service'. Those who wish to attend a service are more likely to go to a large congregation with the best music or preaching. But it is much easier to start to belong to a small fellowship than to a large one. Small fellowships may, therefore, be more culturally appropriate just now. Fewer people now prefer a large church to a small one because what they aspire to get out of church has changed: once it was teaching and inspiration, now it is belonging.

3. Stress and busyness

The stress and busyness experienced at work and, often, in the home have increased markedly in recent years. Even leisure is now pursued more energetically than in the past. On average, people come to church more stressed out and exhausted than used to be the case. More people feel the need to receive, and fewer people have the capacity to give. Take schoolteachers, for example, who are present in numbers in many larger churches. Once they had time and energy to be church leaders and run the children's groups. Now, typically, they are only just surviving the stress and workload of their jobs.

Lay leadership in larger churches is much more demanding and time-consuming than in small ones. Large churches have had increasing difficulty in finding leaders with the time and energy required for the major jobs. Vicars of large churches spend many hours trying to fill vacancies for wardens, PCC members, Sunday school teachers, worship group members, home group leaders, and so on. Many people today are only prepared to commit themselves to a Sunday duty once a month. This is not just because they are exhausted by modern living but also because they don't want to be tied to going to church every week. In a small church or fellowship, things have more chance of happening naturally without the need to appoint people to onerous jobs. But large churches are finding it hard to appoint people who are able to put in the time and organizational effort needed to make them work effectively week by week.

4. The newcomer

Larger churches suffer from the practical problem that newcomers are harder to spot and integrate. If a new churchgoer has not made several friends within the first month or two, they will probably stop coming. Typically, someone new will not come every week, which compounds the problem of keeping in touch with them. Many existing members are, anyway, paralysed by the fear of asking someone if they are new, and being told snootily that they have been coming to this church for 35 years. Newcomers also tend to feel that a large church does not merely not notice them, it also does not need them. There seems little point trying to break into the fellowship.

5. The drifter

In a small church, everyone knows that Mrs Smith was not in church this week, and one of her friends will probably either know that she is away visiting grandchildren, or will call round to check she is okay. Spotting someone's absence is much harder in a large church, and the problem is again compounded by irregular attendance. If the leaders of the church manage to notice that Mrs Smith is not in church today (itself quite a feat in a large crowd), they will not know whether she is absent because she only comes about one week in two on average, or because she is poorly. If she is poorly, she may be thinking to herself, 'Those people at that church don't care about me.' And so Mrs Smith may easily drift away. In an era when people no longer come to church out of a sense of duty but rather for they what they get out of it, they are much more likely to drift away from a large church which fails to follow their movements. Large churches today may still have more attractive front doors, but they have wide-open back doors. And members of large churches are more likely to walk out through the back door both because they feel they will not be missed and because, thinking like consumers, they have less of a sense of loyalty.

6. Children and young adults

Large churches tend to have a higher proportion of children in their congregations than small churches do. For example, in York Diocese in 1999, children under 16 made up 16 per cent of the congregations of large churches (150+ adults), but only 7 per cent of the congregations of the smallest churches. Since the Church is losing children more rapidly than it is losing adults, those churches with more children, that is, the larger churches, are declining more rapidly. The same can be said about younger adults, including the parents of the children.

7. Transience and absorption capacity

Large churches in suburbs tend to have a faster turnover of members than do small ones in villages. This is partly because of the age distribution – job moves have little impact on congregations who are all retired. As society has become ever more mobile, so transience has increased accordingly. Christian Schwarz has shown that the capacity of a church to absorb new members does not vary a lot with the church's size. One reason for this is that all new members need to develop some sort of relationship with the church's leaders.

8. Leadership style and burn-out

The leadership style that is needed to maintain and grow large churches today is very different from what is needed in small ones. The hands-on pastoral leadership model of a small church is likely to have been the one that was implicitly assumed at theological college. In today's complex world, the minister of a large church may need a range of skills that were not considered at ordination selection or theological college, or acquired later. Many clergy in charge of larger churches feel themselves to be under-prepared and under-supported for the task. The job of the incumbent in such a church is not to do the ministry but to ensure the ministry happens. The minister must move from being a hands-on foreman to being a managing director, or even chairman of the board. The appropriate way of life for such a role is quite different, and alien to many clergy. The incumbent in really large churches has to work with leadership teams and a range of paid employees, to direct activities rather than do them. But the expectations of the congregation, or of the incumbent, may not have changed enough to enable this to happen without stress or conflict. Members of large churches appear, on average, to be less happy with their minister than members of smaller churches.

Caught in this situation, running short of lay leaders, with a mountain of management work and a small to medium business to run as well as a huge amount of pastoral and teaching work to get through, and feeling ill appreciated and out of his or her depth, a minister is liable either to burn out or leave prematurely, or both. After all, the pay and conditions offered for a relatively small and easy job are just the same – why should the vicar risk his or her health and family life for the sake of an impossible job? It is perhaps not surprising that some large churches then have difficulty finding a suitable replacement who is willing and able to take on the workload and the responsibility.

9. Hitting the glass ceiling

Examination of the attendance returns of many parishes over a period of years shows that there is a typical pattern to the adult attendance figures in growing churches: 1992 – 68; 1993 – 79; 1994 – 97;1995 – 121; 1996 – 140; 1997 – 93; 1998 – 68; 1999 – 79; etc. etc. This suggests that there is a sort of 'glass ceiling' beyond which churches do not usually grow. This glass ceiling is normally in the area of 100–150 adults, and never lower. There are one or two other glass ceilings at much higher numbers, but far fewer churches ever encounter them. It is a glass ceiling because most churches cannot see it coming and do not understand clearly what it is they have bumped into.

What happens is that a healthy church gets together with an enthusiastic incumbent and begins to grow. All is well for some time but, eventually, a stage is reached at which the incumbent can no longer sustain the momentum. There are now too many people to pastor, and the paperwork has increased. The numbers of 'occasional office' contacts just keeps on growing. The old hands are having trouble coping with the influx of new people. The church building is pretty full on some Sundays. One or two lay leaders 'burn out'. Conflicts bubble up. The vicar gets ill through overwork. Suddenly the tide turns, people leave, and the church is quickly back down to where it started. Very few churches ever manage to grow through this glass ceiling and very few clergy succeed in changing their leadership style, and finding enough support, to enable them to lead the church through the ceiling. The result is that, although numbers of larger churches have shrunk in recent years back into the 'small' or 'medium' categories, very few have grown to replace them.

10. Conflict

Many clergy in charge of large churches testify that conflict is one cause of decline. Conflict can arise because the leader brings about much-needed change, which usually brings winners and losers, and conflict. It can arise, equally, because there has been no change – some members of the PCC have become frustrated, and the lack of change has led to numerical decline so that morale has slumped. A large church has far more individual personal relationships within it, each with the usual human capacity for going wrong. In a group of four people, there are only six relationships (A–B, A–C, A–D, B–C, B–D, C–D). In a group of 7 there are 21, and in a tiny church of 10 people there are 45. In a church of 200 there are potentially about 20,000 interpersonal relationships, any one of which can go wrong at any time. When people attended services out of a sense of duty, this was not quite so important. Now that people belong to a fellowship out of a need for high-quality relationships, it is critical.

Breakdown of communication, or of inadequate relationships, is another common cause of conflict. In a large church where people may attend different services and may not attend every week, communication is a real problem. Many clergy and administrators spend hours producing church notice sheets, only to receive complaints from those who never bothered to read them that they did not know what was going on.

11. Money

Generally speaking, it is true that parish share payments take a smaller proportion of a large church's income than they do of that of a small church. It is, therefore, hard for those from small churches to sympathize with or understand the problems large churches have with money.

Large churches have replaced the Church Commissioners as the source of subsidy funds for paying stipends to ministers of small churches. Through the parish share mechanism, many larger churches have therefore increasingly paid over to dioceses far more than they receive back in respect of stipends and parsonage upkeep. A large church can easily feel that the main impact of the diocese on its life is to drain it of its resources.

At the same time, the increasing experience of large churches is that they can only run well, avoid decline, and grow further by employing their own paid staff team. Secretaries, administrators, youth workers, pastoral care managers, evangelists and associate vicars have multiplied. Just when it has become more and more costly to maintain the ministry of a large church, dioceses have been demanding larger and larger net payments. Some large churches, experiencing a rapid increase in parish share, have been pressurized to lay off their own staff in order to pay the share. Others find that the extra money they have raised to pay for much-needed new parish staff has the following year been taken into account for the share. They have raised £20,000 a year for the new post, and then find that the diocese wants an extra £8,000 a year from them as a result. If they then raise the extra £8,000, the next year the diocese will ask for a further £3,200, and so on. Churches that have begun to grow through evangelism have found themselves 'taxed' by the system before their new members have had time to learn to give realistically.

The degree to which money has been a factor in the comparative decline of the larger churches varies between dioceses, not least according to their very different parish share allocation mechanisms and formulae. But it is a general truth that overburdening larger churches with financial demands is not a recipe for long-term future growth.

If these are the main reasons for the decline of our large churches, what can be done about them?

Solutions

1. Having an aim

A large church is unlikely to turn around its numerical decline unless it tries to. The same applies to a diocese. The first step for a church may therefore be to face the facts of its own decline, to investigate them to discover where and when that decline has been taking place, and to frame some policies with the aim of growing again. Often, the initial impetus for this can best come from a diocese – it can bring its large churches together, show them that they are facing common problems, and get them to discuss solutions together. The aim of the Larger Church Projects in York and Lichfield Dioceses was to turn the whole diocese around by moving the large churches from decline to growth. Having a clear and realizable aim is the first step to actually achieving something.

2. Imitating the small

As we have already noted, it is a remarkable feature of contemporary Church life that tiny churches are, on average, growing. The popular image of the tiny rural congregation about to expire could not be more wrong. In York Diocese more than 200 churches each have an average adult attendance of less than 20, yet in the last decade only one of them has closed. If these 200 had all been in decline, dozens of them would have closed down. The strengths of these small congregations include great commitment to each other and to keeping the church going. Everyone knows everyone else and everyone has a job to do. Everyone is needed. Any policy that involved closing tiny rural congregations as a response to overall attendance decline would therefore hit completely the wrong target. Rather, diocesan policy towards small churches should include at least four elements: first to encourage them in their growth and help it continue, second to help them do together the things they cannot do on their own (e.g. process evangelism courses, youth work), third to help them prosper in a future where they will have little or no access to a paid priest, and fourthly to enable the larger churches of the diocese to learn from their success.

One obvious lesson is that larger churches need effective small-group structures to enable them to recreate the relational advantages of small churches. A large church should aim to create a place for every member where they will be immediately missed if they don't turn up, where they are well known, where they have a job and are needed, where they meet their friends. House groups, interest groups, working groups like choirs, and cell groups are an increasingly necessary part of the life of large churches. It takes quite a high level of organizational ability and a big time commitment from a leader to build up and oversee a small-group structure in order to give a large congregation its relational glue. The incumbent may not be the best person to be directly responsible for this, but someone needs to be charged with this key task.

Whereas home groups were the cutting-edge small-group idea in the 1970s and 1980s, today it is increasingly cells. Cells can mean different things to different people and can simply boil down to home groups by a new name. This is about as helpful as renaming the Post Office 'Consignia'. At least home groups 'do what it says on the tin'. Cells may also bring their own problems in relation, for example, to leadership demands, the difficulty of ensuring unity and consistent teaching, what to do with people who do not readily fit into cells, and the commitment required to cells which may cut across other valuable church ministries and activities. A move into cell structure needs to be well researched and clearly thought out, but little of lasting value comes without hard work and sacrifice. However, it is interesting to observe that the name and idea of cells is not new to the Church. Back in 1983 the Tiller report advocated at some length the use of cells in church life: 'It is the life and work of Christian cells in the community which are designed to overcome some of the weaknesses in the missionary capability and individual care of the parish churches.'[2]

The essence of a cell church is that its members are invited to form small cells of at most six to ten people. Four or five is a very workable number. Each cell meets weekly and is the primary church commitment of the members, even ahead of Sunday worship. Cell is seen as being just as much 'church' as Sunday worship. This is the reverse priority to that of home groups, which are often seen as optional extras to the main church service. The basis of the cell meeting is open, honest sharing at as deep a level as possible. A variety of activities is possible, including Bible study, prayer, meditation, discussion, and working together in a specialist piece of ministry. Cells are kept small so that it would be impossible for someone to drop away without being noticed, and everyone has a voice and is listened to. Cells give members of larger churches their pastoral care support and relational glue. They enable a larger church to combine the loyalty pull of the corner shop with the scale advantages of the supermarket.

Cells are also the primary evangelistic unit of the church. Members of the cell should help each other to pray for their non-Christian friends, and hold each other accountable for their Christian witness. Friends might normally first be brought to the cell, with its informal friendship grouping that will be familiar to today's spiritually aware younger adults who are used to talking about spirituality with others. Only later will they be asked to undergo the more alien-feeling experience of public worship. Cells can have a sense of subversive, even underground, evangelism in tune with a postmodern world that is suspicious of the institutional Church but open to the relational spirituality of the small group.

Essential to the idea of cell is the concept of growth and splitting. In fact, this is a major aim – to draw enough new members into the cell that it is able to split and form two new ones. The church, therefore, grows because the cells are growing and splitting. In fact the church is not a church *with* small groups but a church *of* small groups. At their best, cells are dynamic, close-knit units of committed people, dedicated to evangelism, worship, mutual growth and real fellowship, with God at the centre. As they are still part of a wider church, they are resourced by it and have access to its larger-scale fellowship, teaching and worship opportunities. And the times of worship together become opportunities for sharing and celebrating what is going on in the small-group life of the church.

The Thame Valley Team Ministry in Oxford Diocese is one church that for the last few years has been journeying into 'cell mode'. It had grown to a Sunday attendance size of about 500 adults, but then stopped as the organizational life of the church had become too onerous to keep going. The church wished to change from being programme-orientated to being people-orientated, from grind to gifting and from organization to organism. A new staff member was appointed to set up the cell structure, and many other programmes were closed down to make room for it. The cells were each given six core values to live by: magnify (worship), membership, maturity, ministry, mission and multiplication. Not every church member was expected to join a cell, though all were encouraged to do so. It was recognized that the church would continue to operate on two levels – the big and the small. After two years the church had 38 cells containing 360 people, and some were beginning to split. The main growth points so far have been in the general depth of individual discipleship and in the strengthening of relational support within the cells. The church is now relationship-driven rather than agenda-driven. There is also now an expectation that the church is ready to grow again through the life and witness of its cells.

The Church of England, mercifully, has little in common with the Provisional IRA. However, the latter's ability to re-invent itself is the key to its survival since 1916, and its use of cell groups is instructive. The IRA did not emerge from the ether at the start of the Troubles in 1969 all tooled up and ready to do battle with the British army. It had been in decline for some time, membership had fallen away, and some units had ceased to exist. Its main tactic in the 1970s was the orchestration of acts of mass civil disobedience. But this 'large crowd' tactic failed because it was so easy for the army to infiltrate and subvert. So were its – fairly large – battalions. Eventually, new, younger leaders from the North who understood the realities on the ground ousted the old-guard leadership from the South. The new National Command first met under Gerry Adams and Martin McGuinness in 1976. They restructured the IRA into cells instead of battalions. Each cell would consist of four members and specialize in a particular activity – sniping, executions or bombings, for example (perhaps this is where the comparison with the C of E begins to break down). Only the leader of each cell would have contact with the wider leadership. The level of members' commitment to the cell was far higher than it had been to the larger and more loosely structured battalion. Security leaks were greatly reduced, and the IRA, which had been staring at possible extinction, became an effective fighting force. The goal (getting everyone into a united Ireland) was what mattered to the new, ideologically motivated leadership – they had no loyalty to old methods.

The IRA cells are also known as 'Active Service Units', a term that seems accurately to describe what a church cell group should be. The leader of the cell reports to the church leadership, and cells may be invited to specialize in different aspects of the work of the church. The IRA went into cell mode in order to fight a long war of attrition in a hostile social climate. Perhaps this is the most interesting thing about cell groups – they seem most successful in times and places where the ideologies of those forming them have been under severe threat from society around them. The Church of England, while still the established Church, now faces a hostile, actively pagan mission field. The Church as institution, at battalion level, is increasingly unwelcome, irrelevant and outmoded. The long war of attrition for the soul of the nation needs to be fought on many fronts. Cells, each with a clear mission and an efficient command and supply line, may be just the active service units the Church needs for its foot soldiers in the battle ahead.

There are other reasons for supposing that cells may become increasingly appropriate for the Church of the future. One has already been touched on – that younger adults and young people are typically more comfortable in open discussion in a small group than when taking part in a large-scale, controlled event. For older generations the opposite was the case – it is usually easier to invite a pensioner to church than to a soul-bearing discussion group. If that is so then to be true to our ideologically motivated aim (getting everyone into a united kingdom of heaven) we must change or broaden our methods to attract younger generations. Certainly, one large Anglican church that reorganized its youth group along cell lines saw a large increase in membership as a result.

Another reason why cell structures might suit the present time better is found in the changing nature of some congregations. Typically, an Anglican congregation is much less well defined than those of other denominations. It is much less clear who is in and who is not. The level of commitment demanded in order to be a full member is less. It may be easier to persuade the entire congregation of a Baptist or house church to join cells than the average Anglican congregation. However, the nature of some congregations is changing as Christendom recedes. More have the hallmarks of a geographically dispersed, gathered company of believers rather than of the religiously minded members of the local parish. Such relational, gathered churches may find cell groups much more natural than a traditional parish church.

So today's Christians in today's churches in today's world might take to cell groups more readily than experienced Church leaders imagine. But cell is only one way of large churches acting small. Another way to recreate the advantages of the small is by changing the nature of the worshipping unit. The congregation may not fill the building by any means, but it may still be too large for its own health and effectiveness. The advantages of a multi-congregation approach for large churches were argued in Chapter 10. For this reason I will spend less time here on multiple congregations than I do on cells, although the former may be a more widespread practical possibility at the moment. Many congregations are divided between those who aspire to tradition, dignity and calm and those who aspire to modernity, reality and enthusiasm – or even between those who can get out of bed on a Sunday morning and those who blunder in at two minutes past ten still half asleep. Congregations stuck in uneasy compromises can sometimes be divided up, with gratifying consequences for growth. Also, in a world where Sunday trading, Sunday working and Sunday leisure activities are on the increase, looking for opportunities for new congregations to meet midweek sounds a sensible idea. A church can aim to build a network of quite modest-sized congregations that will each avoid the health and relational problems, the missing of newcomers and the loss of drifters that hamper large congregations. Kept together, a network of small congregations keeps the advantages of the strong – sizeable mission ambitions, 'celebration' size when occasion demands, a wide range of gifts and talents, and financial strength. A church that is a coalition of small, interlocking communities, each with its own identity but finding unity through shared vision, ethos and leadership, can combine the advantages of the small and the large.

3. Organizing pastoral care

We now move to approaches that do not involve either breaking up the large congregation or refocusing on small groups. These are about how to make the large congregation work better while it stays large or grows larger. A welcome team can be appointed to watch out for newcomers and fringe members and help them to integrate. The welcome team can consider its job is done when someone new is settled in a small group, is attending regularly, and has made four new friends in the congregation. Different welcomers may be given different age groups to look after, or different rows of pews, but they must each be on duty every week, for the job is rarely done in one contact. A different pastoral care team may be given the job of noticing when regular members are not there, and following them up, at least to find out if they are ill. Members of both teams will need to be well trained, supported and led for their ministry to be effective.

4. A people-shaped Church

Leaders of large churches may need to stop trying to stuff square pegs into round holes in order to keep the show on the road. A better approach may be to fit the life and activities of the church around the gifting and inclinations of the people. Square pegs in square holes exude more energy, enthusiasm and happiness. They are less likely to burn out and more likely to be regular attenders. Another aspect of this approach is to recognize that the best sort of professional leadership team for large churches today is usually a set of specialists, all trained and with expertise in a particular area of church life. The era of the omnicompetent clergyperson may need burying.

5. Doing a few things well

Busyness and burn-out problems are best tackled in two ways. One is to take a hard look at priorities and to stop doing those things that come low down on the list of priorities. Large congregations should not feel guilty that they cannot do everything that it is possible for a church to do. Instead, they should aim to do a few things well. In this way they can offer a higher-quality product in their key areas while safeguarding their members from burnout. The other way is to use the increasing prosperity of church members and therefore, one hopes, of churches to employ professionals to do what the amateurs no longer have the time, skills and energy for.

6. Leadership style

This may be the most important thing of all to look at. Incumbents should not feel threatened by such a review. On the contrary, a review of a church's leadership style and structure should be designed to make the incumbent's job description more realistic, to relieve him or her from some unrealistic expectations, to strengthen the team around them, and to provide them with increased training and resources to enable them to do their job well. Is the vicar the best person to be the church manager? Or could someone else do that to release the vicar to give vision or be a parish priest? How can co-operative ministry best be forwarded, in which people will have their own spheres of responsibility, and leadership will come from teams rather than one person?

The required leadership style does keep varying with the size of the church. There is not one simple divide between 'small' and 'large' churches. Up to 100 or so, the vicar as foreman in constant pastoral contact with the flock can be an effective model. Above that, the vicar needs to become a departmental or middle manager, delegating and learning to trust the staff while keeping a fairly close personal eye on things. By 300 or so, the vicar needs to start operating like a managing director, where the principal function is oversight of those charged with front-line delivery; and by 750 the minister becomes the chairman of the board, where the primary function is strategy and vision. In normal business life, the middle managers may still be proving themselves, but they are likely to be receiving ongoing management training. This is doubly important for clergy who may not only lack relevant experience but also a natural aptitude for the task of leading a medium-sized organization.

In the specific case of the glass ceiling, unless leadership style and structures change then every church that struggles up to the threshold of being considered a large church will drop back down again. Such churches should not be left in isolation by dioceses to discover this unpalatable truth afresh for themselves and to reinvent a wheel that others have already discovered. It is better that dioceses alert their growing churches to the issues, and ensure that they have some training and help to overcome them. A good way of reviewing leadership teams, organization and style is to bring in an outside consultant experienced in such matters and ask them to produce a written report for the PCC to consider. Another is to get churches of the appropriate size together, perhaps at a day conference, to consider how, for example, to grow through ceilings There is now a body of knowledge concerning the organizational and cultural changes required for breaking through the ceiling on which to draw. Such a conference or exercise would also include stories from churches that have broken through the ceiling.

7. Being radical

Many of the above solutions for improving the prospects of larger congregations lie mainly in the area of being church as we currently know it, only better. They are less radical than the cell or multi-congregation responses. Some churches are able to adopt radical solutions; for others the practical possibilities are more limited. These may well be worth doing and have gratifying results, but they should not be used to edge radical thinking off the agenda. Many new ways and forms of being church are emerging, and larger churches seeking new strategies should be prepared to consider them. For example, one of the largest churches in the Church of England, St Thomas Crookes in Sheffield, has discovered two new growth dynamics – a counter-culture service in a city nightclub, and area cluster groups (made up of clusters of cells) around the city that are turning themselves into church plants. Experience suggests that there are no automatic blueprints for the turning around of our large churches, and that every case is likely to be unique with its own unique solution. But we can learn from each other. This is why it is important for dioceses to help large churches explore the range of possible responses and develop their own solutions. That there are solutions, some modest, some radical, is beyond doubt. When large churches go looking for them with prayer, determination and a little help from outside, they tend to find them.

Finally, it is worth reiterating that leaders of larger churches (even those of only 100+) need encouraging in the difficult, though not impossible, job they have. Beset by many problems and issues, their churches are not so much the 'sick men' of the Church of England as the powerhouses and potential saviours of it. But dioceses need to work through how they can help rather than hinder the growth and development of the larger churches, and the churches individually and together must think through their strategies for growing in a changing world. Laissez-faire is not a survival option for the large churches, but active, visionary leadership at parish and diocesan level can help them grow and prosper in powerful new ways.

Practical actions for a larger parish church

1. Find out the truth about attendance trends in your church and aim to start growing again.
2. Adopt a cell model of being church.
3. Adopt a multi-congregation model.
4. Start or reorganize a welcome group for the larger congregations.
5. Start or reorganize a pastoral group for picking up members who may be drifting away.
6. Make one or two key new staff appointments designed to give a new growth capability to the church.
7. Give up trying to do some of the church's present activities in order to concentrate on the priorities.
8. Rewrite the incumbent's job description to enable him or her to concentrate on what matters for the growth of the church.
9. Add a new congregation to the existing range.
10. Think up your own really radical idea and give it a go.

12

Planting churches

St Mary, Mary, quite contrary, how does your garden grow?

Oaks and primroses

Paul's picture of the Church as a garden in 1 Corinthians 3 was mentioned in Chapter 3 of this book. The Church has a God-given dynamic for growth. It will grow automatically, like any garden, as long as the gardening is halfway appropriate and keeps the weeds at bay. With good propagation, it will also look beautiful. Some plants in a garden are able to grow to a great size as individual specimens and to live nearly for ever. Fifty years ago, your author planted an acorn in his parents' back garden. Today it is a large, spreading oak tree. Unless it is pruned it will take over the entire neighbourhood in another 300 years. Some of the neighbours are starting to worry. But other plants reach their maximum size much more quickly, and have a more limited life. It is futile to attempt to fill a flowerbed with one single, enormous primrose. Better to keep on dividing the roots and so multiplying the primrose plants into new places in the garden.

It may be that the greatest failure of the Church of England's gardening in the twentieth century stemmed from a fundamental horticultural mistake. We treated our churches as though they were all oak trees – able to grow to any size and live virtually for ever. One plant could fill the whole parish garden more or less permanently. But most congregations are primroses – they have a limited, vigorous individual life, and they grow and spread to fill the ground by division into large numbers of individual plants. God has done his part – he has given the Church a natural, inbuilt capacity to grow. But our gardening has been so clueless that we misdiagnosed where that growth capacity lies. It lies not in the Church's growth hormones but in its reproductive organs. Of course there are a few oak trees in the Church of England garden, but most churches are primroses, not oaks, and always will be. There is no point trying to make oak trees out of primrose cuttings.

New wineskins for new wine

The findings reported in Chapter 11 demonstrate the difficulty of growing most churches beyond a certain limited size. Many hit the glass ceiling just as they are beginning to get large. Those that are already large have a distressing tendency to wither. In many areas of the country the church garden has had no new plants added to it for centuries. It is not surprising that decline has set in. Imagine trying to keep alive your back garden at home if you are not allowed to plant anything new, ever. The number of worshipping Anglicans in a parish varies very little with the population of the parish once it reaches 2,000 or so. Congregations in parishes of 2,000 are nearly as large, on average, as in parishes of 20,000. The number of worshippers varies, as it always has done, not with the population of an area but with the number of churches that area has. Areas such as South Yorkshire and Hull, which have very low churchgoing rates, actually have larger congregations than the national average. Their low churchgoing rates are not because they have small congregations but because they do not have many churches. The average Anglican congregation size in South Yorkshire is 76, compared with a national average of 60. But the population per Anglican church is 5,500 compared with a national average of only 3,000. The implication is that the planting of new congregations sounds a more likely way of generating new church growth in such areas than trying to increase the size of existing congregations, many of which are elderly and have lost their vigour.

The history of the growth and development of the Christian Church throughout the world bears out the simple truth that church planting and church growth are almost the same thing. The periods of the growth of the Church in England were the periods when most churches were built – the early Middle Ages and the mid- to late nineteenth century. If the ancient parish churches in the expanded towns and cities of the last century had not planted lots of daughter churches and new parishes, these churches and their people would not exist today.

Church growth and church planting

In countries where the Church is growing today, the normal means of growth is not the emergence of super giant churches but the planting of many new ones by pioneer evangelists or, more usually, existing local churches. Nepal has one of the fastest church growth rates in the world, and hardly any large churches. Rather, new, small-scale fellowships spring up in response to small-scale evangelism across the country at a rate far too fast for the national Church to keep up with. As soon as churches begin to grow they found daughter churches in the next village or at the other end of town. In Peru the Anglican Church has had a strategy of starting house-fellowship churches with just ten people. The house may be specially adapted with a large open-plan area upstairs for meetings. The church is given five years in which to grow to 100. Groups of ten are then split off to start the process all over again. Church growth and church planting are the same thing.

Research in the USA shows that, typically, newer churches grow faster and produce more new Christians than settled older churches. Figure 12.1 is taken from an unpublished PhD thesis by Gavin Wakefield (1998). It shows believers' baptism rates per 100 existing members among 20,000 Southern Baptist churches. Churches ten years old or younger have nearly three times the rate of baptisms than those that have been around the longest.

It is no surprise that the same pattern is found in the New Testament. When Paul wrote to the Christians in Rome and other great ancient cities he did not write to some great cathedral where all the Christians met for worship. He wrote to a whole network of churches that usually met in houses – such as that of Priscilla and Aquila in Romans 16.3,4, Nympha in Colossians 4.15, and Philemon in verse 2 of that letter. That the New Testament Church grew by dividing and spreading into new houses was inevitably the case, if only because there were no purpose-built church buildings for large numbers of people to meet in regularly. This bit of history teaches us that we should not

Figure 12.1 Southern Baptist churches in the USA: baptisms p.a. per 100 members (grouped by age of church)

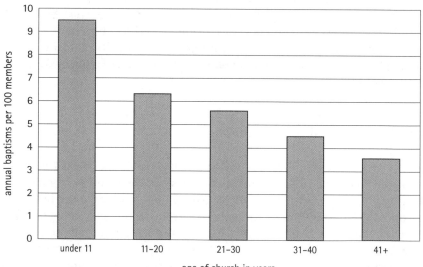

be so exclusively 'church building and Sunday congregation minded' that we fail to recognize that small groups meeting in houses can be being authentically 'church'.

Missed opportunities?

For the last century, the Church of England has not had a policy of planting new church fellowships. In fact, there have been some discouragements to such enterprise. Those that have begun have usually resulted from local initiative, and been few in number. In many areas, the thought of starting new congregations has not even occurred to the Church. This is an odd way to tend a garden. In the vigorous planting years of the nineteenth century, the idea of a new congregation was synonymous with that of a new building. Some of these buildings today are seen as millstones round our necks, but they all still witness to the vigour of the Victorian church-planting movement in the towns and cities of England. In the early years of the twentieth century, however, church building almost ceased. Something similar was happening simultaneously in other denominations. Local circuit preaching rotas in the nineteenth century show that Methodist meetings frequently began in new places, some of which lasted only a little while as the attempt at church planting failed, others of which resulted in buildings and settled churches. All this stopped around 1905, after which the rotas stabilized as there were hardly any new churches or speculative mission situations. For the first period of its existence, the Salvation Army vigorously pursued the planting of new corps, with missionary groups of young soldiers touring the country. As a matter of policy, this was stopped in 1905, in order to consolidate what had already been achieved. The church planting missionary movement was never resumed. It may be no coincidence that around 1905, the very time that church planting seemed to come to an end in various denominations, was also the peak time of churchgoing in England, from which point decline continued for the rest of the century.

A new church planting movement

However, something much more like a coherent church planting movement has got under way in the last 20 years or so. Those who were involved in it from early days have been disappointed at its impact because their expectations were very high. Particularly following the Dawn Conference in 1992, which set ambitious planting targets for each denomination by 2000, disillusionment set in as the targets were missed by spectacular amounts. But this attempt to turn around national Church decline through planting did not fail in the 1990s because church plants did not succeed and grow when they happened. Rather, too few of them were attempted to turn national decline on its head. The achievements of those plants that were made form impressive statistical evidence that starting new churches or congregations is a central piece of good practice leading to church growth in Britain today.

The Sheffield Centre for Church Planting attached to the Church Army College holds a database on Anglican church plants over the last 23 years. There are 369 plants on the database, each one a planted fellowship meeting in a separate place from the parent congregation. It does not, therefore, include those churches that have simply added another service time in their existing building. Planting new congregations in the existing building is just as much church planting as using different buildings, but data is harder to obtain. The database is not complete, but it is thought to include the great majority of church plants in the Church of England, together with some by episcopal churches in other parts of the UK. The database records both the number of people who came together from the existing congregation – the planting team and original founders – and the attendance at the last known date (which is often not the present, but on average three to four years after the planting date).

New churches grow fast!

The stunning evidence from the database, summarized in Figure 12.2, is that

Figure 12.2 Old churches shrink, new churches grow

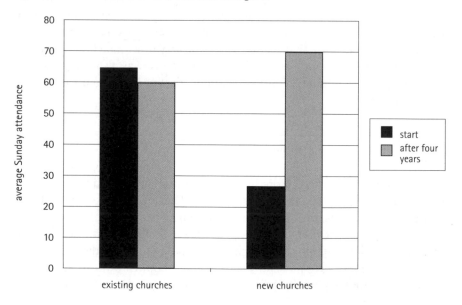

in total almost 10,000 people were involved in planting these 369 churches – an average of about 27 people per church. Three or four years later, their combined attendance was about 26,000, making an average of about 70 people per church. Growth averaged somewhere around one-third a year, making an increase of more than 250 per cent in the period. This figure includes those plants that did not thrive and closed down. There is no statistical evidence on what happened to parent churches after the plant began. However, much anecdotal evidence suggests that churches are likely to recover their numbers after a plant. They are smaller and more eager to grow back to what they once were. The estimate of 16,000 extra people may therefore be a minimum – there may be some to add to that from new growth in the parent church.

There remains the question of whether church plants grow mainly by transfer from other, less exciting, churches. In an unpublished MA thesis from Exeter University in 1996, entitled 'The impact of church planting on the local community', M. A. Bing analysed a sample of 90 church plants containing 6,087 adults and 2,389 under-18s. These churches therefore contained a total of 8,476 people, an average of 95 each. Figure 12.3 shows the composition of these churches. Twenty per cent of the people were the original planting team and a further 16 per cent transferred from other churches. But the remaining 64 per cent were mainly not transfers. A significant proportion of people stop going to church when they move house. The fact that we have become a more mobile society is a major reason for the overall decline in

Figure 12.3 Composition of newly planted churches in the UK

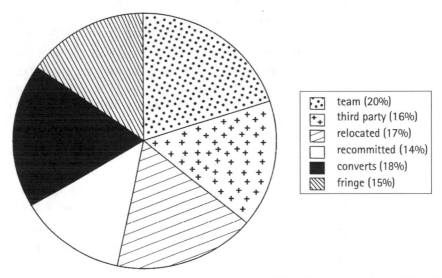

team (20%)
third party (16%)
relocated (17%)
recommitted (14%)
converts (18%)
fringe (15%)

Source: M. A. Bing, 'The impact of church planting on the local community', unpublished MA thesis, Exeter University, 1996.

church attendance. Only some of the 17 per cent who relocated would have looked for another church if they hadn't found the one that did attract them. If we divide this 17 per cent into two equal halves, we find that a fifth of members of very young churches came from the original planting church, a quarter came from other churches, and well over a half were new to churchgoing. It seems that church planting certainly does increase total church attendance.

But do church plants sustain their growth, or do they fade away with time like a sunflower at the end of summer? The figures in Table 12.1 suggest that, typically, growth continues as plants mature, though at slower rates than at the beginning. However, the results are not as compelling as they might immediately seem because the date of the latest information on which the numbers of 'extras' is based varies with each example. The latest date on the database for churches planted in 1978–84 is sometimes not much further away from the planting date than for those started in 1992–9. Some of the explanation may, therefore, be that the growth rates of recent plants are a little less than for earlier ones. This is one of those research areas where some further work is needed.

Table 12.1 Growth of Anglican church plants (by start date of plant)

1978–84	39 plants	1,032 planters	2,592 extras	2.5 extras per planter
1985–91	175 plants	4,692 planters	8,895 extras	1.9 extras per planter
1992–9	155 plants	4,295 planters	4,837 extras	1.1 extras per planter

Source: Sheffield Centre database.

Who has the resources to plant new congregations?

But how many churches have the strength to make a successful plant? If only strong churches that can spare a large, talented planting team can make a successful plant, then planting as a growth strategy will have severe limitations. However, the clear evidence from the database is that large teams are not necessarily required. Very small teams in fact have greater percentage success than large ones, as Figure 12.4 shows. (It should be added that the result for teams of less than 5 has been omitted from the chart in order that the other bars should not be rendered invisible. However, on average the 42 planting teams of between 1 and 4 people attracted 57 extra people, an increase of 3,000 per cent. This is the ultimate church growth figure in the entire book!)

So the number of new people attracted to a church plant is not influenced by the number of planters until the size of the planting team gets very large indeed. A team of three is likely to attract the same number of newcomers as a team of 73. The bigger the plant, the slower it grows – just like the existing churches that we looked at in Chapter 11. Tiny plants, like mustard seeds,

Figure 12.4 Percentage growth of church plants (by size of planting team)

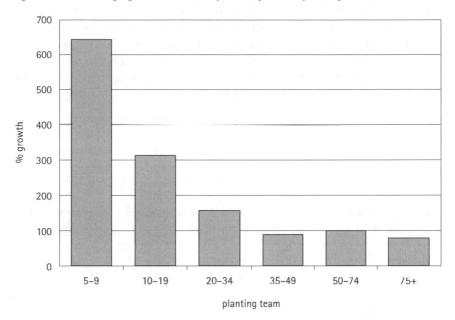

grow at incredible rates. Large plants, though not matching these rates, still grow fast. It seems that churches only have the capacity to absorb a certain number of new people each year, whether they are new plants or existing congregations. In fact, seeing that a church already has a lot of people in it may actually put people off. The difference with church plants is that we are dealing not with genteel decline but with growth performance varying from 'only' 80 per cent up to 3,000 per cent. These are not growth rates in some culture far away – they are the performance of a large group of Church of England churches in the recent past. In fact, the group is so large that it is the size of an average diocese. The Church of England has planted the equivalent of a new diocese in the last 20 years. Perhaps a few more would not come amiss.

Three policy implications are clear from these astonishing findings. First, any size of church except the very smallest should be capable of planting an offshoot, especially if the ideal size of planting team seems to be about three! Such an offshoot need not, of course, be in a separate building – it could be a new congregation in an existing building. Second, any church planting policy should bear in mind that the most productive use of the most precious resource – people – may be to encourage them to plant large numbers of new congregations in small groups. Growth is by number of plants, not by the number of people starting each plant. This means that the scope for growth by planting is gigantic if the planting is arranged in the most effective way.

Large numbers of primroses will fill the garden more quickly than a few oak trees. Third, dioceses interested in reversing their decline can do so by including a proactive planting policy as part of their overall strategy. As long ago as 1991, the Archbishop of Canterbury, George Carey, wrote: 'The time will shortly come when bishops will have to develop a strategy for church planting.'[1] A few limited attempts at such a strategy have emerged since, but surely the time for strategic mission thinking in the Church of England is now.

What's in a name?

'Church planting' may not be the most helpful name for the activity of giving birth to new expressions of the worshipping Body of Christ. It can imply that church plants are a breed apart from existing churches. Existing churches are respectable and safe, church plants are risqué and not quite 'Anglican'. Yet every church, from the first one in Jerusalem on Pentecost Sunday, was born at a point in time. There is no such thing as a church that is not a church plant. It may have been 1,000 or 100 years ago, but every parish church was founded by somebody. Every church is the result of mission before it can be an agent of mission.

To other minds, a church plant is more of a clone of the original than the needful new expression of what it means to be the Body of Christ. The very word 'church' is a turn-off and is what the radical Christian is trying to get away from. In some minds, moreover, it implies the construction of buildings. But most modern plants start in homes or rented rooms in schools or community centres or pubs, or in existing church premises. And the definition of what it means to be church should be as rich as the creativity of God himself.

'Church planting' certainly seems to imply the creation of a separate organizational unit. Yet the planting of a new congregation within the orbit of an existing PCC, perhaps in the same building, is the most common way of creating new worshipping units. The debate about whether multiplying congregations is the same as planting new churches is perhaps one of arid semantics, but, if not identical twins, the multiple congregation model and the church planting model of reaching out to new groups in the community are at least siblings.

So, is there a better term than 'church planting'? Circumlocutions such as 'giving birth to new expressions of the Body of Christ' are understandable but may not be memorably snappy. 'Congregation planting' is a useful title, and retains the rich theological potential of the 1 Corinthians 3 picture of the Church as a garden. But this may fail, in some eyes, to make the distinction needed between multiple congregations and 'proper' plants. And many new groups would not like to be thought of as traditional congregations – passively sitting in pews while a 'minister' talks at them. A new name for the activity of church planting may be needed that reflects the aspiration of many modern Christians to be followers of Jesus rather than an organization of religious people. Perhaps, in recognition of the timeless fundamental that all expressions of church must involve meeting together, we could simply talk about 'new groups'; and perhaps, in recognition of the original name for Christians as followers of 'The Way', and of the need for finding new ways of doing church, we could talk also of 'new ways'. The springing up of new groups of Christians and of new ways of being Christians together may be what we are aiming for in these changing times.

New ways and new forms

Many examples of new forms and new ways of being church already exist, either independently or as part of one denomination or another. Probably the most common are specialist churches catering for a niche market. These include ethnic churches, which cater for one ethnic or language group, youth culture churches, children's churches, pub churches, club-land culture churches, sports and other common interest group churches, and work-based churches. The multi-congregation model of being church can be applied to these independent niche churches as it offers a range of specialist congregations within one existing church structure, each catering for a different grouping. There are, of course, dangers in creating fellowships restricted to 'people like me', but pragmatically they meet the need most people feel to have fellowship and worship with 'people like me'. They are not so different from the large number of traditional Anglican churches that have become essentially 'pensioner churches', or at least 'churches for the middle-aged and elderly'. The Church of England used to be called 'the Conservative Party at prayer' – it is now in danger of being the National Trust at prayer. Linkage and ways of securing some interdependence with a broader based church life can get around the restrictions of the niche fellowships. In any case, 'church' is much more than the single congregation. If all congregations in a town were mainly for young people, this would be just as much a travesty of the Body of Christ as present-day situations where most congregations are mainly for the elderly. But if 'church' is thought of as the totality of all congregations in the town, then there is much less ecclesiastical problem in the existence of specialist congregations.

Other new forms and ways of being church have been initiated by existing churches with a specific missionary aim and are modelled on what seems to have worked elsewhere. Seeker-sensitive services aimed at people who have become dechurched, cross-cultural plants into a community different from that of the sponsoring agency, and café-style churches where everyone sits around tables with food and drink are three types that are currently having some success. For yet others their defining characteristic is their small scale. This coheres with our findings about the suitability and success of small churches in today's society. Cell churches, household churches where the small units are much less programmed and more independent, and table-based churches where everyone eats around a large dining table while praying, reading the Bible and talking together are three models. In each case the size of the individual unit quickly reaches its natural limit and growth comes through multiplication.

Other new ways and forms are more likely to cater for the disenchanted, to help people reconnect with church. These might include 'alternative worship' groupings, and meetings of Christians so disenchanted with church as they have known it that they prefer to meet together informally. They may pray and read Scripture together, but may not want to be labelled as a new sort of 'church' because 'church' is the thing they are trying to escape from. Some existing churches have also been deconstructing themselves – removing their existing programmes, meetings and organizational structures in order to clear the ground for a new, relational, way of living. Finally, some new ways and forms are defined by their lack of a geographical focus. These include relational Anglican churches with no geographical parish, Web-based fellowships, and new congregations meeting at different times of the week and day where the thing people have in common is that they are free at that particular time. The growth in attendance at cathedrals in recent years is a related phenomenon – these Anglican churches without a parish seem to offer a distinctive way of being church that is in tune with the lives and culture of some people. The growth of retreats, the desire for spiritual direction and the popularity of visiting monasteries and convents are other examples of specialist non-geographic movements.

It is clear from all the above that there is no one prototype or model for churches to copy when thinking about how to promote new groups and ways of being Christians together. Parish churches with a heart for mission must clearly consider carefully the options available, and would probably do best to invent their own. They should identify groups or areas where the church needs to develop its mission, and seek out the opportunities and subcultures in which a new way or form might be effective. They should then pick a team to develop the scheme, looking for people who are keen to be involved and recognizing that the church may need to commit some of its best people to this enterprise. Most churches should also invite an experienced consultant to help them develop their plans and avoid the pitfalls that others have encountered in the past. And they should do a thorough, rather than a fast, job of preparing for the risky step of giving birth to their new expression of the Bride of Christ. It takes nine months to make a baby, no matter how many people you put on the job. And each new expression of the Bride should have its own unique features and beauty that reflect the never-ending creativity of Christ. The main thing is not to adopt a rigid programme but to get involved in the creative process.

Dioceses and denominations need to give a lead

Dioceses can play a vital role in the success of new groups, and in new vision for the future growth of the Church of England. In other Churches, the denominational leaders are playing a key role in promoting and steering the planting movement. In the Elim Pentecostal Church, for example, where a town has been identified as a possible place for a new church the national leadership will visit, assess the possibilities, seek out a building, and arrange initial funding. In the case of the Salvation Army, plans for new churches come from top-down strategy. In other denominations the emphasis is more on offering general vision and encouragement to bottom-up initiatives. In the Church of England, both ways are needed. Dioceses should certainly consider how best to prompt, encourage and resource parishes and deaneries in their new groups and new ways. The spread of new ideas, and news of good new practices, requires contact between churches. But too many of our churches lead very isolated lives. They do not know what is going on in the churches around them. Some believe that every church is in decline like themselves. It is society that has turned against the Church and there is nothing that can be done about it, therefore we are released from any obligation to try anything new. Others would like to try something, but need help to find a vision. Dioceses are uniquely placed to put churches in touch with each other, to give church members new experiences of what it can mean to be church by arranging visits and exchanges, to organize consultancy help to parishes, and to connect once isolated churches to the national scene, to news of good practices and to patterns of thriving, healthy church life.

But dioceses also have a role to play in framing directly the sort of new way and new form that individual churches are not capable of by themselves – such as a town-wide, Web-based relational church, or a city-wide youth or counter-culture congregation. The Church of England centrally, as well as individual dioceses, needs to consider how to resource and finance new initiatives on a much greater scale than hitherto. There is a great need for on-the-ground training for potential leaders and team members to new groups and new ways. And clergy selection and training desperately needs to broaden out from the pastoral model to that of mission growth. As with the church planting movement of the nineteenth century, that of the twenty-first needs to be a fruitful partnership between parish, diocese and denomination. A garden full of identical primroses will not look its best for most of the year. Instead, in the Church that is God's garden, let a thousand flowers bloom!

The involvement needed from denominations centrally and from dioceses lies not in issues of 'faith and order' – of ensuring that experimental forms stick to the creed, and are controlled by diocesan authorities. Attempts at 'faith and order' control are the kiss of death. Rather, the pioneer movements and the Church in inherited mode actually need each other for resources, support and inspiration. New forms and ways of being church benefit from having a secure, accepted place within the denomination, and the denomination is enriched, and perhaps even in the longer term saved from extinction, by those new ways and forms. Some of today's way-out experiments may become tomorrow's traditional church life. So the job of a diocese is to encourage new forms and ways, but not to control them to death. Instead of faith and order control, diocesan and denominational authorities can helpfully offer nurture and discipleship assistance, trusting the faith to grow healthily through the authority of Scripture, the power of the Spirit, and the guidance of affirmed leadership.

Encouraging young pioneers

As a general rule, it is difficult for the older generation of leaders to envision and lead new ways and forms of being church that suit the changing world we are moving into. Those with wide experience may not have the instinct for what is needed to re-imagine church that connects with those much younger than themselves. There are still some young adults in the Church with a passion for their own generations. We need to trust these people to lead the next stage in the church planting movement, to drive the new forms and ways of being church that the Church of England will nurture in the future. Yes, they will need experienced advice and other resources in the background, but if appropriate new ways and forms are to emerge for the newer generations in the Church they must be devised and run by those generations themselves. The leaders of a new church plant aimed at people in their twenties should be that age themselves. In many places, the Church has become a gerontocracy. It is time to leap the generations and offer freedom to create and lead to those few crucial Anglicans who have the instincts, energy and enthusiasm of comparative youth. The Church that has the courage to support the young wherever they lead is the Church that will conquer the future. The re-imagination of the Church in new ways and new forms comes from the rejuvenation of the Church in new leaders and generations. Let a thousand flowers bloom, and let the young do the gardening.

Practical actions for a parish church

1. Compile some facts about both the church and the parish in order to identify any appropriate new church or congregation plants.
2. Take advice from the Church Army Sheffield Centre for Church Planting about how best to go about things.
3. Appoint a planting team.
4. Join with one or two other churches to plant a new church together.
5. Support a young adult with a vision.
6. Try a new congregation either in an existing church building, or in a suitable secular venue.
7. Ask the diocesan authorities (a motion at diocesan synod?) to adopt a church planting strategy.

13

Growing younger

Don't let anyone look down on you because you are young,
but set an example for the believers in speech, in life, in love,
in faith and in purity. (1 Timothy 4.12 NIV)

The ageing of Anglicans

Anglicans are getting older. In 1980, it is thought that the average age of Anglicans was 36, the same as that of the population. Today it is 47, compared with 38 for the population as a whole.[1] Around 1980, one-fifth of Anglican churchgoers were aged 15 to 29; today, the proportion is just one-tenth of a much-reduced total. At the other end of the scale, in 1980 just under one in five were aged 65 or over, today it is nearly one in three.[2] The recent Church Life Survey conducted by the Churches Information for Mission (CIM) suggests an even higher proportion of pensioners.

The ageing of congregations has been matched by the ageing of the clergy. Around 1980, a quarter of the clergy were under 40; today, it is only about one in six. There is an old theory, borne out by a lot of hard experience, that clergy tend to attract to their churches people aged up to ten years either side of them. Half of all incumbents are now over 51, and many of them find it increasingly hard to relate to younger adults and to young people. The trend towards ordaining older people after they have had some sort of secular career and experience has a (debatable) rationale in terms of maturity for pastoral care and leadership. But perhaps we overlooked the implications for church growth along with those for pensions, and now we are paying the price.

Growing older, growing smaller

The trend to older congregations greatly exacerbates the problem of declining total attendance. The fact that it is the younger generations that the Church has been losing means that decline is likely to continue for purely demographic reasons unless new generations of young adults and young people can be won back. This is the principal evangelistic challenge for the Church of England today. But there is another reason for worrying about ageing congregations, and for thinking about what can be done to reverse the trend. The research on the churches that responded to the questions of the 1989 census and 1998 survey shows that the strongest correlation of all between growth/decline and church characteristics is that with the age structures of congregations. Churches with an unbalanced age structure are far less likely to be growing than those with a broad and healthy mix. The evidence for this is shown in Figure 13.1. Only one in eight churches with nobody in them under the age of 45 grew between 1989 and 1998, but churches where most, but not all, people were aged under 45 were just as likely to grow as to decline. On the other hand, churches with nobody over 45 did badly as well. It seems that churches thrive best when there is a wide spread of ages, with most people at the younger end. Growing churches are much more likely to be churches where the majority of members are under the age of 45. This is not only because of the importance, already brought out in Chapter 9, of having a broad coalition and so gaining entry into a range of subcultures in the area, it is also because of the energy, enthusiasm and relevance to the largest contemporary mission field that younger Christians can bring. Their presence in numbers can of itself so change the feel and culture of a church that it becomes more relevant to younger adults generally without any specific 'policy' changes. So the 1989 and 1998 databases reveal that the Church of England must learn to attract younger adults in greater numbers if a new growth dynamic is to be generated.

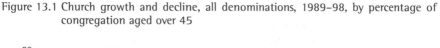

Figure 13.1 Church growth and decline, all denominations, 1989–98, by percentage of congregation aged over 45

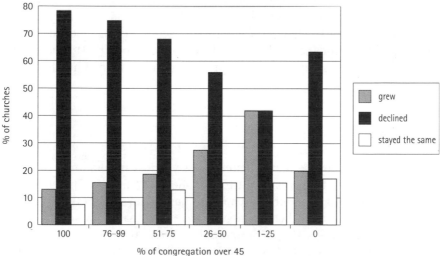

Part of the reason for differences between denominations in their attendance trends is connected with different rates of ageing. The average Methodist, for example, is now 50 years old but the average Baptist is only 41. It is no coincidence that the Methodists have been losing people faster than the Anglicans, and the Baptists have not been losing people at all. Part of the causation process goes one way – denominations lose the younger people so their average ages rise – and part of it goes the other way – denominations that are ageing find it harder to attract new people to their ranks. Numerical decline and ageing together form a potent downwards spiral. The continuing rapid decline in Sunday schools suggests that the ageing of Anglicans will continue to feed decline unless it is tackled head on.

Older members are not the problem – they are part of the solution

In general terms, this should not be done by putting off the older people. The figures show that churches with nobody over 45 find it hard to grow. This may be not just because they have no access to this segment of the population, but also because the wisdom and experience of grey hairs, and the time commitment made by many active retired people, is badly missed. Closing down provision for pensioners will not of itself attract any young adults to the church. Rather, the faith, time availability, financial strength and wisdom of the pensioner church need to be harnessed for the sake of new generations before it too starts to seep away. The right question to ask, therefore, is how can this church or deanery or diocese or denomination win back the younger half of the population? And the older members of the Church, far from being part of the problem, should be made to feel that they are part of the solution. Those, of course, who simply wish to defend what they have in church life against the changes needed to attract others may indeed be part of the problem. But those who are willing to work together to reach new generations for the sake of the future of the kingdom and the Church may be the key to success.

Not just the very young

It is a fallacy to suppose that reclaiming the younger generations back into church life involves leaping straight to teenagers. The English Church Survey data suggests that about one church in ten has nobody aged under 45 in its congregation, and a further one in six have less than a quarter of their congregation under 45. Overall, in more than three-fifths of all churches the majority of the congregation is now over 45. Widening the age range of the adults to include a full representation of those aged, say, 18 to 45 is the principal challenge. Many of these will be parents themselves, and so will bring their children with them when they enter the life of the church. Adults in their 30s may look just as grown up as those in their 50s, but their generational attitudes, background and culture are usually very different, even though they are less visibly obvious than those of teenagers.

Ideas for growing younger

Find out the facts

Local churches that are anxious to grow younger can respond to this challenge in a variety of ways. Many of these have already been mentioned in earlier chapters in different contexts. The best place to start is to find out the facts. General feelings and impressions may, in fact, be quite misleading. 'What is the age profile of this church?' is a good first question. It may be helpful to break this down between the different congregations. There is no problem in having a predominantly elderly congregation in a church that, overall, has a good age spread. Having a Prayer Book congregation that is mainly elderly, and a family service where most people are under 45, might be perfectly good practice. In some churches it will not be difficult to ask people to fill in a simple questionnaire and tick their relevant age group (say 30–39, 40–49, etc.). This is the best way to get accurate information. If this could cause offence, however, someone could hover discreetly at the church entrance and make a guess at the age group of everyone coming in. Or an incumbent or warden can make similar guesses from the electoral roll list. Children's ages should be available from their group registers. Note that the average age of members may differ from the average age of attenders, as members of some age groups may come less regularly than others.

The second key question to ask is, what is the age profile of the catchment area? This can be done from census information, from local authorities, and from school roll information. How does the age profile of the church fit that of the catchment area? Are there any missing, or thinly represented, age groups in the church? Suppose, for example, the congregation's age profile is older than that of the catchment area, and the main missing age group is people aged 15 to 35 (this is a common finding). The church can then decide to try to attract the missing age group back, which in turn will lower its own average age and should start a healthy 'growing younger – growing bigger' cycle. The age profiling exercise should be repeated every couple of years so that progress towards growing younger can be measured and monitored.

Appoint a 'growing younger' team

Once the facts have been established and target age groups identified, the church needs to discern which of its members have the vocation, vision and energy to be involved in the process. This is probably better than devising a grand plan and then looking round for reluctant arms to twist to implement it. As there are no 'one size fits all' ways of growing younger, it is important to be guided by the insights and inclinations of the team that is brought together to devise and implement the 'growing younger' strategy. Such a 'growing younger' team could be appointed by the PCC and report back to it periodically.

It is, of course, essential that this team includes as high a proportion of younger members as possible. And it is important that they make contacts and do some listening to their peer group who do not come to church. What are the ways in which this church could make meaningful connections with younger adults? Some quite radical ideas outside the experience and imagination of the older members may emerge from such an exercise. The existing church may be in for some unwelcome surprises, because few people will be found who will be keen on joining in exactly what is on offer now. For example, what if a survey of adults aged under 40 in a 'professional' neighbourhood revealed that their idea of a helpful church made no demands on them on Sundays whatsoever? Instead, their primary need was the growth of their own spirituality, they would communicate by email, meet in small groups for dinner parties with Christian input when they could, and spend six weekends a year getting together to deepen their faith with Christian teaching and meditation exercises. They would be willing to act as helpers in a Christian club for their children on Friday evenings. Could the local church cope with the idea of a new congregation along these lines, and would it see it as 'church' or not?

Develop existing contacts

There are also, of course, steps that can be initiated by the church leadership as well as those that are suggested by outsiders. One policy that has been found to work is for lay people as well as clergy to be involved in the creative use of baptism and wedding preparation contacts. The legal requirement to attend church for six months in order to get on the electoral roll of a church other than the parish church of a couple's place of residence must have led a number of people into faith and churchgoing in recent years. This evangelistic opportunity may be lost in the proposed changes to the marriage laws, and it may be worth thinking about the evangelistic opportunity of marriage preparation under the new arrangements. This is not taking unfair advantage of people – after all, they have come to the church voluntarily to share with it and with God the great moment of marriage. If we truly believe we are custodians of good news, it is unfair to hide from couples the fact that we have something even better to offer them than a God-centred wedding service in an impressive building.

In general, neither a completely open infant baptism policy, with no questions asked and no demands made, nor a closed policy, with baptisms effectively restricted to the children of believers, or to those who have jumped through some pretty demanding hoops, have proved to be the best ways of encouraging churchgoing. This is not the place to go into the theological arguments about the appropriateness of infant baptism in different circumstances, but it is worth noting that the best and most productive evangelistic consequences are most likely to come from policies that include warm, immediate welcome, well-thought-out preparation, an explanation of the Christian faith, some modest prior churchgoing, and sensitive follow-up.

But no one policy is likely to work in isolation. For example, a church is only likely to encourage baptism families to start worshipping regularly if, as well as offering good baptism preparation and pastoral follow-up, it also has a suitable service for young families to attend. Paying attention to, or setting up, appropriate all-age, child-friendly or family services is often a key ingredient. Today, such services may be better held on weekdays than on Sunday mornings. A parent and toddler service at the end of the playgroup that meets in the church hall, or a parent and child service timed for going home time at the local school, are two examples of recent successful good practice. In some communities, 4 p.m. on a Sunday afternoon has proved to be the best time for an all-age service.

Help younger people belong

Other churches anxious to integrate younger adults may need to look at their fellowship and social programmes. Many churches have persisted with women's meetings in the daytime long after most women under 60 have been going out to work. The older ladies don't want to come out at night but the younger ones are only available in the evening. Impasse! Often, the result has been a withering and ageing of the daytime group because it would not change its timing to suit new members. It has effectively excluded the younger women. Twenty years ago they might have set up their own rival meeting; today they are less likely to bother. Generally speaking, churches serious about lowering their average age need to time their programme to suit younger adults.

Content may be even more important than timing, of course. The women with jobs may not wish to come out to a women's meeting even in the evening because such a single-sex group is not part of their culture anyway. Perhaps a spirituality group open to all, or a series of short-term courses, or a special interest group, or a cell structure, are more likely to attract younger adults and so lower the average age of those involved in the life of the church.

Respect younger people and allow them to lead

It is also important for churches anxious about their age profile to involve the younger people they have in their leadership team. Younger people may need to be introduced to leadership positions on the PCC, or as wardens, or in charge of church activities, as a matter of policy rather than chance or waiting for the existing group to get too old to carry on. As well as looking at the average age of the congregation, a church also needs to pay attention to the average age of the PCC. If there are older teenagers in the church, at least two should be on the PCC, and their perspectives taken very seriously. One token teenager is not enough – he or she is likely to feel isolated and out of their depth, and they may also turn out not to be representative of the other young people.

Employ younger staff

Churches thinking about employing new staff should also consider their ages. For example, a staff member in their twenties, as well as doing their own job, may also be someone around whom begins to cohere a group of young adults. Perhaps this used to happen a lot in the days when there was a generous supply of young curates, especially when they were unmarried! It seems likely that the dramatic fall in the number of young curates, and therefore of young adults in positions of church leadership, in the second half of the twentieth century has contributed to the drop in the numbers of young adult church members. The increase in the average age of people being ordained was more by design than accident: in effect, younger Anglicans were told that they were not wanted as leaders. This was no way to encourage them. No young leaders may also mean no young followers. Churches able to employ their own staff can rectify this deficiency up to a point, but perhaps the Church of England needs a wholehearted return to the old policy of ordaining the young if it wishes its clergy to understand, attract and minister to the generation in their twenties and thirties. After all, Paul's star church leader, Timothy, was a young man who set an example to all. Jesus had completed his ministry by the time he was 33. If we now see as a prime criterion for church leadership the ability to grow the community of believers such that it again becomes a power in the land, then we may find that this facility is more common in the young than the middle-aged. Also, it is by no means necessarily the case that someone in middle age with good general life experience, but only recently ordained, will have the particular skills needed to lead a church well. Perhaps the best training for the increasingly complex, technical and demanding job of leading larger churches in Britain today is actually many years' experience of church leadership itself.

It is very much a sign of hope for the future that churches are beginning to employ younger staff again, especially as youth or student workers. Younger people should also be considered for other positions, such as vergers, organists and administrators. There have also been moves to attract more younger ordinands. Such trends need to be sustained in order to make a significant impact on the age structure of church leadership and so of the whole Church.

Getting started

The key element a church needs in order to attract younger adults into membership is other young adults. This is especially true for single people. A church with an easily visible and lively group of young single adults is highly likely to attract others. This, of course, begs the question of how a middle-aged church gets started. Much attention may need to be paid to the first one or two folk in their twenties or thirties. Perhaps they can be linked socially in some way with members of their own age group in other local churches. This may be a key area in which churches can work together. A deanery or an ecumenical 'twenties group' may be a key resource that sustains younger adults attending a variety of churches where they are in a small minority. Such a group should be given a high profile and be seen as part of the life of all the churches involved. There is now an interdenominational contact and networking organization for younger adult Christians, based in Staines, called 'Twenty Thirty'. Its aim is to facilitate social events that enable Christians under the age of 40 to come together from a variety of local churches. The events are designed to be non-threatening to others so that Christians can also invite their friends. Often an existing church group can form the nucleus of a network of this sort, not only for its own benefit but also as a help to other churches trying to attract and hold on to small numbers of younger adults.

Sometimes it is possible to arrange a link between two local churches, one a strong one with young adults and one lacking younger adults. A small team from the one could be seconded to the other in order to form a committed nucleus around which a new and younger grouping could form.

Perhaps a central focus of prayer for growth should be that these nucleus people would appear in that unexpected way that is so typical of God's planning and provision. Perhaps older church members could be asked to form a group praying specifically for God to draw an initial group of young adults into the life of the church.

Other good practices

Other policies for growing younger were discussed in Chapter 7 and Chapter 8. A church that starts to attract children or teenagers is likely to bring its average age down with a bump, not just because of the children but also because of the involvement of their parents, most of whom will be under 45. Some of the measures suggested in Chapter 11 will also reduce the average age of the Church of England because the average age of large churches is usually less than that of small ones. If we can stop the large churches declining, we will be helping to stem the loss of the young. Those trying out churches for the first time are likely on average to be younger than the person who has been going there for the last 30 years. A strong welcome group that includes as many young adults as possible may be a key strategy for churches that do sometimes get newcomers trying them out. Similarly, planting new churches (see Chapter 12) brings down the average age as members of new churches tend to be younger than those of long-established ones. This applies also to the planting of new congregations within the existing framework or buildings. It is sometimes easier to start a new service aimed specifically at younger adults than it is to modify an existing one that really suits pensioners. And perhaps it is fairer to the pensioners not to rob them of their service in order to reach out to new generations.

Working together

Church leaders who adopt a policy of attracting younger people into church life may sometimes need to do this quietly and diplomatically. But usually it is best to enlist the older members as allies in this endeavour. 'The Vicar doesn't like us much, he's only interested in young people' is usually untrue but is also easily imagined. Better to have a coherent church policy, agreed by the PCC, than to limp along with a half-resented vicar's pet programme. Sometimes, of course, for the sake of the future of the gospel, the vicar will simply have to endure the disappointment of the elderly that they don't get all the vicar's time. Part of the journey of reorientating a church towards attracting young adults is the changing of the expectations that are laid upon the clergy and other leaders by the existing congregation. They should not be expected simply to add on new targets and involvements to already crowded lives. Rather, what is needed is a mutually acceptable reorientation of their time commitments to free them up for the new, agreed priority.

Growing younger dioceses

If church congregations are older than the population at large, it seems generally true that diocesan staff, synods, boards and committees are even older than the congregations. It can easily be the case in a diocese that almost all the senior staff are in their sixties and are beginning to think about retirement, and all the rural deans are over 55. It is also likely that the majority on the bishop's council, the board of mission and the synod are over 60. How many people under 30 are there on patronage boards? It is not impossible, but it is very difficult, for such groupings to have the right instincts for making the church relevant to the young again. Ways need to be found of bringing younger adults into diocesan positions. A diocese can conduct its own age structure analysis just as well as a parish, and then devise ways of reducing the average age of its staff and committees. Young adults do still exist in numbers in the Church of England in certain parishes – the talent and faith is there if only dioceses have the will and the imagination to find and use it. Large churches rich in young adults also need to see themselves as resource churches for the whole diocese, and share the life and insights of their younger members generously with the rest of the church. One or two places are using the concept of 'turnaround teams', where a team gathered by the diocese from other churches will be seconded for a period of time to a struggling or elderly congregation in order to form a nucleus for future growth. Holy Trinity Brompton has sent a number of large groups to join existing churches in order to help their rejuvenation and renewal. Such transfusions, of course, require the agreement of the receiving church. In a similar way, churches blessed with young adults could encourage them to involve themselves in diocesan affairs. Sometimes bodies like bishops' councils and boards of mission are viewed in the same light as boards of directors – as the preserve of those in senior positions who have worked their way up through the system for many years. But the Church is not organized in that sort of way – such bodies have few executive powers but they do have mission influence. The young and inexperienced may make existing members feel slightly uncomfortable in meetings, but relevance is more important than gravitas in missionary England today.

The same point can also be made about the Church nationally. Serious attempts have been made to include younger adults on the Archbishops' Council, and perhaps similar efforts would bear fruit on boards and councils and evangelistic agencies, not just those involved with young people. A national board of mission on which over half the members were aged under 35 might give a very different lead from the usual middle-aged grouping.

It may appear at first glance that the strong influence of average age on church decline and growth is a particularly thorny problem because it is not something that can be changed very easily. However, this chapter has given sufficient examples of processes and policies that can reverse the ageing of the Church to demonstrate the possibilities. We need not only to pay attention to provision for young adults but also to promote the involvement of young adults within the life and leadership of the Church. If a church or diocese sets a five-year target for reducing its average age, adopts a range of tailor-made policies for doing so, and monitors its progress, it will succeed!

Practical actions for a parish church

1. Foster a desire among the existing older members to make attracting younger people into church life a priority.

2. Discover the facts about the age profile of the church and the parish.

3. Appoint a 'growing younger' team to plan and take forward the strategy.

4. Start a tailor-made worship and social event for young families as the next step to which to invite baptism families.

5. Start a new child-friendly worship event at the end of the playgroup, or ten minutes after the local school finishes.

6. Reorganize the small-group life of the church so that people in work are able to attend.

7. Appoint and elect the youngest people possible to key leadership jobs in the church, such as churchwardens and PCC members.

8. Employ a young staff member to do youth work, run the process evangelism, or as the curate.

9. Start a twenties group jointly with two other local churches.

10. Plan with a neighbouring large church for them to send out a group of their younger members to form a nucleus in your church around which others can coalesce.

11. Give the youngest people the most visible profile at church services, e.g. as the welcome team.

12. Ask the older members whose youth-working days are over to find the money to employ a young youth worker to begin again.

14

Supporting the clergy

Elders who direct the affairs of the church well are worthy of double
honour, especially those whose work is preaching and teaching.
(1 Timothy 5.17 NIV)

The central role of clergy skills

When it comes to the growth and life, or the decline and death, of the Church,
the clergy are key people. Therefore, a Church that wishes to grow and live
needs to invest in the well-being of its clergy, in their practical resourcing,
and in the renewal of their faith, vision and skills. Good clergy on their own
do not make for growing churches. Other factors are needed as well. No clergy
should be criticized simply because their congregations are declining. It may
not be their fault. They may be achieving great things in other dimensions of
church life.

However, in the Church of England, there are probably few examples of
churches that are growing but do not have good clergy leadership. Good clergy
appear to be a necessary but not sufficient condition for church growth. The
evidence throughout this book, moreover, leads us to the very hopeful
conclusion that clergy skills are more important than clergy talent. By talent
I mean that which is inbuilt and cannot be taught or learnt. By skills I mean
things that can be taught and learnt that enable clergy to do their job
effectively. In today's world, for example, it may be more important for the
vicar to know how to organize process evangelism than to be a naturally gifted
preacher, to have the skills for developing team leadership rather than the
talent for doing everything alone. There will always be a sense in which effective
clergy are born as well as made, always a role for God's innate and special
gifting for individuals, but there may never have been a time when acquiring
the skills of good practice was more necessary for clergy who wish to see their
churches grow. If this is so, then the scope for growing the Church by equipping
the clergy is immense. Clergy who do not feel that they are as talented as their
neighbours need have no inferiority complex – all are capable of acquiring
and deploying the necessary skills.

Reminders of the key role the clergy play in the lives of their churches are scattered through the pages of this book. In particular, we have seen how important it is to update clergy selection criteria and training methods in order to provide the Church with men and women who are able and equipped not just for the old role of pastor to a stable flock but for the new roles of missionary to a lost society and church builder for the growth of the kingdom. One implication of this (brought out in Chapter 13) is the need for more clergy and other Church leaders to be in their twenties and thirties. Figure 14.1 shows

Figure 14.1 Age profile of recommended ordination candidates, 2000

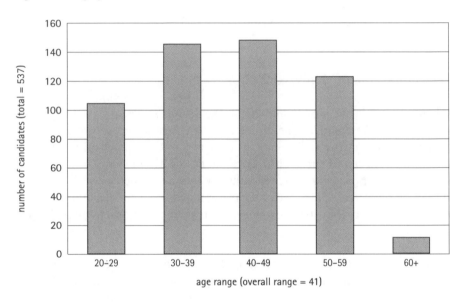

age range (overall range = 41)

the age profile of recommended ordination candidates in 2000, a profile that is much the same as it was in the 1990s. It is likely that the majority of those in the 20–29 age bracket will have passed the age of 30 before they are ordained priest. In 2000 there were just four clergy in the whole of the Church of England under the age of 25, and just 150 (1.5 per cent) under 30. It is these clergy that have the best chance of relating to young adults today, and also of acquiring the needed range of skills and experience while they are still young enough to have the energy to lead a large church successfully in the future. What a contrast to the nineteenth century! In 1849, Charlotte Brontë wrote: 'Of late years, an abundant shower of curates has fallen upon the north of England: they lie very thick on the hills; every parish has one or more of them; they are young enough to be very active, and ought to be doing a great deal of good.'[1] Surely the Church should be seeking to engineer a new shower or two in the current desert.

Clergy characteristics matter

Three pieces of statistical evidence illustrate the crucial role of the clergy. Figure 14.2 shows that attendance trends do vary with the age of the minister, and that older incumbents are more likely to be associated with decline and less likely to be associated with growth. 'Stayed the same' means an attendance change of less than + or – 10 per cent. The difference between the percentages growing and shrinking for younger clergy is 37 percentage points (61–24), for middle-aged clergy it is 46 percentage points, and for older clergy it is 52 percentage points. Decline is always more common than growth, and although some of the older clergy have growing churches, attendance growth is clearly more likely for the younger clergy and decline for the older. When it comes to rapid growth or decline (here defined as + or – 60 per cent), 9 per cent of younger incumbents were associated with each – younger clergy are just as likely to have rapidly growing churches as rapidly shrinking ones. However, only 6 per cent of older incumbents had churches experiencing rapid growth, and 15 per cent had rapidly shrinking ones.

This evidence, apart from once again indicating the urgent need to seek younger candidates for ordination as a matter of policy, further shows that the personal characteristics of the incumbent are important determinants of the direction of church life.

Figure 14.3 yields similar evidence, this time of the impact of length of incumbency on attendance growth and decline. It can readily be seen that

Figure 14.2 Attendance growth and decline in Church of England churches, 1989–98, by age of incumbent in 1998

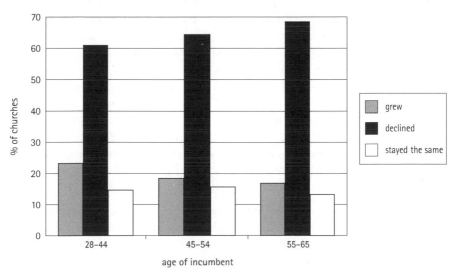

Figure 14.3 Attendance growth and decline in Church of England churches, 1989–98, by length of incumbency by 1998

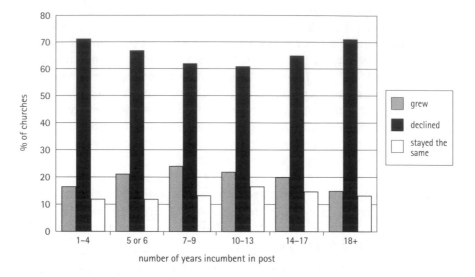

both short and long incumbencies are more often associated with decline, and medium-length incumbencies with growth. It would seem that, on average, from a purely church growth point of view, the best length of time for an incumbency is between 7 and 13 years. The chances of attendance growth get slimmer and slimmer for incumbencies both shorter and longer than this. Once again, this finding does not mean that some clergy cannot see church growth very quickly, nor that others cannot preside over growth towards the end of long incumbencies. There may also be good reasons to have short- or long-term incumbencies for other than church growth considerations. However, if the Church of England is serious about halting its own decline, it does seem that encouragements to medium-length incumbencies are a good thing. Five-year contracts and withdrawal of freehold may be important for reasons of financial caution, or perhaps desired for reasons of central control, but moving people on after five years does not look like a good church growth option. Short incumbencies and frequent vacancies can be damaging, yet the average length of incumbency in the Church of England is between six and seven years. This is clearly too short, and clergy should be encouraged by their own PCCs and by their diocese to stay for a fairly long time, but not for too long! An average of ten years looks about right.

A final piece of evidence for the importance of the personal characteristics of the clergy in determining growth and decline comes from two similar dioceses. In one diocese it was discovered that wherever there was a large fall in attendance in a parish this was almost always associated with a pastoral or personal breakdown. Either there had been some breakdown in the incumbent's health or family relationships, or a breakdown in relationships between the incumbent and a large section of the congregation. In fact, so striking was this finding that it seemed to account for a substantial proportion of the total attendance decline in the diocese. By contrast, another diocese seeking explanations for its comparatively good attendance trends, which included a significant growth in attendance in 2000, realized that it had, either by accident or design, experienced hardly any pastoral or personal breakdowns among its clergy. It therefore had virtually no parishes with steep or sudden attendance falls.

Recruitment, selection and training

If, as suggested above, it is true that clergy with the appropriate characteristics and mindset are likely to lead churches into growth, then recruitment, selection and training become significant long-term determinants of the growth potential of the Church of England. In particular, the old pastoral model whereby clergy are selected on the basis of pastoral sensitivity rather than gospel enthusiasm may need an overhaul. In the post-Christendom world of the future, the Church will need fewer pastors and more missionaries.

Furthermore, if it is true that the possession of the appropriate church leadership skills is key, then the content of clergy training may also need an overhaul. An academic theological education may not be the best preparation for the job the clergy are actually called to do. When a new incumbent is called upon to turn around a failing operation with a turnover of £200,000 p.a., half-a-dozen paid staff, a crumbling medieval building, a parish share debt, and a complex interaction of activities, her detailed knowledge of the book of Habakkuk may not be her most potent weapon. She may have learnt to rejoice in the Lord whatever pastoral disasters may happen, but she will also need to know *how* to get the flock back in the fold and the herd in the stall (Habakkuk 3.17,18).

If greater emphasis is to be placed on actually training ordinands for the realities of their future jobs of growing churches in difficult times, then more of the trainers will have to be experienced parochial clergy themselves. It is not realistic to expect academics without this experience to impart skills they do not possess, nor to train ordinands for a life they themselves have not lived and may not properly understand. There is, of course, the theory that the 'practical' training comes with the experience of a curacy. There are many problems with this expectation. One is the hit-and-miss nature of curate–incumbent relations, another is the expectation of the parish that they have acquired another pair of hands, not a full-time trainee, a third is the narrow, and possibly outdated, wisdom and experience base the curate has to draw on in this apprentice model, and a fourth the fact that busy incumbents do not have time to train curates.

There is a wide variety of training colleges and programmes for ordinands in the Church of England. Some offer more academic courses, some are more practical. Some are full-time residential, some are part-time non-residential. Some are clearly associated with one church tradition or another, others are not. Are the graduates of some colleges or courses more likely to lead churches into growth than the graduates of others? The data from the 1989 census and 1998 survey yields a sample of 3,009 Anglican clergy from about 40 different training institutions. A number of comparisons were made, including residential colleges v. courses and charismatic-evangelical tradition v. others. No statistically significant differences were found whatsoever between the different groups. In other words, someone from an area ministerial training scheme was just as likely to have charge of a growing church as someone from one of the heavyweight evangelical colleges.

This startling (to some) result could mean one of a number of things – that all training methods are equally effective or ineffective, that the skills imparted were less relevant than the (fairly randomly distributed) innate talents of the clergy, or that the skills were not imparted in the first place. However, it does seem safe to conclude that no one college or style of training should complacently assume its superiority over others in this regard. There are two important caveats to all this, however. First, this data refers to incumbents who were trained in the 1980s or earlier. Perhaps we would see greater differences between more recent ordinands. Second, those graduating from the evangelical residential colleges are probably more likely to be incumbents of larger churches. On average, surveys suggest that congregations in the evangelical tradition are 50 per cent larger than the others. But the larger churches of all traditions are much more likely to be in decline. So, if we could compare like for like in terms of church size we might find that the graduates of these colleges are more associated with growth. But the most important conclusion remains – there is no evidence that any one training style or tradition enables clergy to buck the declining attendance trend. In this lies a major challenge for clergy formation and training.

Maximizing clergy effectiveness

It seems from our findings on the age of the clergy, the length of incumbencies and effectiveness of training courses that the old gut instinct of parishes to look for a new vicar, wherever he or she might come from, aged 35 to 40, who will stay for ten years, have a stable family life, and not fall out with anyone, is pretty sound! More importantly, what is also clear is that clergy need to be looked after and supported if they are to stand the best chance of delivering the growth goods. Diocesan support structures that can give early warning of potential problems, and help the incumbent sort them out before it is too late, are a key ingredient in any anti-decline strategy. All too often, the first a diocese hears of a problem is when the bishop reads the local paper. All that is then possible is a damage limitation exercise. Better by far to have good pastoral care for the clergy in the first place.

Parishes similarly cannot afford to neglect the well-being of their incumbent and other staff. How can we help the vicar focus on her key strategic tasks? What office and secretarial resources can we give her to enable her to do her job effectively? According to a recent British Gas SME Time Survey, three out of four owners and managers of small businesses feel they spend too much time on non-core activities. Many incumbents feel exactly the same. Clergy and PCCs have a responsibility to talk through together how the vicar will spend her time, and how she is to be supported practically and emotionally to help her sustain the very draining job she has taken on. A shared vision and a shared understanding of roles and expectations can make for good working relations and for healthy, growing churches.

If it is true that skills matter more than talent, and that in a fast-changing world new skills and knowledge are needed all the time, then the ongoing training of the clergy is a vital part of equipping them to lead churches into growth. This is one of those areas in which the Church has made some advances. Details of training opportunities are now more often circulated by dioceses to the clergy, and training officers and training budgets have become accepted norms. However, some would say that the content and relevance of training events to the key agenda of turning around the declining Church often leave something to be desired. Also, in times of budget cuts training budgets are often vulnerable, and dioceses might find it advantageous to consider more stringently which training opportunities will actually increase clergy effectiveness at their core tasks. There has been some waste of resources due to duplication of opportunities already provided by established para-church organizations. Dioceses have got in the habit of paying twice over for training – paying a training officer to organize it and an outside body to do it. It may sometimes be that training budgets for useful courses can be safeguarded or enlarged by finding ways of managing with fewer diocesan organizers.

Recent research for the EU, which has formed the basis for new maximum hours regulations, suggests that, on average, people who work longer than a 48-hour week find it counter-productive. Forty-eight hours is the average maximum it is sensible to work because effectiveness is greatly diminished beyond this point by tiredness and staleness. Most people can achieve more of real value in 48 hours than they can in 58. If working hours are too long, physical and emotional exhaustion, and all sorts of illnesses and breakdowns, become more common. Relaxation and recreation, time for maintaining family ties and for attending to the human soul, are vital restoratives for those with demanding jobs. Another headline from the same British Gas survey is that 'Owner/managers are overworked and stressed out, putting in over 60hrs per week.' If the secular working world recognizes that a 60-hour week leads to overwork and stressed out managers, so should the Christian working world.

And yet the culture of the Church of England is that its clergy, from bishops to curates, work cripplingly long hours. Working weeks of 60, 70 and even 80 hours are commonplace. After a full working day, parish clergy turn out for evening events and meetings most nights of the week. Whereas almost every other job in the country is based on a five-day week, clergy are asked to work six full days. There is no respite even at Christmas and Easter. Most conscientious clergy are constantly tired. Emotional and physical exhaustion is at the root of many breakdowns. This situation has got worse, not better, as the number of stipendiary clergy has dwindled, good practice becomes more demanding, and the average age of the working clergy increases.

Measures to enable clergy to live a normal life within the confines of a sensible 48-hour working week have to be at the core of any policy for supporting the clergy. These can be put in place by individual parishes, but they may also be needed from the Church centrally and from dioceses. Of course, not all clergy are hapless victims in this process. Many willingly put in the hours for the sake of the kingdom of heaven, and receive much job satisfaction. Others are driven to overwork by their own internal emotional needs. The job invades the home, it is hard to switch off, there are few clear outputs and success criteria, guilt at visiting left undone is rife, the list of important things to do never ever comes to an end. Self-justification by work is endemic. And it is self-defeating. The EU research applies to all – clergy are likely to achieve less of real value in their 70-hour weeks than they would in a 48-hour one. Dioceses need more proactive sensible and compassionate employment policies for their clergy to help them develop proper balance in their working lives. In this way the clergy will stay fresh and keen, with the energy to contemplate new developments, the ability to give of their best throughout their working week, and a greater, fairer chance of avoiding breakdowns.

Choosing the right clergy

In the old way of doing things, Revd Quiverfull wanted a bigger vicarage following the latest arrival in the family, and the bishop offered him something to suit. This did not always ensure that the parish received the most appropriate incumbent. Neither, incidentally, did it do the clergy many favours. Preferment by casual patronage often means that the new incumbent is remarkably ignorant about what he or she is taking on. One of the most hopeful pieces of better practice in the Church in recent years has been the development of ways of helping parishes find clergy that suit them. The systems of parish profiles, parish reps, incumbent profiles and job descriptions have made the whole business more professional and more likely to attract round pegs to round holes. Where parishes advertise and appoint from a shortlist they are far more likely to get the sort of person they want than if they simply wait for a patron to present them with someone.

However, the tendency of some dioceses when they hit a financial crisis to restrict the filling of new posts to internal candidates can clearly derail this advance. In an attempt to cut clergy numbers as fast as possible a diocese can easily give a further twist to its own decline cycle by appointing less than ideal candidates to parishes simply because they are already on the payroll of the diocese. Such a policy, by taking away from parishes their freedom to seek suitable candidates by open advert and interview, can also harm diocesan–parish relations. Better for dioceses to plan their staffing over the long term, attract the best clergy they can, and so be strengthened in the battle to reverse decline.

Increasingly today, when the Church is fighting for its life, when reversing or avoiding decline must be a major priority, parishes must look for a leader who can help them do this. 'How would you attract young adults into the life of this church?' 'Where do you see the possibilities for growth in this parish?' become key interview questions. Some bishops have quietly adopted a policy of finding new clergy for their dioceses who have a heart for growth and an idea of how to achieve it. It would seem that, over a period of years, such policies pay off in the diocesan attendance statistics.

Choosing the right bishops and archdeacons

As this book has pointed out, some dioceses have been better planned and less conservatively run than others. This matters from the point of view of the growth or decline of the Church. Chapter 15 suggests ways in which the effectiveness of dioceses can be, and is being, greatly increased. Just as the selection and training of parish clergy matters to the growth or decline of the Church, so does the selection and training of senior clergy. Diocesan bishops are largely chosen from the ranks of suffragans and archdeacons. These in turn are largely chosen by diocesans. Such a circular system can work perfectly well, but there are dangers in such self-perpetuation, one of which is that it is bound to be treated with suspicion in the postmodern world. The Church is anxious to avoid the perception that keeping the right tradition, knowing the right people, and being a compliant colleague is the route to preferment. It is therefore recognized that objective criteria should be applied when identifying potential candidates. Today, the whole future of the Church of England is in the balance unless attendance decline can be reversed. One key objective criterion should therefore be to look for clergy who have successfully led parishes into significant growth. Senior clergy with this background will be best equipped to lead others to do the same.

Being realistic

We have now considered eight key ways of turning around the decline of the Church that have emerged from statistical enquiry: facing facts, nurturing faith, welcoming all, taking risks, acting small, planting churches, growing younger, and supporting clergy. All of them offer hope for the turning around of decline. However, it is important not to underestimate the extent of the challenge. In many cases all that a single favourable factor appears to do is to slow down the overall rate of decline. For example, a rich ethnic mix means that 27 per cent of churches are growing instead of 20 per cent, or youth provision means that 39 per cent of churches are growing instead of 18 per cent. Only tiny churches and church plants had a majority of growing churches among them. Churches may need to look to a combination of strategies for future growth – doing process evangelism, employing a youth pastor and planting a new congregation, for example. The Church of England as a whole may expect to slow or even halt decline with such measures, but radical new forms and ways of being church may be required before significant national growth can be contemplated.

So, although we have identified many specific actions and strategies for parishes, deaneries, dioceses and the national Church that will help to turn decline around, no one action is likely to be sufficient in itself. Rather, some joined up thinking leading to the arranging of all sorts of policies around the growth objective is likely to be required. But neither should it be assumed that unless we are tackling the problem on all fronts at once we are failing. Sometimes very modest first steps yield surprisingly gratifying results. It is important to be realistic about what can be attempted in any given time scale, and to believe that God will honour the priorities we discern. Similarly, there is no one formula that will work like magic in every situation. We all have to make our own discoveries suited to our own unique situations. What I hope to have done over these eight chapters is to offer ideas and inspiration, and to increase confidence that there are practical, realistic and effective answers to the decline of the Church.

It is important to reiterate that new activities and initiatives should not be bolted onto already overstressed churches and over-busy clergy lives. The section above about maximizing clergy effectiveness calls for less to be attempted, not more. Healthy churches and healthy Christians on the whole aim to do fewer things but to do them better than most of us manage at the moment. Wise leaders seek to develop people more than programmes. Often the key actions to be taken are those that withdraw churches and individuals from commitments in order to free them up for new priorities. Having thought through the things that may be most appropriate for turning a church around, the first (and the most painful and contentious) task may be to agree the things that the church should cease to try to do. The pace we set ourselves should be one that a marathon runner can sustain – for in the end the marathon runner will get further than the sprinter. We must pray for wisdom as we set our priorities so that we can maximize our long-term kingdom impact in God's world.

Practical actions for a parish church

1. Appoint a young incumbent to your parish.

2. Use the advertising and shortlist interview procedure in order to discover the candidate most likely to lead your church into growth.

3. Encourage the clergy to stay for 8 to 12 years.

4. Send your vicar on at least two training courses a year, and send other staff and leaders also.

5. Find the vicar a secretary.

6. Appoint a church administrator.

7. When reviewing the job description of your church staff, give an indication of the maximum hours they are expected to work.

8. Make it your priority to help your clergy and their families be happy and fulfilled – clergy who receive much from their church are able to give much in return.

15

The vital role of the diocese

> When the number of disciples was increasing, the Grecian Jews among them complained against the Hebraic Jews because their widows were being overlooked. (Acts 6.1 NIV)

The evidence and arguments so far suggest that dioceses are key units for determining the future decline or growth of local churches, and that the ethos, culture, structure and policies of a diocese will partly determine its own future growth or demise. By 'diocese' is meant the senior staff and other diocesan post holders, synods, boards and committees constituted at diocesan level. This is an optimistic conclusion because it means that decline is not pre-ordained either by the changing environment in which the diocese operates or by the nature of its parish churches. Its future lies at least in part in its own hands. Good practice in a parish church that has known decline can turn it round, and the same is true for a diocese. If every diocese determines to implement good practice for the growth and strength of its churches then there is every chance of turning around the national trend.

Future significance of dioceses

There are reasons for supposing that the cultural change we see taking place around us today is making the diocese more important than it was in the recent past. Anglican ecclesiology has always acknowledged the importance of units of aggregation greater than that of an isolated, individual congregation. In part this is connected with the role of a bishop, in part with the importance of belonging to the historic apostolic Church, and in part with the mutuality in giving and receiving so commended by Paul among the New Testament churches. Anglicans are not natural congregationalists, and will not willingly abandon their mission to the whole nation, maintained as it is by the mechanism of the strong parishes in a diocese supporting the weak through the parish share. But if our theology has always indicated the importance of the diocese, it is now strengthened by practical argument. The greater significance of the diocesan unit, for good or ill, in the growth or decline of the Church comes from the increased need for the Church to keep up with today's fast-changing world by changing itself. In many areas of church life, the unit and instigator of change can only be the diocese.

This is true, for example, of the way in which the people of the diocese are divided up between the churches for the purposes of pastoral care and evangelism. For centuries they have been divided up geographically. This arrangement suited a medieval rural economy. Between them, the clergy, each licensed to a specific geographical location, were responsible for the spiritual care of all the citizens of the land. But geography was not fundamental to the intention of the parish system – the fundamental principle of the 'cure of souls' was to ensure that no one was left out of the spiritual care network of the national Church. The geographical parish was simply the best means to that end. In order better to meet that unchanging aim of reaching the whole nation, dioceses may now need to change, or at least to supplement, the means.

The parish system has not always been 100 per cent geographical anyway. Some cathedrals have had little parish to speak of, yet have cared for large numbers of worshippers who live in many surrounding parishes. Minsters and monasteries provided other models from an age before that of the settled parish. In the minster model, instead of the countryside being divided up into parish units each looked after by one man, groups of clergy or monks and their disciples would journey around a wide area tending to the needs of the villages and preaching the gospel. Church buildings were not involved – the focal point was often an outdoor stone cross. Today, once again, most rural churches no longer have their own exclusive priest, and rural incumbents are beneficed to impossibly large numbers of parishes. Perhaps the minster model suggests a better way of exercising cure of souls in the countryside, but experiments in this direction can only be instituted by dioceses.

In today's urbanized, mobile and relational world, people vote with their feet anyway. They pick the church that suits them best. There are usually several within driving distance. Whether or not they live in a particular geographical parish does not even occur to many churchgoers as a significant factor in their choice of church. About 50 per cent of Anglicans worship in only about 15 per cent of the churches. The idea of an even spread of people and parishes and clergy across the land sharing the load along geographical boundaries ordained from on high has little correspondence with reality today. People divide themselves up in their own way, in relational and cultural groupings – the Church cannot force them into its own parishes. People will typically join in worship not with 'people who live near me' but with 'people who are like me'.

So, if it is the duty of the diocese to ensure that all the people of the diocese are covered by the pastoral and evangelistic life of the churches, then the diocese may need to make some changes to the way it achieves that objective. In fact our very Anglicanism seems to demand that dioceses supplement their geographical parishes with some relational ones in order to reach those who are currently overlooked, whom the geographic parishes cannot touch. Take, for example, a town-wide youth church. The 'parish' here is composed of the relevant age group who live in and around the town in question. The aim is to offer 'church', including both worship and relational glue, that is suited to the culture of the 'parish'. This requires a specialist team and skills not normally found in the average geographical parish church. It also involves a greater number and concentration of teenagers and young adults. Other examples of non-geographical parishes could include a Wednesday night church; a Web-based congregation relating in a mosaic of different ways and coming together periodically for celebrations; an inner-city 'children's church'; a sport- or activity-based church; and existing cathedral congregations.

Just as only a diocese can be responsible through its pastoral committees and bishops for changing geographical parish boundaries and creating new geographical parishes, so only a diocese can take ultimate responsibility for the setting up of new non-geographical parishes to cater for the emerging postmodern world of relational community. Sometimes a dominant local church, or a far-seeing local leader, is able partly to replicate the diocesan role (e.g. in the setting up of a town-wide youth church), and they may have the advantages both of being on the ground to start with and being able to work ecumenically rather more easily. A diocese may be able to encourage, authenticate and contribute to the pioneering work of a parish. However, these conditions do not exist in most places, and initiatives easily falter when key personnel move on. The way the Church of England is organized, only the diocese can offer the continuity and oversight needed for the long haul in each area.

Changing the ecclesial model

Our inherited ecclesial model relies mainly on the local church to both frame and deliver the church growth goods. The bishop used to be seen as a high-status figurehead who was not expected to interfere with a stable set of parishes except to disapprove of or discipline them if they stepped out of line or tried something new. Those in authority in a diocese may not have expected to be held responsible for its decline, growth or success. In an era when parishes formed an unchanging single society around their parish church (if such a time ever truly existed), this model may have sufficed. One local priest and church could deliver Christendom to all in the parish. Acts of Uniformity would hopefully bring dissenters back to the fold. Canon law restricted (and still restricts) the freedom of the clergy to bring about change – 'I will use only such forms of services as the canons allow ...'. But this model of everything being left to the parochial clergy was always less true in theory than in practice – the cure of souls has always been the joint responsibility of the bishop and the incumbent.

And this 'one size fits all in a stable world' parish church concept cannot possibly deliver the church growth goods in today's culturally fragmented and fast-changing world. Increasingly, people view themselves not as part of a community to which they must conform, but as sovereign consumers in their own right. Today, we no longer think: 'I must fit the world about me' but 'the world about me must fit me'. This world-view applies equally to our choice of motor car, holiday, shampoo, and spirituality provision. Religion perceived as conforming to an inherited set of rules is increasingly unpopular. Spirituality as an individual project is the new norm.

And so a parish church offering worship and church life in only one form and subculture, often one from the past, is almost bound to be in decline. The numbers of people who fit easily into virtually any and every subculture in an area will decline as cultural fragmentation proceeds. A parish church in one 'fine tradition' is increasingly no longer good Anglicanism. Anglicanism is not about one worship or church style – that would be to mistake the medium for the message, the means for the end. Anglicans do not aspire to live in a subcultural ghetto, to become a small sect in a pluralistic society. Rather, Anglicanism in England is about making the gospel and the kingdom accessible to all. Therefore the Church must perforce be multicultural in its own expression. Ideally, a parish church should aim to offer worship and church life in and to all the main subcultures of its parish – a traditional service, a youth service, a child-friendly service, a jazz service, and so on. Offering a variety of packaging does not mean that the content must change. This is not a liberal agenda. The creeds and the historic faith of the Church are the baby that should not be thrown out with the ecclesiastical bath water. Anglicanism is also about transmitting the historic faith of the creeds and formularies to present generations. Some large churches in towns and cities may be able to make a reasonable fist of becoming a broad church culturally. Many others, though, are hampered by their own inherited culture ('this is how things are done here' or 'this is what proper Anglicans do'). It is important for these churches to realize that the modern world requires them to broaden their tradition, not necessarily to abandon it. But even many large churches will lack the resources adequately to offer an 'it must fit me' spirituality package to more than a few people. In order to be able credibly to say 'We in the Church will walk with you on your spiritual journey, to help you meet your Saviour Christ' to a wide variety of people, a wide variety of walks needs to be available. This variety is wider than, and not through routes that, most single parish churches can offer.

It is true that many people can shop around different churches to find what they want. It may be that a certain town or area contains all the main types of church that are needed. But this will have happened by chance and accident of history, and it is increasingly not available in most areas as the variety required has increased. Some element of organization is needed where the haphazard vagaries of patronage, local church initiatives and history have left gaps in the provision.

This means that a new ecclesial model is needed, one which redefines the levels at which the Church is responsible for the delivery of church growth, one which includes not just the parish, but the deanery, the diocese, the national Church and other denominations as well. Only at this level can the Church plan and organize the variety and some of the forms the postmodern world demands. In pre-modern society, small businesses supplied local people with their needs, and the parish church model fitted in with this world rather well. In the 'modern' world that followed, big business used economies of scale to supply large national markets with standard products – Henry Ford's 'any colour as long as it is black'. The uniform nature of Anglican liturgical worship to some extent mirrored this phase in economic development. But now, in the new, postmodern world, giant multinational businesses, while garnering ever greater economies of scale, also use their size to offer tailor-made solutions for every individual's 'it must fit me' requirements. A new car range now has an infinite number of specifications so that virtually every vehicle is unique in the combination of details it offers. Giant holiday companies advertise 'tailor-made' holidays to suit individual requirements. The choice in even as simple a product as shampoo becomes ever more bewildering – shampoo to suit different hair colourings, skin types, water hardness, frequencies of washing, shampoos to add volume or shine, with or without conditioner, conveying this, that or the other image. In the Church, *Common Worship* materials have now given each parish a toolkit with which they can personalize the liturgy for their own use. This is helpful, but even *Common Worship* cannot hope to cater for the great spread of people in today's world. So how can a local parish church, or even a collection of them each acting in isolation, deliver the needed array of personalized Christian spirituality solutions? In the postmodern world it therefore becomes the responsibility of the deanery, the diocese and the national Church to use their scale to offer new varieties of worship and church life so that the Church of England again becomes a culturally appropriate Christian movement for the whole nation.

Ways some dioceses work

Disapproval mode

Traditionally, many dioceses have appeared to be in 'disapproval' mode. Innovative parishes moving away from inherited traditions have been looked on with suspicion or hostility. Some churches have felt that conformity to a pattern, preservation of a building, the wording of the liturgy, the clothing of the priest, the gathering in of the quota, or the letter of the law have been more important to the diocese than the spreading of the gospel or the work of the kingdom.

A parish church grew strongly through the increased use of lay ministry. The senior staff of the diocese never complimented the incumbent on the joyous growth of his church but ticked him off for using 'unauthorized' preachers. This example, and the others that follow, of dioceses making progress from unhelpful to good practice, are all real ones taken from around the country.

Disinterest mode

Sometimes a diocese that has stopped giving out disapproving vibes to imaginative parishes simply ceases to show any interest. A parish that has become an exception to the general diocesan decline and has a growing congregation is disappointed that the diocesan authorities never show any interest in why or how this has been achieved. There is never any suggestion that the diocese can either help with or learn from what is going on. This can be most marked in dioceses with serious financial difficulties, for they are in danger of getting to the point where their main priority is to gather in the income. It may be that the only way to get the attention of such a diocese is to underpay the parish share!

Permission-giving mode

Dioceses are increasingly moving out of disapproval or disinterest mode into 'permission giving' mode. Bishops, motivated by the realization that doing nothing in a fast-changing world will not ensure survival, give verbal encouragement to their parishes to experiment and change to engage better with the modern world. In parishes that wish to move forward, taking off the diocesan brakes can be liberating. Dioceses are becoming more likely, for example, to give their blessing to cross-boundary church plants. However, there are limitations. Parishes may actually need not just diocesan permission but also diocesan help. A vicar approaches the bishop with a good initiative for starting a new ministry in the town with young adults. The bishop says,

'I'll back you if you can find the money to get it started.' But the vicar can't, so the idea is stillborn. A little seed-corn money, or the services of a diocesan youth officer one day a week for six months, could have tipped the balance.

Encouragement mode

Some dioceses have gone further, and are now at the next stage, in 'encouragement' mode. Clergy and PCCs are gathered together for training programmes. Parishes are invited to submit their 'mission action plans' to their bishop. Senior clergy visit their deaneries to talk through with the parishes their plans for the future growth and mission of their churches. This can have the effect of galvanizing the more reluctant or unaware parishes into new initiatives suited to changing times. There is some statistical evidence (reported in Chapter 4 in relation to York and Wakefield Dioceses) which suggests that being in 'encouragement' mode can by itself slow decline.

Proactive mode

But there are yet three further stages for dioceses to move towards if they are to be fully effective in generating the new growth of the Church. The first is 'proactive' mode. A diocese in proactive mode does more than simply encourage and goad its parishes into better practice for the future, essential though this is. It also initiates its own programmes for growing new forms of church. Clear and well-resourced diocesan strategies for new forms of church and for church planting will involve dioceses moving on to a challenging but necessary agenda for halting and reversing the decline of the Church. Other forms of proactive action by dioceses and deaneries that are already becoming common include recognizing and training new forms of ministry for rural parishes where stipendiary priests are thin on the ground. Increasingly it may also need to include new forms of organization as alternatives to the nightmare of large-number, multi-parish benefices. City-wide strategies for moving the Church into mission mode as well as pastoral mode may need to be sponsored and implemented by dioceses. Piecemeal closures and amalgamations is simply a minimal effort way of managing decline. A strategy for replacing old buildings and forms with new ways of working, perhaps replacing pastors with church-planting missionaries, gives hope of growth for the future. Ironically, the main motive for such reviews of strategy is often the need to resolve financial difficulties. These have been brought about in part through the drying up of central financial support to parishes as clergy pensions have absorbed more and more of the available money. But they have also been brought about by declining church congregations. If the one in six church attenders who have been lost in the last ten years were suddenly to return, then many diocesan financial crises would disappear overnight. But the need to review activities in order to find more economical, and perhaps more effective, ways of working may actually be the God-given trigger that is needed to enable dioceses to bring about growth through change.

Three dioceses each received some unexpected money from the central authorities with a request that it be directed towards evangelism through new sorts of church. One diocese, without a moment's thought about investing it for future church growth, simply pocketed the money for existing stipends. One used some of the money to finance a new relational church for young adults in a large town. The financial aim of this investment was that the new congregation would start to pay its way and make a contribution to common costs after a few years. A third diocese decided to invest all of the unexpected grant in new forms of church and to match the amount from its own funds.

The range of new styles of church is sometimes known collectively as 'the emerging church'. The idea that as one form of church declines another can arise to replace or supplement it is essential to the Church's future. But the implication of the word 'emerging' is that the process is somehow automatic or organic. The job of the diocese is simply to watch out for the emerging church and encourage it as it emerges. The reality is that new forms of church do not 'emerge'. Visionaries guided by the Holy Spirit plan and plant them. The role of the diocese is not only to observe and encourage the emergence of new church but also to invent and to generate it.

Policy mode

Possibly the most difficult and important step for a diocese to take in relation to discharging its responsibility to grow the Church of the future is for it to move into 'policy' mode. Each diocese has its own unique set of practices in relation to things like employment, preferment, finances, pastoral reorganization, asset management, housing, training, or evangelism. Some of these are not 'policies' strictly speaking because they have emerged as a result of custom and practice rather than having been thought through and adopted as official policy. However, let us call them 'policies'. Typically, there has been little attempt at joined up thinking between different policy areas. These are the responsibility of different boards and committees, who may not appreciate or take account of the needs of other groups when making decisions. Historically, no board or committee or individual has had the responsibility for attending to the issue of the growth and decline of the Church. This is a strange omission as this is the central issue on which all else hangs. With so many dioceses now facing the very real prospect of extinction unless attendance decline is reversed it becomes important for every responsible body and individual to consider the impact of existing and potential policies on the growth or decline of the Church. Otherwise it will be all too easy for a diocese to achieve the opposite of its desire and become an engine of decline.

Examples of this can be found in every area of diocesan life, but perhaps the most obvious are in the realm of financial policy. A diocese is facing a deficit budget and needs to reduce its expenditure. Instead of planning a reorganization of posts, abolishing the least important and creating a few strategic new ones, it simply leaves unfilled all the vacancies that happen to occur. This is because the financial managers have no control of policy, and the policy makers no familiarity with the financial realities. Church of England dioceses tend to set their budgets the opposite way round from everyone else. Most people first work out how much income they can expect, and then decide how to spend it. Dioceses, typically, first work out how much money they would like to spend, and then ask the diocesan board of finance to work out how much income is required from the parishes in order to produce it. Crises occur when parishes are collectively unable to supply this total, an amount that was decided with minimal reference to its impact on their lives and ministries and to their ability to pay. And so financial management and employment policy only get joined up at the last minute, when a crisis has already begun. Parishes large and small become subject to the random vagaries of interregnums which sometimes go on for years. Large parishes can easily be plunged into major decline by such a lengthy leaderless spell, especially if assistant staff start to leave as well.

A parish decides to adopt good practice for growth and pay a youth worker. His ministry is wonderfully effective and the church grows, but the parish share goes up too because of the increased attendance. For a year or two, the parish cannot pay all its parish share. The diocese complains to the parish and asks it to sack the youth worker. The vicar is marked down as disloyal and a trouble-maker.

A parish raises the cost of paying for an evangelist by asking the congregation to increase its giving. The congregation meets its target, and the evangelist begins her work. However, next year the increased income of the church leads to a large increase in its parish share. Because the extra giving was designated, and because new income from new Christians only follows after a time lag, the parish cannot afford the increase. The diocese demands it put its house in order and pay the share instead of the evangelist.

A board of finance is faced with the need to make some budget cuts. It is always easier to cut uncommitted expenditure. It notices a budget for grants of seed-corn money to parishes making growth initiatives in their youth and children's work. This was the bishop's idea. The board cut the budget and tell the bishop the grants can't be afforded any more.

A diocese puts great pressure on all its parishes to pay their parish share in full or let the side down. Parishes start to pour time and effort into fund-raising events. They encourage their members to increase their giving, and make church life uncomfortable for some. Mission, evangelism and church growth become luxury items which are pushed down the priority list by the urgent need to raise funds. Parish leaderships begin to feel their main function is to be tax collectors for an insatiable diocese. Morale suffers. Disputes break out between 'payers' and 'non-payers'.

A parish adopts good practices and its congregation grows, amidst much rejoicing. A year later it is dismayed to find its parish share bill has rocketed. The share is based in part or whole on attendance, and that has gone up. In contrast, the sleepy next-door parish has seen its congregation dwindle but is protected from the consequences of this by its parish share being reduced. The problem for the growing church, which appears to be being taxed for its successful evangelism, is that the new people will take several years to learn to give at the rate of long-standing members. It cannot pay all its share in the next year, whereas the declining parish can. The diocese is cross with the growing church and congratulates the declining one, whose vicar becomes the next archdeacon.

All the above examples are real ones that have arisen in the context of having to raise and pay parish shares. This is of course a many-sided problem with no simple solutions. But too little attention is so often paid to the impact of diocesan policies and attitudes on the growth and decline of the parishes. However, policies can be reviewed with these factors in mind. For example, parish share division methods do not need to rely to any significant extent on attendance figures. When diocesan leaders assess parish data they should look at attendance trends as well as share payment records. People who are considered for key appointments should include those who have led their churches into significant growth. In this way those with first-hand knowledge of how to grow churches will be well placed to enable others.

Another important policy area to review for its impact on growth and decline is that of employment. We saw in Chapter 14 the relationship between length of incumbency and age of clergy on the one hand and attendance decline and growth on the other. Churches appear more likely to grow under incumbencies that last for around ten or twelve years. But the average length of an incumbency is currently only between six and seven years. Dioceses increasingly offer five-year contracts to priests-in-charge. This is done for reasons of flexibility and control because dioceses wish to be able to manage their own decline rather than be clogged up with incumbents they cannot remove. But short incumbencies are themselves one of the causes of decline. However, it is quite possible for a diocese both to retain flexibility by suspending the freehold and to encourage its clergy into staying for an appropriate length of time by renewing contracts where necessary.

That older clergy are more likely to be associated with declining congregations may not simply be because they are less in touch with today's world, but also because their energy levels are reducing. To be the minister of a church today, especially a larger one, has become a demanding and exhausting occupation. It may be that appointment policies and career guidance for clergy should aim to put incumbents aged 35 to 55 in the more demanding jobs. Recent moves to return to the days of ordaining clergy in their twenties should be developed. It is much harder for a deanery to relate to young adults if all its clergy are over 55.

Appointments policies for parochial posts are also changing. The old stereotypes include posts filled through the old-boy network, or by patrons doing someone a favour. But good practice for the growth and strength of the church in question requires that an incumbent be found to suit the needs of the parish. Increasingly, parishes and dioceses are advertising vacancies, and offering job descriptions to go with them. Sometimes, prospective clergy are selected by competitive interview, and questions are asked like 'How would you lead this parish out of decline into growth?' Wakefield Diocese has renamed itself 'The Missionary Diocese of Wakefield', and so attracts incumbents happy to subscribe to that self-understanding. Such good practices, as they gather momentum, can only help in the battle to reverse decline nationally.

Chapter 14 also showed that good pastoral care of the clergy must be central to a diocese's 'policy mode' for reversing decline. This is not only because of the obvious reason that good clergy are a prerequisite for church growth. It is also because of the ever-increasing stresses of modern clergy life, which result in many pastoral problems and breakdowns. The short-term result of such problems has always been a fall in attendance. At one time it was assumed that, once a new vicar was in place and memories had faded a little, people would flock back and normality would be restored. However, the evidence suggests that today this is no longer the case. People behave as consumers. They do not attend a church out of a sense of loyalty to it. When it lets them down they leave it and never consider returning. Losses through pastoral or personal breakdown can be permanent. It is therefore doubly important for dioceses to take pre-emptive action, by putting in place strong schemes of pastoral support for clergy and early-warning systems of potential problems. In other words, pastoral care for clergy needs to be proactive, not reactive.

Strategy mode

If a diocese wishes to see its churches engage successfully in evangelism and to flourish and grow in the new century then it probably will need a strategy for achieving its aim. We see this in all walks of life: the setting of specific aims and targets focuses the life of an organization and gives it criteria for measuring success and failure. An organization that has no aims is unlikely to achieve anything. A strategy involves long-term strategic thinking, joining up every relevant aspect of the life of the organization. 'Policy mode' was about joining up the thinking in various policy areas; 'strategy mode' is about selecting and implementing a small set of key policies for achieving a clearly thought through strategic objective. The key requirement for successful strategy is to have leaders who are capable of strategic thinking. This ability may need to be a necessary characteristic of future bishops.

The publication *The London Challenge*[1] sets out the policy and strategy of the Diocese of London for the period 2002 to 2007. The diocese has set itself eleven 'challenges' that join up policy thinking across the various aspects of its life. One of these is the specific target of encouraging numbers on electoral rolls to grow to 70,000 by 2005 (electoral rolls are more ruthlessly and regularly updated in London than in most dioceses, which means that they measure current membership realistically). It then has five 'commitments' which set out five main themes for the life of the Church. All of these interrelate with each other, but two of them are specifically about evangelism and church growth. These set out the strategy for achieving the goal of 70,000 members by 2005. One is:

> We are committed to sharing the good news of Jesus Christ in twenty-first century London
>
> - by developing a programme in the spirit of Alpha and Emmaus in every parish and chaplaincy by 2004 to help people find faith and grow as disciples of Jesus Christ
> - by experimenting with new ways of being church, in addition to the parish system. For example: youth churches, community-based churches, cell churches, network churches.

The other is:

> We are committed to telling the story of Jesus Christ 'afresh' for this generation and especially for the young
>
> - by strengthening children's work in the parishes
> - by expanding secondary school provision while striving to make our existing schools places of faith and excellence

- by developing youth worship, youth networks, youth events and youth congregations
- by supporting the work of our Chaplains in higher education.

In other words, the strategy for achieving the church growth objective, which will be measured by electoral roll growth, is universal process evangelism course provision (see Chapter 8 in this book), imaginative church planting (see Chapter 12), and adopting contemporary good practices for work with children and young people (see Chapter 10). There is also an emphasis in the document on the encouragement of minority ethnic groups (see Chapter 9) and the deployment of clergy (see Chapter 14). There must be every hope that such a strategy will achieve the desired objective and that the Diocese of London will continue to grow in size, ministry and influence in the capital.

This review of the variety of stages that dioceses have reached illustrates the vital importance of good diocesan practice for protecting and enabling parish church growth. A diocese that is in proactive mode (planting new congregations, setting up new forms of church), in policy mode (shaping all its policies to meet the needs of decline reversal) and in strategy mode (having specific policies for achieving the goal of strategic growth) is likely to succeed. There are many signs that dioceses are becoming more growth-friendly in their cultures and policies. The fact that there is still a long way to go suggests that there is also considerable further scope for reversing the decline of the Church through the good practice of the dioceses.

Growing a healthy diocese

We have established how important it is for dioceses to develop the way they operate, to move from 'disapproval' or 'disinterest' mode through 'permission-giving' and 'encouragement' modes to 'proactive', 'joined up policy' and 'strategy' modes. But we also need to address a perhaps more fundamental dimension of diocesan existence – not just the way they do things, the practices they adopt, but their very soul and nature, their ethos, culture and spiritual health.

Many parishes today are taking a look at themselves with a view to identifying their strengths and weaknesses, ways in which they are healthy and ways in which they are unhealthy. In some dioceses, the bishop is asking every parish to go through such an exercise, using the Springboard Resource Booklet *Growing Healthy Churches* by Canon Robert Warren as a tool. Once aspects of ill health are identified they can be attended to. This is strategically important because it is these limiting factors that are likely to be dragging the church down or stopping it growing. Paying attention to quality aspects is likely to result in quantity growth. The most important of these factors relate to the culture and ethos of the church rather than to its programmes or structures. What is true for the expression of church at one level (parish) is also true for the expression of church at another (diocesan).

To suggest that dioceses, like churches, would benefit from a health check is not to imply any particular criticism. All organizations need to review the way they do things from time to time, and in a fast-changing world, aspects once seen as strengths may now be seen as weaknesses. Examples of weaknesses in the contemporary world identified by *Growing Healthy Churches* include conforming to set ways rather than exploring new possibilities, being hierarchical and structure-bound rather than informal and equality-based, having a controlling rather than a liberating mindset, being nice rather than real, being in survival mode rather than engaging with reality, passionless rather than passionate, inward-looking rather than outward-orientated, looking to the past rather than the future, and resisting change rather than working with it.

The spiritual vitality and energizing faith of a diocese can be renewed by its conducting its own health check on the interrelated workings of its senior staff team, diocesan officers, 'Church House' staff, synods, bishop's council, boards and committees. The healthy church checklist reproduced here (see Figure 15.1) is just as applicable to the church and diocese as it is to the parish church.

So a diocese is far more than just an administrative body needed to keep the parish system ticking over. It can hold the key to the future of the Church of England in its locality. By being proactive, by joining up its policies around a coherent aim, by giving strategic impetus to every local church, by all the ways in which it can itself model the marks of the healthy community of faith and help to multiply new and healthy expressions of local church life, the diocese can ensure that the Church grows rather than declines in the twenty-first century.

Figure 15.1 Seven marks of a healthy church: expressing the life of Christ through the local church

1 **Energised by faith**
rather than just keeping things going or trying to survive
- **worship and sacramental life** move people to experience God's love
- **motivation:** energy comes from a desire to serve God and one another
- **engaging with scripture:** in creative ways that connect with life
- **nurturing faith in Christ:** helping people grow in, and share, their faith

2 **Outward-looking focus**
with a 'whole life' rather than a 'church life' concern
- **deeply rooted** in the local community, working in partnership with other denominations, faiths, secular groups and networks
- passionate and prophetic about **justice and peace,** locally and globally
- making connections between **faith and daily living**
- responding to human need by **loving service**

3 **Seeks to find out what God wants**
rather than letting our own preferences set the church agenda
- **vocation:** open to the Spirit's leading about what we should be and do
- **vision:** developing and communicating a shared sense of where we are going
- **mission priorities:** consciously setting both immediate and long-term goals
- able to call for and **make sacrifices,** personal and corporate, in bringing about the above and living out the faith

4 **Faces the cost of change and growth**
rather than resisting change and avoiding failure
- while embracing the past, daring to take on **new ways** of doing things
- **taking risks:** admitting when things are not working, and learning from experience
- **crises:** responding creatively to challenges that face the church and community
- **positive experiences of change,** however small, are affirmed and built on

5 **Builds community**
rather than functioning as a club or religious organisation
- **relationships** are nurtured so people know they are a part of a community of faith (often through small groups) with opportunities for service
- **leadership:** lay and ordained work as a team to develop appropriate expressions of all seven marks of a healthy church
- **lay ministry:** the different gifts, experiences and faith-journeys of all are valued and given expression in and beyond the life of the church

6 **Makes room for others**
being inclusive rather than exclusive
- **welcome:** works to include newcomers into the life of the church
- **children and young people** are helped to belong, contribute and be nurtured in their faith
- **enquirers** are encouraged to explore and experience faith in Christ
- **diversities:** coming from social and ethnic backgrounds, mental and physical abilities and age differences are seen as a strength and sought after

7 **Does a few things – and does them well**
focused rather than frenetic
- **doing the basics well:** especially public worship, pastoral care, stewardship and administration
- **occasional offices:** make sense of life and communicate faith
- **being good news** as a church in our attitudes and ways of working
- **enjoying what we do** and being relaxed about what is not being done

Source: Taken from *Growing Healthy Churches* by Robert Warren and Janet Hodgson, Springboard Resource Paper 2, 2001, pp. 6–7, reproduced by permission.

16

Renewing the spiritual heart

Jesus declared, 'I tell you the truth, no-one can see the kingdom of God unless he is born again.' 'How can this be?' Nicodemus asked. 'You are Israel's teacher,' said Jesus, 'and do you not understand these things?' (John 3.3,9,10 NIV)

Growth ahead

This book contains many technical and practical ways of growing the Church through appropriate good practices even in the changing and challenging times in which we live. Most of these are not just theories from church growth gurus but tried and tested ways of being church that are already working in many places. The implication of this is that a more widespread attention to what we have already discovered about church decline has the capacity to turn the whole Church of England around. In fact the rate of decline has been slowing considerably in most recent years, perhaps precisely because this is starting to happen. There is not a huge gulf between an attendance decline of 0.5 per cent per annum and a growth of 0.5 per cent per annum. A new cycle of growing numbers, strengthening finances, increasing self-confidence, growing respect, and renewed influence on the life and culture of the nation is within the grasp of the Church too many have written off.

More is needed

And yet! And yet! From deep within the Church of England as we experience it in parishes and dioceses around the country, a new golden age of growth does not always feel just round the corner. We may be able to point the Church of England horse to the waters of church growth, but no power on earth can lead it there, let alone make it drink. Only a large-scale, divinely driven movement of many Christians allied together can speed along change in the Church of England. I have suggested that there may be signs of such a movement gathering momentum already in, say, the return of evangelism to centre stage, the exponential growth of process evangelism courses, the experimental new ways and forms of being church, and the exploding numbers of trained church youth and children's workers. But though we have evidence to suggest that these things are already slowing attendance decline, may have the power to halt it completely, and even to bring about some modest growth, we also have the sense that something else will be needed for the Church to grow again, and flourish, in the longer term. This final chapter, more prophetic than analytic, suggests what this next phase in the resurgence of the Christian Church should and will be like.

Spiritual health the priority

Increasingly today, people aspire to holistic health – the Jewish *shalom* – of body, mind, soul and spirit. The spiritual health of individuals and of churches is an increasingly important subject of study. Fewer churches today seem content to muddle through as second-rate Christianized clubs, and that must be all to the good. More and more churches are seeing the need to pay attention to their spiritual health. I have already argued that an increase in the number of people involved in church life will flow from an improvement in the quality of church life. The natural church development movement is based on this premise. The more parish churches (and dioceses) that conduct their own spiritual health check, perhaps with the help of Robert Warren's Springboard booklet *Growing Healthy Churches*, and implement their findings in order to improve the health of their corporate lives, the greater the chances of the whole denomination growing.

Quality of community

Although neighbourhood and family communities have been breaking down at an alarming rate recently, the need of individuals to find and enjoy community somewhere has not gone away. Increasingly, churches have become the focus of churchgoers' desire for community. People today tend to belong to the church before they believe in the message. Second-rate community in a world of high standards and aspirations is a turn-off. But high-quality community is deeply attractive and satisfies human need. Many of us involved in church life lament the deficiencies of our church communities. They will never be perfect because we will never be perfect this side of heaven. But they may be better than we think. People who compare us with the 'community' of a business that cynically manipulates its workforce, reduces pay and degrades conditions if it can get away with it, and will downsize at the whim of an accountant's sneeze, actually find the church rather warm and accepting. People bruised by the fallout at the sports club or the whingeing on the back row of the local choir can actually find the church a haven of consideration and harmony. Ways of improving the organizational side of a church community have been discussed in earlier chapters, but, of course, the main ingredient in community is love. Love cannot be taught or programmed in by church leaders, only modelled.

The mystery of God is the magnet

Christian community is God-centred or it is nothing. Many people in urban areas live virtually their whole lives in an obviously man-made environment. Prosperity, science, medicine and education appear to squeeze out the wonder and mystery from the world, offering the prospect of lives nicely under control. But, even though churches sometimes try to do this, God cannot be packaged, defined and controlled. The Holy Spirit is untamed and free. A church that is able to inspire a sense of awe, wonder and mystery at the unfathomable majesty of Almighty God will draw many to drink from its deep wells. Some of us have lived through an age of shallow pallywallyness with God. Others have been bored half to death by the trivial predictability of conventional, routine worship. The church that satisfies postmoderns in their search for real spirituality will allow God to be himself – the giant and glorious Trinitarian mystery, never properly encompassed, always unpredictable, and always available to be explored afresh.

Constant renewal

Jesus impressed on Nicodemus, the established religious leader of his day, that even he must be spiritually reborn. Much renewal of human hearts has been happening in the Church of England in recent decades. In fact that is exactly why it is still a force to be reckoned with. But, in an era of accelerating change that is drawing society away from the Church, the established religious leader that is the Church of England must understand that it must be reborn again and again in order to see the kingdom of heaven come to England's green and pleasant land. The only constant for the Church of the future, if it is to remain relevant, will be the never-ending need to change the way it lives and breathes and communicates the unchanging Jesus Christ to the changing world. The Church of the future, therefore, will need a structure and a culture that are designed not to enshrine stability but to handle change.

A competitive market place

The Church began its present life in 1559 as a nationalized monopoly. It still has some features of that earlier life – it is the official 'By Appointment to Her Majesty The Queen' provider of church to the nation. It still possesses some of the bureaucratic inertia that is the perquisite of all monopolists.

However, over the centuries, competitors appeared – the Puritans in the seventeenth century, the Methodists in the eighteenth, the Roman Catholics following emancipation in the nineteenth, and the Pentecostals and house churches in the twentieth. On each occasion, the Church of England learnt from its competitors and matched their strengths. The Evangelical Revival matched the 'horrid enthusiasm' of the Methodists, the Oxford Movement positioned the Church of England in the same segment of the market as the Romans, and the charismatic movement mirrored the Pentecostals.

But now the nature of the market place that the Church is in has widened and changed, probably forever. It is no longer exclusively Christian. The market is no longer 'church', it is 'spirituality provision', and church is just one option among many religions, 'isms', New Age practices, philosophies and therapies. This market has expanded, not contracted. It is the churches' market share that has gone down. And together with its market share the Church's image as the repository of goodness and right morality has also taken a battering. It is hard, for example, to overestimate the damage caused by recent highly publicized cases of child abuse. Many now see themselves as morally superior to the churches, which are perceived as narrow-minded and hypocritical. Churches are seen as repressive, hierarchical and exploitative, alternative spiritualities as life-affirming, freedom-giving and tailored to individual requirements.

Despite the backlash, figures of Christian authenticity – Mother Teresa, for example – are universally revered. The Church will need more and more leaders and members of authentic holiness and transparent goodness if it is to regain its rightful place in the public eye.

An unbeatable product

In this great new market place, the authentically Christian Church has one unique and potentially overpowering advantage over the panoply of other 'isms' – its product. The packaging might sometimes be shabby or the marketing shaky, but once the product is unwrapped it is life and health and peace. It is nothing less than the glorious mystery and overwhelming love of God, supreme meaning and purpose to life, the gift of forgiveness, status as God's children, resurrection life, the Spirit of Jesus Christ in human hearts, and a place at the heart of the potentially most caring, God-infused community there is. It is the real thing, not a fake, a cheap imitation or a hollow promise. Some Christians have wanted to tamper with the product, as though a competitive advantage would be gained by making it more like the others. The manufacturers of Coca-Cola would not dream of watering down their product to make it more like a bland, cheap rival – 'Econo-Semi-Fizzi-Cola' – they *know* they have the real thing.

Market-aware

But what Christians have to offer is much more complex and multi-faceted than a soft drink. We have answers to the difficult questions of life, but in order to satisfy the contemporary thirst for answers, we need to listen to contemporary questions and answer them. It is no use scratching where people used to itch, we need to scratch where they itch today. Ancient Athens was also a great market place of ideas and gods. Paul did his homework about Epimenedes and the unknown God, and then, having got the measure of the crowd, he was able to plunge straight in. In today's Areopagus, today's market place of ideas, fine theological constructs and arguments do not scratch where most people itch. The sharpest questions now are 'how can we find relationships, meaning, religious experience, transcendence?' People today may not respond to the authority of the Bible (Billy Graham's 'The Bible says – so it must be true') but they do respond to the authenticity of Christians' lives. This is not to argue that there is no longer a need for apologetics, because every theological question will still get asked somewhere by someone, and because apologetics is always needed to interpret authentic Christian lives. Nor is it to argue that sound learning and accurate theology are no longer important. The theologians guard and polish the crown jewels of the faith. Although the premium now is on relevance rather than truth, the Christian faith is ultimately only relevant because it is true.

Self-giving

The Church that a few generations ago evangelized half the world – there are now 36 Churches in the Anglican Communion – in the twentieth century lost its ability to talk about God in the pub, or even, amazingly, in the Church. It has been possible to spend a lifetime in the Church of England and never once be asked to talk about God except in the words of hymns or liturgy written for you by someone else. God-talk became the province of the professionals – the evangelists and the clergy. Personal faith – something real and relevant – became private faith – something that should be kept hidden. This is suicide for the Church in an age when people respond less to the propaganda of professionals and more to the opening up of the lives of ordinary Christians. When Jesus was asked what was the most important of all the commandments, he replied: 'Love the Lord your God with all your heart and with all your soul and with all your mind and with all your strength. ... Love your neighbour as yourself' (Mark 12.30,31 NIV). Such holistic engagement with God and with one another is 'the real thing' that satisfies human thirst. Moreover, when Paul wrote to the church in Thessalonica, he reminded them, 'Being affectionately desirous of you, we were ready to share with you not only the gospel of God, but also our own selves' (1 Thessalonians 2.8 RSV). Not just verbal proclamation but also, crucially, the sharing of our very selves – it is no longer enough for evangelism to be 'mind to mind', it must also be 'life to life'.[1] Easily the best-selling of my previous books has been an autobiography – an account of the death of our son Matthew, and how a Christian family found the resources to handle their bereavement.[2] Fifteen years after its publication, letters still arrive from readers thanking us for opening up our lives to their lives. Evangelism needs Christians who are ready to give an account of the hope that is set before them, for whom faith is personal but not private.

Of course, most people will not come to Christians to ask them to share their inner selves – Christians have to go to them and show how God has mended broken hearts and given joy, meaning and hope to human lives. Evangelism is about reaching out rather than pulling in, about going into the market place of spiritualities and demonstrating, living out, sharing the real thing in a land of fakes and hollow promises. And the days of evangelism being the preserve of specialists – evangelists, missionaries, priests, enthusiasts, Alpha leaders – are over. Evangelism is by the whole Church or it is ineffective. The whole army of ordinary Christians needs to be mobilized for the resurgence of the Christian Church in general, and the Church of England in particular. In peacetime, a professional army may be enough. In wartime, ordinary citizens have to be mobilized in order to secure victory. The battle for the spiritual health, for the soul, of the nation is now a full-blown war requiring every Christian to volunteer or be conscripted into active sharing of their very selves.

Mobilizing personal faith-stories

Progress towards this has already been made. Process evangelism courses like Alpha often require ordinary Christians to share their inner selves with those exploring the faith. Some Anglican churches are learning to include interviews and testimony in their weekly services. Where this happens, these are almost always the most powerful and memorable parts of the service, inspirational for fellow Christians and powerfully attractive to others. Cell churches provide a setting where Christians can talk through their everyday experiences in a natural environment in keeping with the spirit of an age where it is normal to share spirituality ideas.

Perhaps the main task now for church leaders and clergy is to unlock the evangelistic potential of the faith-stories that are already there, often locked inside the private world of individual Christians. We said earlier that constant renewal of the inner heart is needed for the Church to succeed in recapturing the culture. But that is not to suggest that such renewal is not happening. In fact, many clergy think that the reality of Christian experience has grown more widespread and powerful in recent years. It is quite likely that the Spirit has already been at work within the Church to prepare it for this time. Now the evangelistic task is to make public what already exists in private, to bury once and for all our unease and embarrassment at talking about the supernatural, about Jesus, and to mobilize the testimony of every Christian, warts and all. Although we do rejoice over the occasional extraordinary life story, by and large the more ordinary the Christian and the more humdrum the life, the more relevant and compelling the story becomes. But, until now, these stories have not always been properly respected, listened to and broadcast. Clergy have been taught to talk to Christians and to feed into their minds the truths of God through their preaching, but they have rarely been encouraged to listen to Christians and to draw out of their hearts their experience of God. We have been trying to *give* God *to* people at times when we should have been trying to *find* God *in* them. It is the communicated experience of the people more than the sermons of the clergy that will win the battle for the hearts and minds of the nation.

Using technology

The gospel was not exclusively, or even mainly, spread round the Roman Empire by big-league evangelists like Paul. It was gossiped by a myriad ordinary Christian people travelling around on their daily business utilizing the cutting-edge technology of the times – the Roman road. Without this technology it is hard to see how the gospel could have spread so far so fast.

Today, the very age that demands the sharing of the same gospel through mass communication *from* the many *to* the many also provides the means of achieving this. This is the information age. Now, for the first time, every local church can launch the faith-stories of its members into the market place of ideas. Individuals can be interviewed or invited to write their story down, to commit it to tape or to video. These stories can be collected in booklet form or on videos, tapes, CDs and DVDs, and circulated for home use. They can be posted on the Net using the church's web site, and constantly changed and updated. The booklets or videos or DVDs can be given away to families and friends, to those with some sort of contact with the church, even posted street by street. They can be used in one-to-one meetings, in small groups and in church services, or to invite people to meet Christians, to listen to their spiritual experiences and faith journeys, to see what resonates with them and how they would like to explore their own response further.

The vital role of church leaders in all this is to help the people discover that their own experiences of God are not only authentic but also powerful in an age when 'what works for me' is listened to with respect. It may be that the main pay-off from a local church deciding to hear and deploy the stories of its members is not to the programmes it builds them into but to the everyday witness of the individuals themselves.

Empowering the young

In order to harness developing technology to the full, many churches will need to rely on the skills of their younger members or sympathizers, including children and teenagers. This could be the greatest benefit of all – to learn to rely on the young and so give them a quite natural central role in the forefront of the church's evangelism, which is where they need to be. Each successive generation will be won mainly by the witness and testimony of its contemporaries. Each generation must evangelize its own. The younger people in our churches have technological skills and tools the older generations by and large do not. And they also have a new opportunity in a market place which is increasingly losing old inhibitions, and which no longer sees Christianity as the norm against which to rebel. When open minds encounter the real thing they tend to recognize it for what it is.

And finally ...

And so local churches can deploy the technology of the age into the market place of spiritualities to communicate the authentic stories of the people of God. The age-old problem was brilliantly summarized by Jesus himself – 'The harvest is plentiful, but the labourers are few' (Matthew 9.37 RSV). We have the opportunity now to release a new army of labourers with freshly loosened tongues, their personal stories authenticated, nurtured and promoted by their leaders. The Christian dumb shall speak, and the Christian lame shall walk into the ripe harvest field of this unsettled world where material plenty and spiritual hunger walk hand in aching hand.

> 'Pray therefore the Lord of the harvest
> to send out labourers into his harvest.'

Notes

Author's preface
1. Bob Jackson, *Till the Fat Lady Sings*, Highland Books, 1996.
2. Bob Jackson, *Higher than the Hills*, Highland Books, 1999 (about the Church in Nepal).

Chapter 1 Facing the truth

1. Peter Brierley (ed.), *Religious Trends 2000/2001*, Christian Research, 2000.

Chapter 2 Bums on seats – why they matter

1. See Robert Warren and Janet Hodgson, *Growing Healthy Churches*, Springboard Resource Paper 2, 2001.

Chapter 4 Bringing growth out of decline

1. A. C. Bing, 'The impact of church planting on the local community', MA thesis, University of Exeter, 1996.

Chapter 5 Why should the future be any different?

1. M. Moynagh, *Changing World, Changing Church*, Monarch, 2001; John Drane, *The McDonaldization of the Church*, Darton, Longman & Todd, 2000.

Chapter 6 The Church after Christendom

1. It should be added that Callum Brown, in his book *The Death of Christian Britain: Understanding Secularisation, 1800–2000*, Routledge, 2001, adds a fifth, controlling, aspect, which he calls 'discursive' Christianity. He considers this to be the key that unlocks the four elements outlined above. This refers to the way people talk about themselves, and the perspective they have on their (often unconscious) practices.
2. Grace Davie, *Religion in Britain since 1945*, Oxford, 1994.
3. See, for example, Roger Jowell et al., *British Social Attitudes* (17th report), p. 124: 'there has been hardly any change in belief about God over the last decade'.
4. Anton Wessels, *Was Europe Ever Christian?*, SCM Press, 1994.
5. William Temple, *Christianity and Social Order*, Penguin Books, 1942.
6. *Ibid.*, p. 8.
7. *Ibid.*, p. 7.

8. Alexander Schmemann, *An Introduction to Liturgical Theology*, St Vladimir's Seminary Press, 1986.
9. See Robert Warren, *Being Human, Being Church*, Marshall Pickering, 1995.

Chapter 10 Taking risks

1. Stephen Neill, *Anglicanism*, Mowbray, 1958, p. 250.
2. Phil Clark and Geoff Pearson, *Kidz Klubs: The Alpha of Children's Evangelism*, Grove/Church Army Booklet Evangelism 45.
3. See Leslie Francis, *Religion in the Primary School: Partnership between Church and State?*, Collins, 1987.

Chapter 11 Acting small – whatever your size

1. See Christian A. Schwarz, *Natural Church Development Handbook*, BCGA, 1996.
2. John Tiller, *A Strategy for the Church's Ministry*, CIO, 1983, p. 76.

Chapter 12 Planting churches

1. George Carey et al., *Planting New Churches*, Eagle, 1991, p. 30.

Chapter 13 Growing younger

1. *Religious Trends, 2000/1*, Table 4.9.
2. These figures come largely from the 1989 English Church Census and the 1998 English Church Survey.

Chapter 14 Supporting the clergy

1. C. Brontë, *Shirley*, Chapter 1.

Chapter 15 The vital role of the diocese

1. Available from www.london.anglican.org.

Chapter 16 Renewing the spiritual heart

1. For this phrase, and for some of the ideas in this section, 1 am grateful to John Drane's CMS lecture in 2001.
2. Bob Jackson, *Matthew*, Highland Books, 1987, 2nd edn 1993.

Index

Note: Page references in *italics* indicate tables and figures; references in **bold** type indicate maps. Where more than one sequence of notes appears on a page, notes are identified by the addition of a, b, c. etc.

administrators 42, 122, 167
age structure: of clergy xii, 3, 100, 146, 152–3, 158, *158*, 159–61, *159*, 164, 167, 177–8
  of congregations 10–11, 88, 120, 146–9, *147*,
  lowering 15, 149–53, 156
  of dioceses 155–6
Alpha courses 59, 67, 73, 81–3, *82*, 84–5, 179, 188
Anglo-Catholicism, and growth 51
archdeacons, selection and training 165–6
attendance: and characteristics of clergy 159–61, *159*, *160*, 177–8
  decline *see* decline
  diocesan variations 36–42, *37*, *38*, 39
  frequency 5–6
  growth *see* growth
  impact of 60–61
  midweek 8–10, 73, 99–100, 106, 128
  and morality and values 20
  other denominations 14–15, *14*, 31, 41, 64, 109, *147*, 148
  and population change 38, 120, 137–8
  and social change 30, 32, 36
  statistics 2–6, *2*, 34–5, *50*, 58–9, 71–4, 96, 104, *109*, 131
  and women priests 47–8
  see also children; October count; usual Sunday attendance
authenticity, renewed 63, 64, 67, 186–7

baptisms: preparation for 150–51, 156
  statistics 2, 2, 6, 64
Baptist Union: and age profile of congregations 148
  and Alpha courses 83
  attendance figures 14–15, *14*, 41, 64
  as gathered churches 58
  and organization 15, 95
Bath & Wells diocese, attendance statistics *37*, *38*
behaving 18, 59–60, 80
believing 18, 47, 59–60, 81, 184
belonging 18, 47, 59–60, 67, 80, 110, 118, 184
  and young adults 151–2
Bing, M. A. 137
Birmingham diocese, attendance statistics 37, *37*, *38*
bishops: and ecclesial models 170–71
  selection and training 165–7, 179
  see also dioceses
bishops' councils, age profile 155
Blackburn diocese, attendance statistics *37*, *38*, 45
boards of mission, age profiles 155
Bradford diocese, attendance statistics 37, *37*, *38*, 45
Brierley, Peter 34
Bristol diocese, attendance statistics *37*, 38, *38*
Brontë, Charlotte 158
Brown, Callum 61–2, 191 n.2b
Brunner, Emil 47
burn-out, in large congregations 127–8

Canterbury diocese, attendance statistics *37*, *38*
Carey, George, Archbishop of Canterbury 140
Carlisle diocese, attendance statistics 37, *37*, *38*
cathedrals, role 142, 169, 170
cell churches 52, 90–91, 124–7, 129, 131, 142, 188
Centre for Youth Ministry (CYM) 100–101, 107
change: in the Church xiv, 33, 51–3, 54–5, 95, 122, 168–9
  social 19, 27, 30, 32, 36, 55, 56–69, 94–5, 171
Chelmsford diocese, attendance statistics *37*, *38*
Chester diocese, attendance statistics *37*, *38*
Chichester diocese, attendance statistics 37, 38
children: and Church Schools 105–6, 107, 179
  coordinator for 73
  decline in attendance 2, 8, 10–11, 12, *12*, 15, 37, *38*, 40, 41, 46, 70, 97
  in large churches 120, 154
  mid-week provision 9, 99–100, 106, 107, 150
  and Sunday Schools 96–8
  and use of statistics 78
  worship clubs 91, 100, 103–4
  and youth workers 100–102, 184
Children Act 97, 100
Christendom: definition 56
  erosion of 56–69, 127
  quality *v.* quantity 19–20
Christian Research 34, 41, 81, 83
Christianity: as counter-cultural 64, 89, 130
  and culture 27, 41, 57, 61–3, 103, 171
  diffused *see* folk religion
  as way of life 66, 68–9, 141
Church: and acknowledgement of decline 1–16, 22
  and care *v.* mission 20–21
  central authorities 76–8
  as faith community 18, 60, 66, 68, 89, 170, 184–5
  indifference to 27, 30, 32, 59, 126
  as inflexible and immobile 29, 30, 94–5
  and kingdom of God 17–21, 23, 31
  and mission as central activity 22, 47, 68
  models 170–72, cell 52, 90–91, 124–7, 129, 131, minster 169, multi-congregational 90, 93, 103, 127–8, 131, 140, 141, multi-cultural 87–8, 91–2, 171–2
  new ways of being church 52–3, 66–9, 130, 135, 140–44, 175, 179, 183
  and quality *v.* quantity 18–19, 23–6, 41–2
  reform *v.* revolution 30, 51–3, 69, 95–6
  renewal by God 53, 95, 188–9
  and repentance 31–2
  as servant 67, 68
  and 'small is beautiful' 19–20
  and social change 27, 36, 66–9
  and State 57, 58–9, 62, 65
  see also change; schools
Church Army 93, 136, 145
Church Life Survey 60–61, 146

church planting 52, 73, 130, 132–45
  and age profiles 154
  composition *137*
  and diocesan input 140, 143–4, 173–4, 179–80
  and growth by transfer 35, 137
  other denominations 15, 41, 143–4
  teams 138–9, 143, 145
  for young people 103, 105
churches: buildings open 2, 4–5, 12–13
  and coalition-building 88–9, 147
  evangelical-charismatic 49–50, 162
  gathered *v.* parish 57–9, 65, 127
  growth of newer churches 134, 136–8, *136*
  healthy 25, 42, 109, 117–18, 167, 180–81, *182*,
    184
  and local community 110
  as multi-cultural 87–8, 89, 171–2
  niche churches 141
  relational 52, 76–7, 142, 143, 170, 175
  rural 53–4, 76, 91–2, 108, 110, 114, 123–4, 169,
    174
  and tradition 86–7, 127, 171
  Web-based 142, 143, 170
  youth provision 35, 88
Churches' Information for Mission (CIM) 60, 146
churchmanship: and clergy training 162
  and growth 49–51, 85
  and welcome 86
clergy 157–67
  central role 157–8, 159–61
  deployment 42, 164–5, 167, 169, 178, 180
  and length of incumbency 159–60, *160*, 167,
    177–8
  maximization of effectiveness 162–4, 167
  non-stipendiary, increase in number 3, 42
  and occasional offices 64–5, 121
  rural 76, 169, 174
  selection 52, 143, 158, 161
  stipendiary, decline in number 2, 3–4, 5, 42, 164,
    retirements 3, sense of personal failure 22, and
    smaller churches 42, 108, 110
  and stress 4, 121, 164, 178
  training 152–3, 158, 161–2, 163, 167
  working hours 163–4, 167
  see also age structure
collaboration, inter-church: and church planting 145
  and nurture courses 85, 124
  and provision for all 91–3, 153, 156
  and youth and children 98–9, 103, 105, 107, 124
Common Worship 68, 172
communicants, Christmas and Easter 2, 5, 6
Confessing Church, Germany 20, 30
confirmations, statistics 2, 3
conflict, in large congregations 121, 122
congregations: counter-cultural 89, 130, 143
  multi-congregational model 90, 93, 103, 127–8,
    131, 140, 141
  optimum size 90
  planting 35, 90, 96, 105, 136, 139, 140, 145, 154,
    166
  see also age structure
congregations, large: and age profile 120, 154
  and children 120, 154
  decline in 4, 21, 42, 71, 76, 89, 96, 108, 109
  and evangelicalism 62
  and lay leadership 118–19, 121
  and nurture courses 82
  and parish share 108, 116, 122–3, 168
  reasons for decline 117–23
  reversing decline 43–4, 50, 73–4, 111–17
  and small groups 124
  strategies for growth 123–30
congregations, small: growth in 4, 15, 35, 42, 43–5,
    53–4, 108, 109–11, 116, 123–4
  as healthy churches 117–18

and stipendiary clergy 42, 108, 110, 124
courses 53, 80–85, 179–80, 183, 188; *see also* Alpha
  courses
Coventry diocese: attendance statistics 37, *37*, *38*,
    117
  and children *38*, 102
  large churches 116
Credo course 82
Crusaders' Union 99, 107
culture: and Christianity 27, 41, 57, 61–3, 103, 171
  fragmented 87, 171
  multi-culturalism 87–8, 89, 171–2
  see also change, social
curates: and practical training 161–2
  and young people 100, 152, 156

Davie, Grace 59–60
Dawn Conference (1992) 135
deaneries: and multi-cultural approach 91–2, 93, 172
  and process evangelism 84
  and use of statistics 74, 76, 79
  and young adults 153
Decade of Evangelism 46–8, 53, 85
decline: acknowledgement of xi–xiii, 1–16, 17, 22,
    27, 31, 33, 56, 113, 123
  addressing 15, 17–26, 52
  and church size *see* congregations, large;
    congregations, small
  and despair 1, 21, 27–8, 33, 56, 81
  as patchy 15, 22, 25, 31, 33–4, 35
  rate of 2, 8, 11–14, *11*, *12*, *13*, 183
  and repentance 31–2
  reversing 42–5, 112–13
Derby diocese, attendance statistics *37*, *38*
despair, and decline 1, 21, 27–8, 33, 56, 81
dioceses: and age profiles 155–6
  central role 143, 168–81
  and church planting 140, 143–4, 145, 173–4
  and clergy deployment 165, 177–8, 180
  and 'disapproval' mode 173
  'disinterest' mode 173
  and ecclesial models 170–72, 175
  'encouragement' mode 174
  and evangelism 46–8
  healthy 180–81
  and large churches 111–17, 123, 129–30
  and multi-cultural approach 92, 93, 171–2
  and parish share 4, 37, 70, 75, 176
  'permission-giving' mode 173–4
  'policy' mode 175–8, 180, 181
  'proactive' mode 174, 180, 181
  and process evangelism 84–5
  and reversal of decline 43–5, 123
  and risk-taking 95–6
  and small churches 123–4
  'strategy' mode 179–80, 181
  and support for clergy 163–4, 178
  and use of statistics 70, 71, 75–6, 77–8, 79
  variation between 36–42, *37*, *38*, 39, *40*
  and youth work 101
Drane, John 51, 192 n.1f
Durham diocese: decline in attendance 15, 36, *37*, 38,
    38, *45*, 64
  and growth 50, 51

ecumenism, and initiatives for growth 91, 153, 170,
    172
electoral rolls 2, 5–6, 74, 79, 150, 179–80
Elim Pentecostal Church 143
Ely diocese, attendance statistics *37*, *38*
Emmaus course 82, 179
English Church Attendance Survey 33, 34–5, 50, 109,
    147, 148, 162, 182 n.2c
English Church Census 10, 15, 25, 33, 34, 81, 87, 109,
    147, 162, 192 n.2c

establishment 57–8, 65, 185–6
ethnicity: and growth 87–8, *88*, 166, 180
　and specialist churches 141
evangelicalism: and clergy training 162
　and growth 49–50
evangelism: as central 53, 55, 183
　and churchmanship 49–51
　event 80
　as process 41, 47, 53, 80–85, 156, 166, 179–80, 183
　and self-giving 187–8
　strategies for 46–7, 83–5, 112–13
　see also Alpha courses; courses
Exeter diocese, attendance statistics *37, 38*

faith: nurturing 80–85, 98, 103
　re-thinking 66–7
　and self-giving 187–8
faith communities 18, 66–8, 89, 170, 184–5
Faith in Life 60
faith-stories 188–90
folk religion 56, 57, 59–61, 64–5, 66
Francis, Leslie 105
funerals 9, 64–5

Gill, Robin 59–60
giving, levels 2, 5
Gloucester diocese, attendance statistics 37, *37, 38*
Good News Down the Street course 82
Gospel and Culture movement 41
Graham, Billy 80, 187
Growing Healthy Churches 25, 180, *182*, 184
growth 15, 27–32, 132
　and age profiles 88
　and churchmanship 49–51, 85
　and ethnic mix 87–8, *88*, 166, 180
　and 'glass ceiling' effect 121, 129–30, 133
　and 'growing younger' 149–56
　in larger churches 123–30
　as natural 28–9, 30–31
　in newer churches 134, 136–8, *136*
　and nurture courses 81–5, *82*
　in other denominations 31
　and paid ministry 110
　pockets 33–4
　priority setting 166–7
　and provision for the young 104–5
　qualitative *v.* quantitative 23–6, 41–2
　real *v.* transfer 35–6, *137*
　and reform 51–2, 95–6
　resources for 53–4, 83, 89, 91, 93, 101
　and role of clergy 157–67
　strategies 46–7, 78, 112–13, 166, 179–80, neglect of 15,17–26
　and young adults 83, 146–56, 158
　see also church planting; courses
Guildford diocese: attendance statistics *37, 38, 115*
　large churches 114–16

harvest festival, attendance 9–10
Hereford diocese, attendance statistics *37, 38*
Holy Spirit, and renewal of the Church 32, 53, 175, 184, 188–9
house church movement 52, 134–5
house groups 124–5
Hull, church attendance 14

invitation, personal 80, 84, 85
Islam, growth 56

Jowell, Roger, et al. 191 n.4
Just Looking course 82

Kidz Klub 100, 103–4, 107
King, Philip 41

kingdom of God: and the Church 17–21, 23, 31
　and growth as natural 28–9
　and quality *v.* quantity 18–19

leadership: and cell groups 126
　of children's work 98, 100–101, 107
　and church planting 143
　diocesan 38–42, 70, 75
　in large churches 118–19, 120–21, 128, 129–30, 131
　lay 118–19, 121, 173
　national 55
　parochial 42, 52, 71–4, 84, 88–9, 90–91
　and risk-taking 52
　and young adults 91, 144, 152–3, 155–6
　see also clergy
Leicester diocese, attendance statistics *37, 38*
Lichfield diocese: attendance statistics 37, *37, 38, 114*
　large churches 114, 123
Lincoln diocese, attendance statistics *37, 38*
Liverpool diocese: attendance statistics *37, 38, 45*
　children's work *38*, 100
The London Challenge 179
London diocese: growth in attendance 15, 36, 37, *37, 38, 38*, 64
　policy and strategy 179–80
　and process evangelism 84–5

McCullough, Nigel 21, 77
Manchester diocese: attendance statistics 37, *37, 45*
　and children *38*, 106
marriage: preparation for 150–51
　statistics 2, 3, 9, 19, 62–3
media, and Church of England 21–2, 24, 58–9
membership *see* baptisms; electoral rolls
Methodist Church: and age profile of congregations 148
　attendance figures 14, *14*, 41
　and church planting 135
ministry *see* clergy; leadership; Readers; teams
mission: as Church's central activity 22, 47, 68, 183
　and crossing of boundaries 87
　and new forms of church 141–3
　v. pastoral care 20–21, 143
　training for 174
　and use of statistics 77–8
Moynagh, Michael 51
multi-culturalism 87–8, 89, 91–2, 171–2
Murphy O'Connor, Card. Cormack 62

'Natural Church Development' movement 25, 184
Neill, Stephen 94
Newcastle diocese, attendance statistics *37, 38, 45*
Nietzsche, Friedrich 49
Norwich diocese, attendance statistics *37, 38*

occasional offices 64–5, 121; *see also* baptisms; funerals; marriage
October count 8–10, 11–12, 34, 36, 75, 77–8
　and children 106
Ordained Local Ministers 3
Oxford diocese: attendance statistics *37*, 38, *38*
　cell churches 125–6

parish share 8, 37, 70, 75, 176–7
　and large churches 108, 116, 122–3, 168
parishes: and gathered churches 57–9, 127
　geographical 20, 169–70
　and nurture courses 84–5
　practical action 78–9, 85, 89, 93, 107, 131, 145, 156, 167
　relational 52, 65, 76–7, 142, 143, 170, 175
　and use of statistics 71–4, 77–9
　as welcoming 86–93, 96, 119, 128

pastoral care: and infrequent attendance 7
    in large congregations 128, 131
    v. mission 20–21, 143
    time spent in 64–5
PCC: age profile 152, 156
    and strategies for growth 154
    and support for clergy 163
    voluntary income *2*, 5
Pentecostalism 52, 64
Peterborough diocese, attendance statistics *37, 38*
population change, and attendance patterns 38, 120,
    137–8
Portsmouth diocese, attendance statistics *37, 38*
postmodernism 28, 31–2, 49, 59, 65, 94–5, 110, 125, 172
prayer, importance of xiv, 63, 153
prophecy, need for 18, 52, 67

Readers: increase in number 3, 42
    and team ministry 91
reform *v*. revolution 30, 51–3, 69, 95–6
relationships: and cell churches 124–6
    and clergy 160–61
    and growth 54, 68, 84, 89–90, 122, 169
relevance of Christian faith 27–9, 30, 32, 33, 126, 187
Religious Trends: 2000/2001 6, 41
    2002/3 38
Remembrance Day 57, 66
renewal, personal 53, 184, 188
repentance of the Church 31–2
research and development 22–3, 71, 76–7
Research and Statistics Unit 77–8
resources: for church planting 138–40, 143
    financial 4, 70, 77, 93, 101, 174–5, 176–7
    for growth 53–4, 83, 89, 91, 93, 101
    young adults as 155
retreats, growth in 142
revolution *v*. reform 30, 51–3, 69, 95–6
Ripon & Leeds diocese, attendance statistics *37, 38, 45*
risk-taking 52, 94–107
    and work with children 96–9
Rochester diocese, attendance statistics 37, *37, 38*

St Albans diocese: attendance statistics *37, 38, 102,
    115, 116*
    and children *38*, 101–2, *102*
    large churches 114–16
St Edmundsbury & Ipswich diocese, attendance
    statistics *37, 38*
St Thomas Crookes (Sheffield) 130
Salisbury diocese, attendance statistics *37, 38*
Salvation Army, and church planting 135, 143
Schmemann, Alexander 66
schools, Church 105–6, 107, 179
Schwarz, Christian A. 41–2, 109, 117–18, 120
secularization 18, 51–2, 56–7, 61–2, 65
Sheffield Centre for Church Planting 93, 136, 145
Sheffield diocese: attendance statistics *37, 38, 45*, 80
    and church size 111, *111*, 130
Sodor & Man diocese, attendance statistics *37, 38*
Southern Baptist churches (USA) 134, *134*
Southwark diocese, attendance statistics 37, *37, 38*
Southwell diocese, attendance statistics *37, 38*
spirituality:
    as individual project 171–2, 186
    new interest in 27, 67, 68, 84, *84*, 125, 150, 184
Springboard initiative xii, 34, 47, 50, 81, 114, 184
Statistics: A Tool for Mission 22, 77
statistics: and randomness 34–5

using xi–xiii, 1, 70–79
Sunday, changing patterns of 6, 10, 63, 97, 99–100
Sunday schools 11, 96–8, 148

teams: church planting 138–9, 143, 145
    'growing younger' 150, 156
    local ministry 4, 41–2, 91, 120, 128
    'turnaround' teams 155
    welcome teams 128, 131, 154, 156
technology, use of 189–90
teenagers *see* young people
Temple, William 20, 62
Thame Valley Team Ministry 125
There Are Answers xii, xv
Tiller report (1983) 124
Truro diocese, attendance statistics 15, *37, 38*
'turnaround' teams 155
'Twenty Thirty' group 153

urban priority areas 30, 53–4, 100, 101, 108, 114
USA, growth of newer churches 134, *134*
Usual Sunday Attendance figures 8–10, 12, 36, 37,
    37, 39, *44, 48*, 75
    children 8, *38*, 40, *97, 99, 102*
    large churches 114

Wakefield: attendance statistics 7, *37*, 38, *38, 44, 45*
    and church tradition 51
    as 'Missionary Diocese' 21, 25, 44–5, 178
Wakefield, Gavin 134
Warren, Robert xi–xiii, xv, 68, 180, *182*, 184
welcome: and inclusiveness 86–93, 96, 119, 151
    welcome teams 128, 131, 154, 156
Wessels, Anton 61
Winchester diocese, attendance statistics *37, 38*
women, ordination to the priesthood 3, 47–8, 51, 53
Worcester diocese, attendance statistics 37, *37, 38*
worship: 'alternative' 142
    and church culture 86, 89–90, 171–2
    importance of 60–61, 68
    midweek services 8–10, 73, 74, 106, 128, 151
    patterns 73–4, 86, 89–90
    for young families 102–5, *104*, 151, 156
    for young people 52, 88, 99, 102–5, *104*, 107, 180

York diocese: attendance statistics *37*, 38, *38, 45*, 76,
    112, 113
    and child attendance *38*, 98–9, *99*, 120
    and large churches 111–13, *112*, 120, 123
    reversal of decline 43–4, *43*, 50–51, 108, 112, 117
    and small churches 110, 123
young adults: and age profile of congregation 147,
    148–9
    attracting 65, 150–54, 155–6, 158
    and cell groups 125, 127
    and church planting 144, 145, 173–4
    decline in attendance 10, 96, 100, 120
    and leadership 91, 144, 152–3, 190
    and nurture courses 83
    and social programme 151–2, 153, 156
    and worship 102–5, *104*, 151, 156
young people: and leadership 91, 152–3, 155–6, 190
    and relational parishes 65, 170, 175
    and worship 52, 88, 99, 102–5, 107, 180
youth work 53, 92, 93, 100, 106, 107, 122
    and church growth 35, 42, 101–2, 153, 184
    funding 101, 156, 174
    youth ministers 92, 166